Humanity and Nature

Humanity and Nature
Ecology, Science and Society

Yrjö Haila and Richard Levins

PLUTO PRESS

First published 1992 by Pluto Press
345 Archway Road, London N6 5AA

British Library Cataloguing in Publication Data

A catalogue record of this book is
available from the British Library

ISBN 1 85305 041 5 hb
ISBN 0 7453 0669 1 pb

Library of Congress Cataloging-in-Publication Data

Haila, Yrjö.
    Humanity and nature : ecology, science, and society / Yrjö Haila
  and Richard Levins.
      p. cm.
    Includes bibliographical references (p.   ) and index.
    ISBN 1-85305-041-5 : £35.00. — ISBN 0-7453-0669-1 (pbk.) : £10.95
    1. Ecology. 2. Man—Influence on nature. 3. Ecology—Political
  aspects. I. Levins, Richard. II Title.
  QH541.H233 1992
  574.5'01—dc20   92-3426
                                                                 CIP

Acknowledgements

We are grateful to New Direction Publ. Corp. for permission to
reproduce the extract from Lawrence Ferlinghetti: *Open Eye, Open Heart.*
Copyright © 1973 by Lawrence Ferlinghetti; and to Methuen Children's
Books for permission to reproduce the extract from A.A. Milne: *The
House at Pooh Corner* (1928)

Typeset by Stanford DTP Services, Milton Keynes
Printed and bound in the United Kingdom by
Billing and Sons Ltd, Worcester

Contents

Preface:
The Multiple Faces of Ecology

Through most of its history ecology has been a minor discipline among the biological sciences, living a shady life at various university departments such as zoology, botany, geography, soil sciences, forestry, agriculture, microbiology or limnology. But a drastic change has happened, originating with the environmental crisis that surfaced in the 1960s. Suddenly ecology has come to appear as a major integrative core of biology, a discipline everybody ought to be interested in and know about. The change has been very rapid indeed and the low profile of ecology among biological disciplines only a few decades ago seems absurd.

However, the term *ecology* has several meanings:

- ecology *the nature*: nature's economy as a material fact, and as a material basis for human existence;
- ecology *the science*: the biological discipline investigating nature's economy;
- ecology *the idea*: prescriptive views of human existence, derived from what is known or believed about nature's economy; and
- ecology *the movement*: political activities trying to transform society to agree with ecological ideals.

These dimensions of 'ecology' arise from relatively independent backgrounds and are widely disparate in content. Each one is important, however, and an understanding of their mutual connections is a most urgent task.

This book is about the interfaces of the different aspects of 'ecology'. As both authors are ecologists, we will focus on the ability of ecology 'the science' to answer important questions.

Being both of us simultaneously committed to radical transformation of society in accordance with the interests of the oppressed, the aim is to establish a connection between ecological knowledge and radical politics. We should be able to view nature both as a foundation and a constraint of human culture, and develop practicable ways of relating society with the potentialities and imperatives of nature. This challenge brings forth a huge number of unsolved problems. It is clear that ecology has joined the traditional issues of class, race and gender on the agenda of radical politics, but it is less clear what this means in practice.

We begin our exploration by discussing in Chapter 1 some slogans that have become established as parts of modern ecological folklore. Such slogans, although ingenious metaphors, are surprisingly often misleading or false. This is because ecology does not give us prescriptions; all rules apparently derived from nature are ideological and political and should stand on their own without claiming endorsement from nature.

In Chapter 2 we describe basic features of ecological systems we have ourselves studied. The descriptive narrative starts from Kevo, Finnish Lapland, way beyond the Arctic Circle, and proceeds through more southern environments to general issues of ecological theory. Although ecology 'the science' strives toward generalizations that are not tied to the particularities of specific environments, admiration and respect of nature's detail is at the very heart of ecology.

In Chapter 3 we continue with ecology 'the science' on a more abstract level by relating ecological research to underlying constraints. Science must be viewed in a context. This is true on every level from single 'facts' to general theories. Our goal in this chapter is to make visible the most important connections and constraints of ecological science and to give starting points for criticism.

In the next three chapters we discuss the interface between society and nature: first in connection with two specific social practices, namely, health (Chapter 4) and agriculture (Chapter 5) and then from a broader ecohistorical perspective (Chapter 6). Humans are products of nature and, accordingly, natural beings. Thus it is impossible to assume that culture and nature be somehow 'essentially' in contradiction. One implication is that the ecological crisis cannot be solved once and for all. As a matter of fact, it is impossible to imagine a situation in which there were no problems in the society–nature relationship. Another implication is that a view of 'nature' as a straightforward material entity giving rules to be followed in constructing society lacks any clear meaning. A more appropriate response to the ecological crisis is to modify specific social practices, but this necessarily entails modifications in the whole social structure. Our discussion of health and agriculture in Chapters 4 and 5, and the broad outline of ecohistory in Chapter 6 thus belong closely together.

The last chapter is on ecology 'the politics'. We are not promulgating a universal program for 'ecological politics'. Such an enterprise would contradict the conclusions drawn in the preceding chapters: ecological knowledge does not translate into politics through universal programatic statements but through detailed, creative, innovative and collective efforts in specific historical, political and cultural situations. We discuss general challenges all political movements taking ecological issues seriously must confront one way or another. We argue that it is possible to formulate general principles of radical response to environmental issues, while simultaneously respecting the specificities of historical, contingent situations. The outcome depends on the creative initiative of people confronted by specific problems and challenges.

* * *

The idea that we might write this book together was originally conceived by Steven Rose a disturbing number of years ago. The project simply proved much more complicated than we originally thought. Some extra delay is, no doubt, due to the Atlantic Ocean separating Cambridge, Massachusetts, and Helsinki from each other; however, the Academy of Finland helped to overcome this barrier by financing Yrjö's three visits to Cambridge, as well as supporting his work during the whole project, which we gratefully acknowledge. Our thanks are due to several friends who read and commented on parts of the chapters in draft (Pekka Niemelä, Chapter 2; Marja-Liisa Kakkuri-Knuuttila, Chapter 3; Peter Taylor, Chapters 3 and 6; Tapani Hietaniemi, Chapter 6). Yrjö published some of the ideas in Finnish in *Tiede & edistys* and got fruitful, critical response. Päivö Somerma helped with the figures. Rosario Morales kept asking Dick, 'Have you been working on the book?' On a longer time scale she shared in the development of many of the ideas. Without continuous encouragement and inspiration from Isadore Nabi, Casimiro Fuentes and Leo Rybak this project might never have seen the light of day.

1

What Program can Ecology set for Society?

Let us not, however, flatter ourselves overmuch on account of human victories over nature. For each such victory, nature takes its revenge on us. Each victory, it is true, in the first place brings about the results we expected, but in the second and third places it has quite different, unforeseen effects which only too often cancel the first ... At every step we are reminded that we ... belong to nature, and exist in its midst, and that our mastery over it consists in the fact that we have the advantage over all other creatures of being able to learn its laws and apply them correctly. Friedrich Engels[1]

Modern environmentalism is a product of the late 1960s and early 1970s. At the beginning we find events such as 'Earth Day' in the US, a nationwide teach-in celebrated on 22 April 1970. Similar demonstrations and happenings were commonly organized all over Western Europe.

The demonstrations had their harbingers and stimulators. Of particular importance were influential books such as Rachel Carson's *Silent Spring*. A new environmental consciousness took shape gradually. This happened largely independently of traditional conservation organisations although later these adopted much of the thinking of the activists of 1970.

Two lines of thought, largely missing from traditional conservation movements, were characteristic of the new environmental consciousness. First, emphasis was put on the total human environment, in addition – and partly in opposition – to an older concern of nature protection. The new concern also covered the productive potential of nature. Second, the new movements viewed environmental issues in a social and political context, and began to explore alternative

1

political perspectives. The slogan 'political ecology' was coined by Hans-Magnus Enzensberger (1973).

The development since 1970 will be familiar to readers: first gradual consolidation of new environmentalist organizations and journals and finally, toward the 1980s, establishment of green parties in electoral politics. Awareness of environmental issues has grown in tandem with the sharpening of problems that are genuinely global. The egalitarian mass character of environmental movements has been clear from the beginning despite recurring accusations of elitism from conservative quarters. The early controversies between old and new conservation movements have also been largely overcome.

However, straightforward as this short narrative may appear, there are many fundamental problems and contradictions in environmentalist thought.

Many people filled with new environmental consciousness have turned to ecology in the hope that it would provide some objective rules for how to organize the world, that it would be rooted in nature and therefore be above human fallibility and narrow-mindedness. Suggestions such as those which follow have received currency.

[1] Nature is a complex integrated system in which networks of feedback and the recycling of elements maintain a rough balance, a harmony in which each species has its place. Therefore the appropriate goal for humanity is harmony with nature. Feminists have argued that since the goals of exploitation, conquest and domination have been linked to Euro-North American ideology of masculine success, this change of goal requires the adoption for all of society of beliefs and attitudes of nurturing and community traditionally assigned to women. Feminists disagree as to whether these characteristics are inherently male or female, or socially assigned through gender rules and roles.

[2] In complex ecosystems each part plays a unique role that cannot be assumed by other components. In order to carry out these functions, all members of the system receive and give in a rough pluralistic democracy, and a community of interests prevails in nature among different species in spite of temporary conflicts between competitors for scarce resources, or predators and their prey.

[3] Resources are limited by the finite size of the earth and the finite though vast amount of solar energy the earth receives. If we use resources faster than they can be replenished, our consumption becomes more difficult, more costly and more painful to maintain. Therefore we need to adapt to living on a strictly limited 'spaceship earth', and the appropriate goal for humanity is not unending increase of production, consumption and population but sustainability and frugality.

[4] The sustainability of the biosphere and of our production system within it depends on complexity and diversity. Therefore the simplification of habitats for economic efficiency, the planting of large monocultures for economies of scale, and narrow specialization in the products that can best be produced in a region are shortsighted expedients.

Diversity and complexity should be preserved both for greater long-term stability and productivity, and as a hedge against the inevitable uncertainty of nature. An appropriate ideology must value nature, its habitats and species, for themselves. This is expressed variously as reverence for life, notions of the sacred, or solidarity with all living things. It is accompanied by an aesthetic which delights in the uniqueness of organisms, their wild spontaneity, their ability to thwart human schemes for them.

[5] The biosphere is being damaged by the release of tens of thousands of historically new substances. The organisms of the biosphere did not evolve to cope with them, so that many of these substances are harmful as poisons, carcinogens and mutagens, in the present and in ways as yet unimagined.

The world trade system imposes criteria on agricultural products of ease of storage and transport which often debase quality. It leads to long-distance transport that pollutes the seas and the atmosphere. And through commercial competition it destroys the productive capacity of many regions, replacing it with dependence.

Therefore appropriate goals for humanity are to reduce the production and release of new substances, to demand that each new product be justified as necessary to human wellbeing rather than be merely marketable, and to make better use of old ones and live simply. An appropriate aesthetics derives pleasure from sparseness, economy, unobtrusiveness and skill instead of opulence and power.

[6] Our knowledge is puny compared to the complexity of nature; even the most authoritative reassurances that some new transformation of nature will have only desired results are more a testimony to our arrogance than our wisdom. Furthermore, in the hundreds of millions of years of evolution all sorts of organisms and molecules and vegetation patterns have been tried and rejected – only the most enduring survive. Therefore, in Barry Commoner's (1971) words, 'nature knows best.' An appropriate attitude toward nature is one of humility and awe, an appropriate goal for humanity is to cause minimum changes, and an appropriate goal for science is to learn how to survive with minimum intervention.

One such line of inquiry is agricultural ecology aiming at natural pest control, and elimination of pesticides and synthetic fertilizers. Another is an alternative health practice based on natural remedies, non-invasive therapies, food production for optimal nutrition, the construction of our living spaces and design of our work processes with good health in mind. In general, an appropriate technology is a gentle technology.

[7] Each ecosystem is unique; what makes sense in one place would be disastrous in another. The emphasis on site specificity is consistent with 'post-modern' suspicion of generalizations and universals. This local site specificity precludes any large-scale central planning and proposes instead a system of relatively autonomous communities producing mostly for their own consumption.

[8] Site specificity also requires the local creation of knowledge as part of daily practice rather than as a separate central elite activity. Such knowledge generation would allow room for the integrated experience of people which is felt as intuition or 'gut feeling' and would be more democratic insofar as it respects everybody's experience.

There is much that is appealing in this program which combines practical and ideological goals. However, it is a human, not a natural program, and should stand on its own without claiming endorsement from nature. Each of the claims and proposals is an ideological position. That is, it is a construct built from natural materials as transformed by particular people from particular positions in particular societies according to their own belief systems informed in turn by their experience and needs. This does not invalidate any of the claims or proposals but is a warning that the self-evident may be merely the collective bias of a shared ideology.

We shall first argue that particular claims about nature are neither true nor universal, and secondly that alternative conclusions can be drawn from nature.

Nature is indeed a complex whole. But its complexity is not like that of the individual organism whose various organs have evolved and have been selected on the criterion of their contribution to the survival and fecundity of the whole. Ecological systems are far more contingent. Some, such as the ensemble of ant species in red mangroves of the Puerto Rican bank, recur with monotonous regularity as the mangrove island develops. But the rodent communities of western North America, the birds on Baltic islands, and ants in northern boreal forests are associations which are assembled from larger pools by the accidents of migration and localized random events in the lives of individuals in small populations. There is in fact no single, unique community which is suitable for a particular place. Species enter or drop out of communities at characteristic rates that depend on the type of habitat and its location in a geographic mosaic of habitats. Thus many species are interchangeable or removable without threatening the integrity of the community. It is not quite true that each carries out a function necessary for the survival of the whole.

There are indeed species which do play key roles in communities; they are often called 'keystone species'. The insect life of a pine forest in the Caribbean is quite different from that of other forests, and depends on the pine. The flies that feed on cactus surely depend on the cactus. Other communities depend on particular species of coral or tree or predator, and removal of these key species could result in complete transformation of the community and its replacement by another community. But there is no general rule that says, 'touch anything and the whole will crumble about you.' And indeed, the principle of site specificity seems to contradict the notion that there is only one sort of nature for each place. There are more distinct communities than there are kinds of places to inhabit; the uniqueness of each site is produced by its history and its inhabitants, but all species are capable of living in more places than they actually use. This is obvious also on large geographic scales; compare, for example, the Galapagos with mainland Ecuador, or Madagascar with southeastern Africa, or New Zealand with Australia.

The feedbacks of natural systems are both stabilizing and desta-bilizing. They arise as a consequence of the immigration, extinction and evolution of the component species each on its own trajectory. The tolerance of physical conditions by each species, the environ-mental conditions it creates, its feeding preferences, microhabitat choices and daily and seasonal cycles all affect the stability and resilience of a community but change without regard to these outcomes. And indeed, while some aspects of the biosphere exhibit remarkable resilience, others change sharply over geological time, and most species that have ever existed have become extinct.

For the biosphere as a whole a few groups of organisms seem to play unique roles in regulating the climate: methane-producing termites, sulphur-emitting microorganisms and temperate seaweed, for example, do exert an influence which apparently cannot be taken up by other species. If a variant termite arises which produces more or less methane, this variant will increase or decrease among the termites depending on whether it is relatively more or less successful in reproducing and surviving than the other variants. We have to emphasize 'relatively', because if a termite variant made life more precarious for all termites but less so for itself than for other termites, it would become the most common termite even as termites decrease in numbers and eventually disappear. Therefore the evolution of the biosphere is no guarantee that conditions favorable for any particular species, including us, will persist. The conception that 'nature knows best' is relativized by the contingency of evolution.

Jim Lovelock (1979) has stressed that over long periods of time life has in fact endured, and that very specific life necessities such as oxygen have varied only within very narrow limits compatible with the kinds of life we have on earth. Many readers have interpreted Lovelock's work in a mystical way and taken it to imply that earth will take care of us. But variations in the environment over a much narrower range than would threaten life as a whole can have a major impact on our species. The advances and retreats of glaciers in the course of the last millennia, or 'Little Ice Age', have changed patterns of rainfall, alternately prevented and allowed settlement at high elevation and high latitude, facilitated and interfered with migration. At present the earth climate is warming up as a result of human activities, but climatic cooling and an advance of ice may very well be on the geological agenda. These are all trivial changes on the cosmic scale but of vital concern for us. There is no reason to believe that naturally occurring climatic change will be for the best or that

Gaia will take care of our needs. In fact she could not do so because we have conflicting needs. Climatic changes will make life much more difficult and even impossible in some parts of the world but more benign in others.

Nor is it clear what living 'in harmony' with nature might mean. All organisms consume, leave waste and affect their surroundings. And all respond, as we do, to physical and chemical processes. Presumably 'living in harmony' with nature would imply as a minimum not destroying it. But of course nature cannot really be destroyed. It can be altered, and what we mean by destruction may be anything from causing local changes in abundance in one or more species to complete elimination of species, to changes in the capacity of the community to maintain itself so that there are drastic changes in vegetation type, soil and topography. Nor does living in harmony reasonably mean obeying natural laws. We have no choice in that regard: the natural processes of energy flow, material cycling, natural selection etc., take place with or without our consent; and our own activities are, of course, subject to the same natural processes that take place in nature without us. What we do changes rates and directions of processes, initial conditions and constraints. But there are always natural processes at work, and our own actions are always part of them; it is often impossible to tell apart what is due to 'nature' and what is due to humanity.

In a word, natural variability and change make it difficult to believe in strict prescriptive rules derived from nature. But ecological guidelines for society are suspect on other grounds, too. Our comprehension of the constraints of nature come from the ecological science, but ecology is rapidly developing. Major theoretical changes and reevaluations are to be expected – as have, indeed, occurred in the recent past – and 'principles' derived from ecology are likely to prove transitory.

Consider the story of 'balance of nature'. The view that opposing forces of nature keep each other in check and a delicate balance results has ancient roots in the history of ideas, and until the 1960s it was a widely held view among ecologists as well. Intuitive arguments in favor of the view were summarized by the conception that community diversity enhances community stability by increasing the number of feedback loops which tend to reverse all changes triggered in the community by external disturbance or human intervention (Egerton, 1973; Levins and Lewontin, 1980). However, Robert

May (1973) showed mathematically that the intuition was wrong: the more there are interconnections in a system, the less stable it becomes. Furthermore, feedback loops within a system may be stabilizing or destabilizing depending on the structure of the system as a whole (Levins, 1974; Puccia and Levins, 1985). A corollary of the idea that diversity bolsters stability is that ecological communities would be most diversified in stable environments, but this is not true either: local species numbers seem to be highest in sites subjected to recurring environmental disturbances whereas communities in stable environments are usually dominated by a few efficient competitors (Connell, 1978).

A similar cycle turned up in views of ecological succession, that is, the regular change in vegetation and fauna of a disturbed site with time; succession takes place, for instance, on a forest plot burned by wildfire, on a mountain slope erased by a landslide, or on a river bank laid bare after the meandering away of the river. In the early half of this century ecologists viewed succession as a perfectly regular process similar to the growth and ageing of an individual organism. Criticism against this view went largely unnoticed until a new generation of botanists collected new field data which showed that succession may be explainable by variation in the requirements of individual species; a stochastic element was also recognized in successional processes (Whittaker, 1953; Connell and Slatyer, 1977).

However, a view that ecosystems fluctuate without any bounds and ecological succession lacks regularity would not be adequate either. A remarkable feature of ecological systems is that they tend to maintain basic structure despite drastic changes in values of individual variables such as the size of particular populations. This property of ecosystems is often called 'resilience', and it is quite different from 'stability' (Holling, 1973). Recurrence and maintenance of basic structure in ecological systems, or 'resilience', can be understood by two types of heuristic arguments: first, no ecosystem is an isolate, that is, the change in any system is influenced by what remains unchanged in the surroundings. Second, the energetics of ecosystem development are constrained by basic thermodynamic principles.

Both the succession theory of the 1940s and the balance-of-nature views of the 1950s imply a 'glass-tower view' of ecological systems as regards options of social development, but they are inadequate. How do we know that views held today are any better?

We certainly feel sympathy with the denunciation of modern science voiced by environmentalists and ecofeminists. This is not only a matter of deficiency of our present theories but a matter of deeper social and conceptual contraints and limitations of our scientific culture. However, we will argue that environmentalists are usually not sensitive enough to the possibilities of modifying scientific practices better to correspond to the demands of an egalitarian society and better to cope with ecological issues.

It is clearly true that application of ecology to practical problems of nature utilization and management has been gravely inept on many counts. Agriculture, pest management, fisheries and forestry have been major fields of applied ecological research since the late nineteenth century, but prevailing research traditions are dominated by narrow, practical interests of increasing production and profits. Applied ecology is in many ways analogous to modern technology and has surprisingly little to say on issues of sustainable resource management. Methodologically characteristic of applied research is blind empiricism and lack of theory.

Ecology is tied to a model of science derived from Newtonian physics. According to the model, systems of nature can be dismembered into elementary parts which are acted upon by one-to-one causal forces, and explaining a phenomenon means deriving it from these elementary processes. However, an alternative is available, namely, a dialectical view of science. Dialectics is no new invention. It has roots in Plato (Socrates) and Aristotle and was developed by dissident scholars during the heyday of Newtonianism and, of course, by Hegel, Marx and Engels. Dialectics is not merely an alternative view of science but also an alternative to Newtonianism in research methodology and provides conceptual tools for analysing interpenetration of organism and the environment, consequences of structural complexity of ecological systems, and contradiction (Levins and Lewontin 1985).

Modern science implies a subject–object view of the relationship between humanity and nature. This view is reflected also in the arts, albeit in a much more ambivalent and contradictory fashion than in the sciences. The development of the arts shows close association with contemporaneous scientific thinking. This is clearly true of the great artistic inventions of the Renaissance, particularly perspectival painting. This is not to say that artists would be copiers and appliers of scientific achievements but rather the opposite: artists often discover new ways of reflecting upon the world and our place in it which are later taken up by other people, including scientists. Consider the chronology of the Renaissance: Giotto was active in the fourteenth century, Brunelleschi in the fifteenth and Macchiavelli in the sixteenth, but it was only in the seventeenth century that the scientific revolution was brought into fruition in the work of Galileo.

Also in our own century modern art has paved the way for new ideas about nature and the relationships of humanity to nature. The breakthrough of abstract painting can be viewed in connection with the breakthrough of abstract methods in the sciences. Systematic investigation of nature was important, for instance, for Paul Klee. However, the early masters, for instance, Wassily Kandinsky and Kasimir Malevich, were also inspired by a search for a spiritualist connection between humanity and nature. We need not agree with the particular views of modern artists – spiritualism easily falls prey to the totalitarianism of being right – but we benefit from acknowledging their achievements.

How does the cultural view of nature arise? In the empiricist tradition a human being was considered an empty canvas, *tabula rasa*, on which the environment would write its facts. 'Nature' was in this tradition a collection of those facts. But this is not adequate: human beings are active subjects in the process of becoming conscious, and the idea of nature accepted in a society is a reflection of human relationships prevailing in that society. The development of basic capacities for sense perception depend on socialization and experience (Grene, 1990).

But if views of 'nature' are primarily constituted within society, if our conceptions of the relationship of human culture to nature are not produced by objectivist scientific thinking, then we need to reflect upon the system of values underlying those conceptions. The values are not *a priori* constructs as assumed by Immanuel Kant, and they are not merely linguistic conventions as assumed by G.E. Moore, but they grow from historical and social experience and are institutionalized in systems of thought adopted in a given culture.

The fundamental values attributed to nature in our Western culture deserve criticism; this is again a point in which we agree with many environmentalists and ecofeminists. In our culture nature is basically regarded as a mere means to be exploited for human ends. This is backed by an ideology of domination of nature (Leiss, 1972; Merchant, 1980). A purely instrumental view of nature is, however, internally contradictory: where can I draw a line between the 'I' and the 'nature' which I use as an instrument? This problem applies to even the dearest concept of our scientific culture, namely reason. If reason is a natural characteristic of human beings, is it not of nature? But if reason is both of 'nature' and of 'myself', what does it mean that I use my reason as 'my' instrument when reasoning about 'nature'? This impasse is even more obvious if we substitute emotion for reason. In what sense can my fears, hate, love, despair and satisfaction be 'instruments'? In other words: human beings have their own internal 'nature' which cannot be sensibly regarded as an 'instrument' to themselves.

Furthermore, it has become irrevocably manifest that human beings are creatures of nature and dependent on nature – so, in which sense is it possible to think of nature as an instrument? How can we regard something which our existence absolutely depends upon as an instrument?

This is a fundamental break. Nature regarded as a mere instrument for human ends is a cultural construct, accepted only in our own culture of all the cultural traditions of humanity. The background of instrumentality is, of course, obvious: the material success in exploiting nature. It is deceptively easy to generalize our relation to specific natural resources and view 'nature' just as a collection of usable elements, a mere external prerequisite of human existence, to be moulded according to our wishes.

To break away from instrumentality feels painfully difficult but is, nevertheless, necessary. An alternative view must build upon appreciation of nature as a value by itself. Such an appreciation should be ingrained in all our interactions with nature.

However, this calls forth yet another distinction, namely, between *ethical* and *moralistic* attitudes about nature. Moralism claiming that humans have no right to intervene with nature is equally unintelligible as claiming that lions are 'immoral' when eating gazelles, or pikes be 'immoral' when attacking roaches, or parasitoids are 'immoral' when consuming larvae of autumnal moths. We are creatures of nature and live of nature, and we simply have no choice in this respect. What matters is not whether we modify nature or not, but how, and for what purpose, we do so.

Thus, one should avoid constructing a cheap opposition between instrumentality and appreciation. We need to use nature to fulfil our needs, and it is clearly a rational goal that we be effective in what we do; it is better to hit the nail than the thumb when using a hammer. But instruments are not the whole life, and life is not an instrument.

We started by criticizing some attempts to derive from nature a program for society. This enterprise quickly led us to deep waters: the problem clearly is not just that some current proposals are inadequate and more appropriate programs are needed instead, but that the culture–nature relationship needs to be addressed from several directions that are apparently at quite a distance from immediate ecological problems and from each other.

Returning back to ecology, we should figure out ways of integrating ecological knowledge with social affairs without constructing prescriptive rules. Maybe the basic obligation is to make conscious choices. Maybe the slogan 'living in harmony with nature' could mean acting in such a way that our actions really support our goals. If we intend to continue producing crops in a region, we have to protect the soil. If we expect to maintain a city, there must be sources of fresh water. The first workable definition of living in harmony with nature is that we recognize in practice a correspondence between ends and means.

But this requires that our ends also be achievable and that different ends are compatible. Not all ends are compatible. For instance, it is not possible to achieve simultaneously slow population growth, a young population and long life expectancy. It is not possible to increase consumption indefinitely beyond the capacity of land to produce. We could calculate absolute limits to growth for particular criteria – for instance, if all the carbon in the biosphere were in human biomass how many people would there be? But these are sterile exercises. The constraints on our goals are both more complex and more flexible.

This line of argument continues Barry Commoner's theme that nature knows best. But there are also counterarguments. Consider for example the tundra, an ecological formation only a few million years old. One might propose that life has not yet had time to adapt to tundra conditions and propose intensive plans to make the tundra more hospitable for life. An evolutionary argument might further note that extant groups of organisms, such as the grasses, are historically new. By clever artificial selection and biotechnology we could help evolution along and create whole new families of plants that would be able to colonize environments now on the margin of life. A geo-climatological argument would point out that the climate of the recent million years or so is abnormal for the earth. If we provoke the 'greenhouse effect', it will be only restoring nature to its normal condition that prevailed before the Ice Age, a few million years ago.

Finally, it could be argued that like it or not we are changing nature, as do all species. The only option we have is to determine how we shall change it, whether by conscious planning based on our best knowledge or capriciously in the service of narrow interests.

Most of us would find such reasoning chilling. It presumes a level of knowledge and understanding far beyond anything ever achieved, planning on a scale greater than has previously been attempted, a communality of interest of all humanity that does not exist, and a consensus that has never been approached even for more modest goals. The point, however, is that nature herself does not tell us what to do. Thus, nature is not immediately given as a factor in social scenarios. Nature is mute, she does not give us explicit advice; she only forbids, sometimes only post festum. We cannot evade responsibility by pretending that our choices are dictated to us from outside or assume that doing nothing is acting wisely.

2

Ecological Patterns

Kevo: Life in the Subarctic

When heading toward the Subarctic, you might take along your whiskey but you need not carry ice.

Leo Rybak[1]

Imagine yourself standing outside the Kevo biological station in Finnish Lapland, about 69.5° north of the equator, far beyond the Arctic Circle. The station is situated ashore a small lake on the side of a gently rising hill. The lake is part of the Utsjoki river system, and the waters flowing by the station ultimately end up in the Arctic Ocean off the Norwegian coast.

The dominating forest type in the immediate surroundings is subarctic birch forest, but bare hilltops are visible in the distance, spotted by snow until late summer. By a conventional definition this habitat might not be called a forest at all: trees are low, 3–5 meters in height, and spaced several meters from each other. The undergrowth is sparse as well, with low willows here and there, decorated with a few odd junipers. The ground is covered by a carpet of low shrubs such as heather, blueberry and dwarf birch. The habitat resembles an orchard more than a forest.

We invite you to adopt the perspective of a curious frog, wanting to inspect from her own perspective what is going on in this particular ecological environment. To facilitate the inspection we present in Figure 2.1 a schematic picture of the landscape.

But are you wondering why anybody should be interested in the surroundings of Kevo? For the frog the answer is simple: she has got to make a living. Lapps, whose ancestors colonized the region a few thousand years ago, would give the same answer. Our answer is related: to succeed in adopting a sustainable way of life on the earth we need to understand ecology, but ecological regularities do not hang

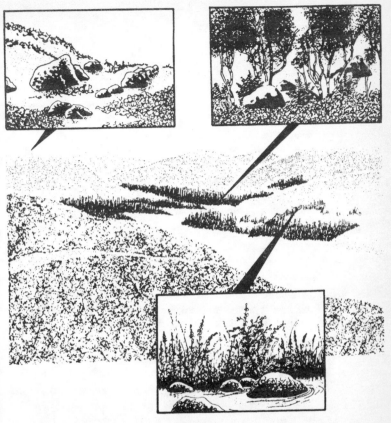

Figure 2.1
The mosaic landscape at Kevo, Finnish Lapland

in the air over a uniform globe, they are tied to specific localities and circumstances. Comparisons of different geographical regions facilitate an understanding of what is general in ecology, valid over a variety of circumstances, and what is unique for each locality.

Taiga – Forest Tundra – Tundra

The birch stands surrounding the biological station belong to the northernmost forest type in Europe. As a matter of fact, here grow the northernmost forests in the whole world, which is due to the ameliorating influence of the northern Atlantic Gulf Stream on the climate in northwestern Europe. The habitat is a part of the *forest tundra*, which is a transition belt between uniform northern boreal forests, the *taiga*, and open arctic habitats, generically called *tundra*.

The physiognomy of the forest tundra is quite uniform over the whole belt from northwestern Europe through Siberia and subarctic North America to Labrador/New Foundland. Tree stands are restricted to more sheltered parts of the terrain such as valleys between hills and mountains. At higher elevations open tundra dominates in its different variants such as dry heath, tundra peatlands, and boulder stone 'fields' on the hillsides.

Plant geographers define the *tree line* as the northernmost limit reached by trees, and the *timber line* as the northern border of continuous forests. The birch is the tree line tree, and pine the timber line tree in Finnish Lapland. These species are unique to northwestern Europe. The tree line tree is larch in Siberia and black spruce in North America. The timber line is made up by spruce on the southern Scandinavian mountains and in western Russia.

An obvious problem a curious frog comes across while leaping around in the Kevo terrain is, which factors determine the location of the timber and tree lines in the north? She readily concludes that the locations have not been constant through time: remains of pines lie scattered in areas covered by pure birch stands today, and old birch stumps are common on heathlands far above present birch forests.

A general criterion for the subsistence of a population at its range boundary is that new births and immigration from other populations compensate deaths and emigration. To begin with, the organisms must be able to survive the hazards of the environment and reproduce. Main factors threatening the survival of individual trees in this environment are physical: climatic stress and lack of nutrients in the soil. The most severe stress caused by the subarctic climate to trees occurs in late winter. It is usually a period of low precipitation and cold, clear weather, and the humidity of the air is very low. As a consequence, all parts of the vegetation not covered by snow face the danger of drying up.

Cold temperature as such is not that critical. Trees can stand low winter temperatures thanks to biochemical changes in their tissues, but great temperature variations in late winter, with warm sunshine in the daytime and extreme cold during the night may prove disastrous. This is true of soil invertebrates as well; temperatures oscillating above and below the freezing point are particularly hazardous. Generalizing, it is an important principle in ecology that often *patterns of variation* are more important than *average values*.

However, the survival of individual trees is not sufficient for the maintenance of a population. The population members must also reproduce; few populations can be sustained on the sole basis of immigration from other areas in the long run. Reproduction of the trees need not be successful every summer. Birch trees are capable of producing seeds for several decades, and pine trees for a couple of centuries. What is needed is that new seedlings compensate mortality among adult trees.

Successful seed production depends on environmental conditions, particularly temperature. Both flowering and getting seeds to ripen require energy that must be available in excess of what is needed for the physiological subsistence of the trees.

Reproductive physiology of pine trees in the north has been extensively studied because pine provides valuable timber. Flowering depends on the weather of the previous summer when buds were prepared. There is great variation among years in this respect, and the variation tends to increase toward the north. Flowering occurs early in the summer, and the subsequent ripening of the seeds depends critically on the temperature during the following summer months. Critical variables can be clumped together into one variable called 'degree days' which simply equals the sum of the temperatures above a certain minimum multiplied by the number of days with that temperature. If the necessary amount of degree days is not reached, seeds will not germinate, however many fertilized seed the flowering season might have produced.

From this observation we can draw a generalization as regards ecological methodology. It is often possible to reduce the number of parameters (corresponding to various environmental factors) that are actually operative in the system by forming a composite *sufficient parameter* (Levins, 1966). Degree days is such a sufficient parameter. A sufficient parameter is an artificial but convenient way to pool together various types of information and ignore some, in order to make the system more tractable. It is a 'many-to-one' description of the original set of parameters. The variable 'degree days' is an entirely artificial construct but is useful for describing and predicting the reproductive success of northern trees. For example, the age structure of northern pine stands is extremely uneven with most individual trees belonging to a few age classes. Using temperature records of the past, the years which produced the age classes can be identified as those with warm summers.

What do we know about factors causing mortality in northern pine populations? Clearly the first few years (or maybe decades in the north) are a critical period in a tree's life. The young seedling may succumb in competition with other plants – for light or, which may be more probable in the open northern habitats, for critical nutrients. It may be tramped upon by a reindeer, or its bark may be eaten up by a vole, or a herbivorous insect may destroy its needles, and so on. However, once a pine reaches a reasonable size, there are two main factors threatening its survival: natural catastrophes such as heavy winds and forest fires, or human disturbance.

Fluctuations in the location of the timber line were probably caused by two main groups of factors: climate and catastrophes, natural or human-induced. The climate of northwestern Europe has fluctuated a lot since the latest glaciation. Four to five thousand years ago the climate was considerably warmer than today. Analyses of pollen deposited in lakes and peatlands demonstrate corresponding changes in the distribution of forests which have retreated toward the south during the last few thousand years. This is presumably not because of climatic changes alone, but increasing disturbance, mainly due to human activities, has also had a role. Forest fires probably became more frequent since the colonization of Lapland by the Lapps. Cutting trees for fuel or household purposes as well as the increasing pressure on forest regeneration by reindeer husbandry are purely human influences of fairly recent origin.

It is next to impossible to separate 'natural' disturbances from human-induced ones among factors that have caused the timber line retreat. This gives rise to another important generalization: human influence on ecological systems has been a cardinal factor even in such a sparsely populated area as northern Lapland for thousands of years. Human influences usually intensify or modify such factors that would be present even without humans, that is, *human beings are natural agents in ecological systems*.

Natural Catastrophes: the Autumnal Moth

What we said above about reproduction of trees is valid mainly for the pine in the north. The birch shares similarities with the pine but it also shows important differences. First of all, successful seed production years are much more frequent in birch than in pine, and the birch also regenerates efficiently vegetatively which pine is not able to do at all. In the Scandinavian mountains birch trees produce some seeds practically every year, and birch is thus able to track climatic changes more closely than pine, an important factor for its being the tree line species (Kullman, 1987). Owing to vegetative regeneration, birch trees tend to be superior in competition for space.

However, birch trees in northern Lapland are threatened by natural catastrophes of another kind: mass outbreaks of the 'autumnal moth' (*Epirrita autumnata*). The larvae of the moth use birch leaves as their food in early summer, and during mass years extensive tracts of birch forests can be completely defoliated. The latest mass occurrence of the autumnal moth in the Kevo region took place in 1965–6: the area of forest completely destroyed has been estimated at 5000 km^2 and a fair proportion of this area (*c.*1350 km^2) will probably remain treeless for decades if not centuries to come, because of the following chain of factors:

[1] The birch trees were unable to regenerate vegetatively, and extensive birch stands died out entirely; this was partly due to exceptionally harsh weather conditions which prevented birch trees from storing resources necessary for regeneration;

[2] following the destruction of trees, water balance in the soil changed and the microclimate became moister than before;

[3] the ground became covered by a thick layer of mosses that grow on moist soil;

[4] mammalian herbivores, reindeer and voles ate up the few birch shoots that sprang up from the ground;

[5] as a consequence, the prospects of germinating are dim for the odd birch seeds that disperse from areas where birch forests survived the outbreak (Haukioja et al., 1988).

A particularly interesting phenomenon observed by ecologists working at the Kevo biological station was the ability of birch trees to build up chemical defense against the moth larvae (Haukioja and Niemelä, 1979). The chemicals involved are mainly phenols that do not naturally occur in birch leaves in concentrations high enough to prevent the moth larvae from consuming them but when leaf damage by larvae begins, phenol concentration begins to rise in adjacent leaves and the growth of larvae is retarded within a couple of days.

A purely mechanical destruction of the foliage is sufficient to induce the reaction.

The term 'chemical defense' implies that the synthesis of these compounds brings some physiological costs to the trees in terms of energy use. Otherwise, why not have the compounds in the tissues all the time? In which case it would be impossible for a human observer to identify their presence as a reaction to the moth pests.

The ability of birch trees to build up chemical defence against the moth larvae is restricted by both lack of nutrients and cold climate. In the short term it is influenced by weather conditions: in a warm summer birch trees damaged mechanically responded more strongly than in a cool one (Haukioja et al., 1985). There is a time lag in the working of the defence mechanism. It takes some time to build up resistence when a new outbreak begins. On the other hand, resistence lasts for 3–4 years once it is achieved whereafter the trees are again susceptible to a new outbreak. This build up of defence and ensuing relaxation is a factor promoting cyclicity in the moth population – the outbreaks occur in the Scandinavian mountains quite regularly in 9–10 year cycles. The defence ability of the trees seems to be genetically determined (Haukioja et al., 1985). This implies that the moth may influence the evolution of the birch on a yet longer time scale – resistant variants survive the recurring catastrophes and their frequency increases in later tree generations (Kallio et al., 1983).

The possibility that such a phenomenon as an inducible chemical defense system evolves in plants obviously requires that mass outbreaks of the pest be fairly frequent. It is not possible to become genetically adapted to unique events. In the case of disastrous events that have a characteristic, albeit statistical, frequency in time (such as pest outbreaks), the genotype of the members of a population subjected to it functions as a kind of 'memory': the ability to respond biochemically to increasing damage by pests is potentially present in an individual plant even though the plant would never *de facto* be subjected to the threat.

This brings forth an important generalization again: ecological phenomena take place in *different time scales* that are interwoven in complex ways. Individuals may respond instantaneously to changes in the environment. Mobile animals move to other places, but plants also have 'behavioral' responses, reactive changes in the state of the organism. Populations are another level of ecological organization, with response times an order of magnitude slower than those on the individual level. In the lifetime of an individual birch tree a moth

outbreak may be a unique event, but in the lifetime of birch populations outbreaks occur with a characteristic frequency (although
single outbreaks are triggered by various combinations of contingent
circumstances).

Biotopes – Habitats – Microsites

When our curious frog turns her attention toward plants smaller than
trees, an important observation that she very soon makes is that the
vegetation tends to vary among different sites although changes
from site to site are fairly continuous. The environment can be
divided into different biotopes, characterized by a particular combination of dominant plant species, such as barren birch forest, alpine
heath, lush woods at sheltered sites along small streams and so on.

Relative differences between different biotopes appear fairly slight
in Lapland compared with temperate or tropical areas. A simple
explanation is that the number of plant species is very low in subarctic
regions: the number of vascular plant species recorded in the Kevo
region is 315. In a tropical forest, in contrast, a few hundred species
of woody plants alone might be found in an area of some tens of
hectares! A few characteristic plants, particularly low shrubs, seem
to dominate all biotopes in Lapland, whereas in more southern areas
dominant species are usually different in different biotopes.

Variations between biotopes within a single region give rise to
another generalization: the relation of environmental variance *between*
biotopes to environmental variance *within* biotopes is critical. In the
Subarctic environmental conditions may show dramatic variations
within each biotope but these variations tend to be synchronous and
similar across biotopes. Snow falling during a midsummer cold spell
covers birch forests, heathlands and lush woods equally. This implies
that once an organism is able to cope with the basics of the environment, it makes a relatively minor difference which particular biotope
it happens to be in.

The fairly high between-biotope similarity is an observation our
curious frog will probably also make at Kevo when she turns her
attention to animals, but here she would have a great opportunity to
make important contributions to ecology: appropriate data on the distribution of animal species across different biotopes are very scarce.

Apparently the difference between forested and open biotopes is
important for many animals, for instance, birds (Järvinen and
Väisänen, 1976). Abundant species of forested biotopes, such as the

willow warbler, occur in all kinds of environments with stands of trees or bushes, but open biotopes have a completely different avifauna and peatlands are dominated by waders.

A frog is ultimately more interested in edible invertebrates than in trees or birds, and our curious frog is no exception. She will not find a rich invertebrate fauna at Kevo compared with what she would find in more southern areas. She can easily find illustrative figures as the Kevo region has been an object of intensive ecological studies since the establishment of the biological station there in 1957 (the investigations are greatly furthered by ability to use the library of the biological station; this is a recent adaptation of frogs to ecology books).

Faunistically better investigated groups include butterflies, moths and geometrids (lumped together under the general name *Macrolepidoptera*), and spiders. The number of species of Macrolepidopterans known from Kevo is 238 and from northern Lapland altogether 522, according to a list compiled in 1980. The figures are very low indeed: a relevant comparison can be made using samples collected with light traps, commonly used for sampling moths and geometrids. Light traps were in operation at the Kevo station through several summers in the 1970s, and the highest abundance was found in 1973 with 22.8 individuals per trap and night, on average, and 112 species in total in three traps (Koponen and Linnaluoto, 1979). Corresponding figures in southern Finland would be a few hundreds of individuals per trap and night, and 200–50 species per season in one trap. Janzen (1988) compared species richness of the whole caterpillar fauna of three reasonably well studied regions, covering about 100 km^2 each, namely Kevo Station, Ithaca (New York) and Santa Rosa National Park (Costa Rica), and gave the following figures: 264, 1577 and 3142, respectively.

Invertebrates are distributed over the habitats similarly to birds: forested habitats (birch and pine forests) tend to be more similar to each other than to open habitats, but individual species show very variable degrees of habitat specificity. Let the ground-living spiders serve as an illustration (all data are from Koponen, 1976): the fauna of birch forests is richer than that of pine forests or open heaths – 82, 66 and 43 species were found in samples collected with approximately equal effort from each of the habitats, respectively – and average densities show a similar relationship – 234, 114 and 89 individuals/m^2, respectively.

The terms *habitat* and *biotope* refer to the environment required by a particular species and to a particular environmental type, respectively. Biotopes are usually identified with plant communities: a subalpine birch forest is a 'biotope', included in the 'habitat range' of the willow warbler. It is often useful to apply yet another term to the specific microscale conditions required by specialized species, namely, *microhabitat* or *microsite*. For instance, microhabitats required by specialized spider species in the Kevo region include particular types of bogs, moist depressions with *Sphagneta* mosses, lake and river shores, and stone belts and cliffs, each one of them hosting several typical species. One species resides in juniper bushes, and one peculiar species lives in the snow, being most commonly caught in March–May.

Through inspecting the spatial distribution of spiders in the environment, our frog is becoming aware of a new important generalization: in defining the habitats of different organisms, the relevant *spatial scales* often differ. What is a basic environmental characteristic for a small species – a moist patch with decaying leaves for a ground-living spider – is usually irrelevant minuscule variation for a larger species such as raven or elk. At any particular site in nature these different scales are simultaneously present. This means that there is no single 'correct' way of defining spatial units but the definition must always be related to some particular organisms. The scale is 'constituted' by the organisms considered.

The smallest scale in terrestrial systems is constituted by microorganisms living in the soil. Our frog has an excellent grasp of spiders and flies, but microorganisms might as well be another heap of dirt under her leaping feet – and yet the microfauna of the soil consists of hundreds of thousands of individuals per m². The two important groups of soil microinvertebrates in the north are mites and springtails. Soil bacteria are far smaller yet than mites and springtails. Bacteria, together with fungi, decompose the organic matter accumulating on the ground; decomposition is indirectly enhanced by the activities of nematodes, mites, springtails, earthworms and the whole range of soil-dwelling animals.

Interactions among Species

Our frog is particularly interested in flies, and in the library of the Kevo station she may come across an exciting example of ecological adaptation in a study on a blowfly species (*Cynomyia mortuorum*) by

Pekka Nuorteva (1972) in another subarctic fell in Finnish Lapland. Blowflies participate in the decomposition of vertebrate carcasses in terrestrial environments. Females lay their eggs in carcasses, and larvae hatching from the eggs feed upon the carcass, which has already been invaded and made digestible for the larvae by bacteria. After a period of growth the larvae pupate, usually on the ground some way from the carcass, and adult flies are hatched in due time. The length of this cycle, the development time of the larvae, is a critical feature in the life cycle of the flies.

Nuorteva had earlier observed that these blowflies are more abundant in the alpine tundra zone on the top of the fell than in birch forests lower down. He made rearing experiments at different altitudes on the fell to find out which are the most favorable conditions for larval development. The experiment was repeated in three consecutive years, and great variation was observed between the years, the development times being 72.3, 46.7 and 50.1 days, on average, in each year. By and large these differences were attributable to temperature. The higher the temperature on average, the more rapid the development.

The relation is more interesting than that, however. Nuorteva noticed that the response of the development time of the flies to variations in temperature was *nonlinear*. The optimum seemed to be at 17°C, the development time being longer at both lower and higher temperatures. The development was *retarded* by cold weather in a nonlinear fashion. Nuorteva noticed that when the daily mean minimum temperature in the soil was +7°C or higher, the development time remained the same, but when the temperature was lower than +7°C the development slowed down considerably.

From these data the frog can draw two generalizations: first, as noted by Nuorteva, the conditions of larval development are indeed important for the distribution of blowflies along the fellside. Adult flies are most active in direct sunshine ('heliophilous'), and the conditions for larval development are optimal in open terrain as well. Hence the preference for open biotopes. An interesting corollary is that the destruction of birch forests due to mass outbreaks of the autumnal moth is expected to broaden the range of optimal habitats for the blowflies – and this is exactly what has been observed. The moth has an indirect positive effect on the blowfly populations.

The second generalization is more abstract, related to the nature of time in ecological processes such as the life cycle of the blowfly. It is often misleading to measure time solely by the watch or the calendar. Time in ecological processes is constituted by the ecological processes themselves, that is, a 'unit of time' has elapsed when a particular process has gone through, whatever its length measured in minutes. In development processes this is often called *physiological time* (Pajunen, 1983; Van Straalen, 1983). By influencing the rate of physiological processes temperature shortens or lengthens the development time of blowflies *relative to the calendar*, but as 'physiological time' the development time is constant. The calendar gives an average measure of the flow of time in the physical environment. The mutual relationship of physiological time within the blowfly and physical time in the surroundings is critical. Either they are concordant with each other, or they are not – in the latter case it is worse for the blowflies.

Let our curious frog next become interested in which creatures can sustain themselves on birch. The autumnal moth was already disclosed as a major pest of the European subarctic birch. The herbivorous fauna living on birch comprises many more species, however. Most of them feed upon birch leaves as larvae, similar to the autumnal moth. This army of herbivorous pests exerts a considerable burden on the birch trees: the proportion of untouched leaves in birch trees was merely 10.5 per cent in an investigation at Kevo (out of 8753 leaves selected at random).

We have already found an indirect dependence of blowflies on the autumnal moth, a herbivore of birch leaves. It is to be expected that more direct interactions exist as well – and that is the case. Important direct interactions occur between birch herbivores and their predators such as birds and small mammals, which feed upon pupating larvae on the ground.

A particularly important group of predators upon herbivores are parasitic wasps called parasitoids; the taxonomic group *Ichneumonidae* is particularly important. Females of these creatures lay their eggs in the larvae (or pupae) of other insects, and the offspring grow by consuming the doomed host 'from the inside'. The degree of specialization in the host selection of parasitoids is variable – some species are generalists, able to parasitize a broad variety of other insects, whereas others specialize in only one or a few host species.

A natural ecological problem is, how rapidly do parasitoid populations respond to abundance fluctuations in host populations? This is also a classical problem of population dynamics, intensively studied since the late 1920s. For species that are scarce in nature collecting an adequate set of data is practically impossible, but the *Epirrita* moth with its parasitoids is an easier object of study. Jussila and Nuorteva (1968) published data on the composition of the ichneumonid wasp fauna in relation to the latest autumnal moth outbreak in Finnish Lapland. The general trend was very clear: the number of wasps per trap and day was of the order of 0.01 individuals in two years preceding the outbreak, 1.6 individuals in the outbreak year, but 11.6 individuals in the first post-outbreak year. Furthermore, two wasp species (*Trachysphyrus albatorius* (Vill.) and *Coccygomimus sodalis sodalis* (Ruthe)) comprised 97.1 per cent and 99.6 per cent of the composition of the catches in the outbreak and post-outbreak years respectively, but were not found at all in the preceding years. It is a fair assumption that these two species specialize in larvae of the autumnal moth.

The outbreak clearly had a cardinal influence on the wasp fauna. What is less clear is the effect of wasps on the moths. They obviously destroy a great number of individual moth larvae, as do birds which also show a marked response to moth outbreaks (Enemar et al., 1984). But here we are confronted by a problem of translating observations from one level of ecological organization to another – an important general problem in ecology once again. The significance or insignificance of wasp-parasitism and bird-predation to the occurrence and dynamics of the moths is determined on the population level instead of the individual level. It is one thing to observe that a willow warbler eats up a few larvae, but another thing to claim that willow warblers control the moth population, although the incident is final for those individual larvae. Direct extrapolations of observations from the individual level to the population level are, as a rule, unjustifiable. In the case of the autumnal moth, the influence of parasitoids and predators on its population dynamics is unknown although some Swedish data suggest that parasitoids may contribute to the population crash following the outbreak in the moth (Haukioja et al., 1988).

There is another insect species that responds strongly and rapidly to a sudden increase in numbers of the moth larvae: the wood ant (*Formica aquilonia* Yarrow); it is the only representative in the European subarctic of the group of wood ants, conspicuous inhabitants of the taiga. The ants are abundant at altitudes below 240 m but not higher, and they are important predators on invertebrates on birch at Kevo. A few years after the latest outbreak an interesting pattern was found in a nearly-destroyed birch forest at Kevo. Sharply limited stands of healthy birches were scattered as 'green islands' in the destroyed forests, and always with an ant mound in the middle. It turned out that the ants can efficiently protect birch trees against the increasing moth larvae by rapidly switching their prey preferences to the larvae abundantly available. However, the radius of the protected area is relatively short, of the order of 20 m from the nest, because of superabundance of the larvae relative to needs of the ants. Ants do not patrol as far from the mound in years with abundant prey as in normal years. In all years, however, the birch trees situated close to an ant mound tend to have fewer traces of herbivores in the foliage than the trees at a greater distance (Laine and Niemelä, 1980).

If our frog compares the different responses of wasps and ants to the increase in numbers of moths during an outbreak with each other, she detects that they are of two different types. The increase in population size observed in wasps is called *numerical response*, and the switch in hunting behavior in the ants, *functional response*. These two types go together when, for instance, willow warblers both increase in numbers in localities with high numbers of moth larvae because a greater number of pairs find it pleasant there (numerical response) and simultaneously include a large proportion of larvae in their diet (functional response).

Let our curious frog continue her investigations of the fascinating ecological processes in subarctic Europe, but her latest findings lead to a generalization again: there are interactions of various kinds in ecological systems, but a major task is to find out which ones among them are critical. The answer is usually not at all obvious from the outset. Who would predict that a moth feeding upon leaves of birch trees has a major effect on the reproductive success of blowflies, living in reindeer carcasses? Thus, the slogan 'everything affects everything' is not strictly correct. Everything affects something, and is affected by something, which is a completely different matter.

The Taiga

These are not Chekhov's cherished cherry trees
that fell down long ago.
This is the eternal taiga now
that still stands up against all winds
dark scars upon the bark.

Lawrence Ferlinghetti[2]

Unfortunately, the perspective of a frog, however inquisitive her personality, is gravely insufficient for understanding ecological processes: her life-span is far too short, and the distances she can cover are far too small. The ecology of any one environment remains a mystery if observations cannot be collected from wider areas and over long periods of time. This, incidentally, is a basic problem in practical ecological research: most research projects run out of funding long before sufficient data sets have been collected.

Lawrence Ferlinghetti began to marvel at the eternal taiga during his trip on the TransSiberian railway. Let us follow his lead and have a closer look at the dominating vegetation zone of the northern hemisphere, the taiga, which, after all, begins just 100 km to the south of Kevo. But a train does not give an optimal perspective to the taiga, being tied to a definite route. Therefore we adopt the perspective of an eagle to complement that of the frog.

Northern European eagles are golden eagles (*Aquila chrysaetos*). They are basically forest birds and construct their nest in trees, usually on hillsides offering a good view over the surrounding landscape, although further south golden eagles usually nest on cliffs. Our eagle has for some time been bothered by the question: how much do forests in the Kevo region differ from those in other parts of the world? Where can one find similar regions, and why are these particular regions more like Kevo than some other ones? This is a classical biogeographic problem that Europeans began to ponder upon toward the late eighteenth century after explorations of different parts of the world had widened their sphere of experience. We reproduce in Figure 2.2 a schematic overview of the Eurasian continent to facilitate the investigation (adopted from Hämet-Ahti, 1981).

Biogeography: Zonality and History

The concept of a *biogeographic zone* is an important descriptive tool used in geographic comparisons. It was a recurring observation made by early explorers that biota tend to form zones. Distinct vegetation zones stretching from east to west are particularly clear-cut in northern parts of both the Old and the New World, from temperate over boreal to subarctic and arctic environments, but mountain ranges break this east–west regularity.

The taiga borders on forest tundra and tundra in the north. Toward the south it grades into broad-leaved forests in maritime climates, and forest steppe and steppe in the arid climates in inner parts of the

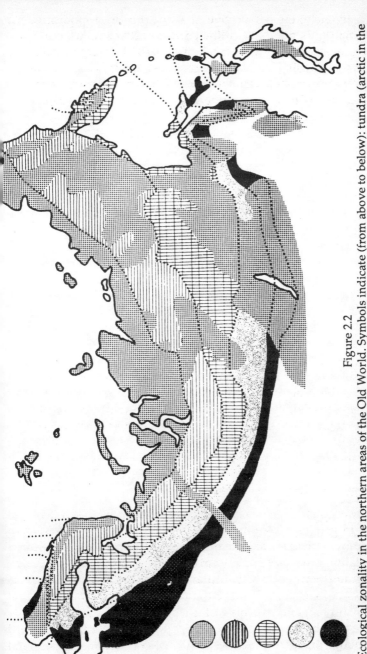

Figure 2.2

Ecological zonality in the northern areas of the Old World. Symbols indicate (from above to below): tundra (arctic in the north, alpine in southern mountains), and northern boreal, mid-boreal, southern boreal and hemiboreal forest zones. Note how mountain regions break the regularity of the latitudinal zonality.

Source: Hämet-Ahti (1981)

continents. Coniferous forests are not restricted to the continuous, northern taiga belt however but also grow at high elevations in southern mountains. A comparison of such taiga 'islands' with the continuous taiga of the north is a fascinating and largely unexplored biogeographic·problem.

How uniform are plant and animal communities in different parts of the taiga? The physiognomy of major biotopes as well as the outlook of landscapes are very similar over the whole taiga range, on both continents, as has been testified by a great number of explorers and voyagers. Our eagle will find very similar landscapes to those in Kevo when she flies far enough to the east and arrives at the biological station of Aborigen in the Soviet Far East, some 200 km north of the city of Magadan. However, the identity of species making up these biotopes varies considerably from Fennoscandia to Magadan. For instance, around Aborigen the dominating tree is larch, with an undergrowth of a mountain pine (*Pinus pumila*) and a dwarf birch (*Betula middendorfii*).

As regards the trees of old, mature taiga, three features deserve particular emphasis (Hare, 1954). First, the number of dominant tree species is low in all parts of the taiga. In northwestern Europe mature forests are dominated by one pine (*Pinus silvestris*) and one spruce (*Picea abies*) species, and half a dozen broad-leaved ones (in the genera *Betula*, *Populus*, *Salix* and *Sorbus*), patchily distributed according to soil conditions and more or less scarce in mature forests. In eastern Siberia and throughout North America the numbers are a bit higher but, nevertheless, very low compared with more southern forests. Second, a change in species identities, or 'species turnover', occurs from north to south, that is, dominating species tend to be different in southern subzones compared with the northern ones although some species occupy a dominant position in several subzones. Third, tree species are different although closely related on the two continents and, in addition, the list of dominant trees of the Siberian Far East is composed of species that do not occur in Europe at all, and the same holds true of New Foundland trees compared with those in British Columbia. In other words, species turnover is complete over the whole east–west range on both continents, presumably due to historical reasons.

The Finnish botanist Ilmari Hustich (1974) used the term 'ecological vicariants' for taxonomically and ecologically related plant species that substitute each other on the two continents; for instance, the Norwegian spruce (*Picea abies*) and black spruce (*Picea maritima*) are 'ecological vicariants'. 'Ecological vicariants' are also readily named in low shrubs which are a dominant element in taiga biotopes, for instance, species in the genera *Vaccinium* on upland sites and *Ledum* on bogs.

But next we follow the natural inclinations of an eagle and turn our eyes toward more attractive objects, birds and mammals. B.K. Stegman studied in the 1930s the distribution of birds over the whole Eurasian continent and ended up with an interesting theoretical hypothesis (Stegman, 1938; the work is discussed at some length by Haila and Järvinen, 1990). He began by investigating distribution patterns of birds particularly adapted to breed in boreal coniferous habitats. These birds number 54 species; he characterized them as taiga species. Stegman noticed that, according to distribution maps, the numbers of birds restricted to coniferous forests are highest in eastern Siberia (42) and decline toward western Siberia (30), northern Russia (25), and northwestern (24) and western (12) Europe.

The explanation Stegman gave to the patterns he found is based on an evolutionary view of the history of the taiga zone. An important notion he adopted is that of a *faunal type*. Species adapted to reside in biotopes that dominate a certain biogeographic zone belong, according to Stegman, to the faunal type of that zone. The species of the taiga belong to the Siberian faunal type, the species of the tundra to the Arctic faunal type, and so on. Stegman further concluded that each faunal type is historically closely connected with the respective biogeographic zone and, for instance, typical taiga birds have thus evolved together with taiga biotopes during the last few million years.

There are several theoretical problems in Stegman's scheme, as discussed by Haila and Järvinen (1990). One of them is that he over-interpreted the data by assuming that the birds of the taiga form a coherent and unified faunistic group. Brunov (1980) has concluded on the basis of more detailed distribution maps that southern parts of the taiga differ from central and northern parts with respect to their bird fauna. The northern subzones host 32 species which probably have their origin in the taiga, whereas the southern subzone has 11 species that have strong connections to other forest types further south.

Nevertheless, with Stegman's work *history* appears as a major element in explaining current distributions of different species of the taiga. This is an important theoretical conclusion. The particular aspect of history that is important in the boreal zone is the Ice Age.

Let our eagle pick up a few natural history books and try to find out what it was all about.

The 'Ice Age' began some two million years ago and has included a number of glacial periods such as the latest one that ended some 10 000 years ago. It is believed that the period of glaciation has comprised some 17 glacial cycles, each one of them consisting of a glacial and an interglacial phase of varying length and uniformity, but it seems that glacial periods have been longer than the more favorable 'interglacial' periods. At present we are experiencing an interglacial period, and the present climatic type is, correspondingly, exceptional on a time scale that extends over the whole age of glaciations.

This means that conditions in the north have varied enormously over the last two million years. Most of the time vast areas have been covered by ice – although the extensions of the continental glaciations have varied from one glacial phase to the next – and every now and then, once in 100 000 years on average, the ice masses have disappeared and new land has become available for colonization by plants and animals.

A natural question to ask next is, how similar has the northern flora and fauna been during different interglacials? Not very similar. The fossil pollen record facilitates a fairly detailed reconstruction of the composition of ancient tree floras as well as of the fluctuations in distribution patterns of individual tree species. Such data from both Europe and North America show great variation in the distributions of different tree species from one interglacial period to the next (Huntley and Birks, 1983; Birks, 1986; Davis, 1986). Paleontological evidence on animals is, unfortunately, far poorer than on plants. G.R. Coope (1987) has analysed subfossil remains of beetles from the British Isles and found remarkable fluctuations in species ranges and composition of local assemblages during the latest glaciations. Beetles tracked temperature changes more closely than trees, being more efficient colonizers of new habitats thanks to their ability to move about actively.

There is clearly a strong element of historical contingency in the composition of northern floras and faunas. The variation in tree species composition of northern forests on a time scale of a few thousand years seems attributable to chance factors in the migrations of individual tree species. The tree that is most characteristic of fertile forest types in Finland today, the Norwegian spruce (*Picea abies*), invaded different parts of the country 5000–2000 years ago and is still advancing westwards in the Norwegian mountains.

But the story of the Ice Age also includes regular, cyclic changes in soil quality during each interglacial period, driven by climate and the influence of vegetation on the soil (Birks, 1986). The soil cycle hypothesis has an extremely important practical implication: *soil quality is not a constant* but, rather, subject to continuous change due to natural processes. Human activities can of course accelerate the process. This is a fact forest managers tend to neglect, with potentially disastrous consequences.

The evolution of the taiga as a vegetation complex has occurred during the Ice Age. A characteristic shared by all plant species growing in the taiga is cold-hardiness, necessary because of the cold winter. The taiga probably originated in eastern parts of the Old World arctic, and coniferous forests have probably most of the time covered larger areas in eastern parts of the Palearctic than in the west. This suggests that animal species adapted to live in the taiga have their evolutionary origin in the eastern Palearctic as well. This brings us back to Stegman: according to his explanation, the number of taiga birds is highest in eastern Siberia because that is where the species evolved. Their success in spreading toward the west has been historically limited because of intervening, unfavorable habitats.

Stegman's ideas relate to basic issues in ecological biogeography which aims at giving ecological explanations to biogeographic patterns. Biogeography deals with distributional data, but in ecology *population densities* are ultimately far more interesting than distribution ranges which, for any given locality, reveal only the potential presence or absence of a particular species. Distributional data and quantitative data can give partly conflicting results in biogeographic comparisons.

It depends on the question asked whether mere distributional data are relevant or not. There is no strict division-line between biogeography and ecology, but the distinction is only a matter of convenience. One can also ask questions about the interface, for instance, about the relation between population distributions and numbers: usually species are locally more abundant, and inhabit a broader array of biotopes, in central parts of their range than close to range boundaries. Data for assessing broad biogeographic patterns are usually not available because ecologists have had few opportunities for conducting censuses in appropriate spatial and temporal scales, but Kouki and Häyrynen (1991) found support for both of these assumptions in a study on the distribution of birds in peatlands in Finland.

Regional and Local Scales

But that is enough of large-scale biogeographic patterns. Our eagle is slowly gliding back toward northwestern Europe and the Kevo region. She has become interested in whether general biogeographic regularities allow insight into the ecology of a particular region such as Fennoscandia.

Being familiar with ice-age dynamics, she is now aware that historical factors are of utmost importance for the biotic composition of northwestern Europe. When studying the present distributions of different organisms within a 'region' such as Fennoscandia, our eagle comes across a new type of spatial heterogeneity of the environment, and a new type of change in time. Ecological communities tend to vary from one place to another, regularly across biotopes but also irregularly and without any apparent correlations with environmental conditions. But communities also change through time. Our eagle may ask the following questions: how regular is the change in time? How does change in time at one site relate to variation over several sites at one moment of time?

Preston (1960) originally suggested that in some situations time and space may be 'equivalent variables' in ecology. This would be true if variation in time at any particular site would go through stages that are (roughly) similar to the spectrum of communities found over the surrounding sites at one point of time.

Preston's idea is useful for envisaging ecological processes in the taiga. Virgin taiga was previously a 'fire ecosystem' both in the Old and in the New World (Zackrisson, 1977; Kuleshova, 1981; Heinselman, 1973; Wright and Bailey, 1982). Vegetation dynamics in the taiga was determined by forest fires which were frequent and followed a 'natural fire rotation'. The frequency of forest fires was in recent centuries in northwestern Europe about once in 80 to 120 years, and estimates from North America are roughly similar. The average area burned at a time was some tens of hectares in northwestern Europe but varied greatly across regions depending on topography. Frequent forest fires created a mosaic landscape of different-aged forest stands (Shugart, 1984).

Following the fire, each burned area entered a process of vegetation growth called *succession*. Let us investigate some qualitatively important features of the process: first, how, and by whom, is recently burned land colonized?; second, what kind of structural changes can be discerned in the community during succession?; and third, how do succession in vegetation and change in the fauna relate to each other?

[1] The first plants to appear in a burned area include some dozens of herbs and grasses. Some of them were probably present on burned sites right from the beginning, having survived in the soil as seeds or root-systems, as documented in northern Finland after natural fires in the 1920s and 1930s (Kujala, 1926; Sarvas, 1937). Other early colonizers are species producing lots of seeds that disperse with wind. Moreover, fire is always uneven and leaves behind less thoroughly burned 'pockets' where some plants survive. As a result, the vegetation is characterized by great mosaic-like variation right from the beginning, different plant species dominating different sites.

The early insects are mainly efficient dispersers. The probability that a particular species arrives at a recently burned area depends on its abundance in the surroundings. Some beetles and bugs actually orient by smoke to newly burned areas where they find rich food resources such as microorganisms or fungi living on burned and decaying wood. Species of old forest may survive the fire inside the upper layer of the soil, but a majority of them succumb due to the greatly changed microclimate.

A set of taiga vertebrates similarly immigrates to burned areas at quite an early stage. Herbivorous small mammals arrive to eat the plants and predators such as weasels or buzzards follow the prey. Insectivorous birds that feed and breed on the ground here find optimal environments. The spatial heterogeneity produced by uneven plant growth is probably reflected in the spatial distribution of the fauna as well, but this is largely an unexplored problem.

[2] After the early colonization phase is over it may take some 3–5 years before vegetation covers the ground again. At this stage the first deciduous saplings get established. Floristic and structural diversity of the growing forest decreases gradually with age. A critical transition occurs with canopy closure, at the age of about 40 years in southern Finland. The amount of light reaching the ground declines, and herbs and grasses disappear whereas scrubs typical of mature forest take over. Shade-tolerant conifers increasingly dominate over broad-

leaved trees. However, these changes are relatively slow, and an old forest is structurally relatively stable. Consequently, the change in forest structure is non-linear in time: change is rapid in the beginning but slows down later on.

For animals this implies that species of early succession can live at any particular site for a shorter period of time than those of mature forest. Pekka Helle (1985) has demonstrated this regularity in birds in northern Finland, but we take up another interesting group of animals, ants (Punttila et al., 1991). Ant species living in the southern Finnish taiga number about 25. A majority of them are denizens of young forests, where (insect) food is originally abundant and microclimate is warm and dry as shading trees are lacking. Several of the species establish colonies rapidly at suitable microsites, and the colonies begin to produce reproductive progeny within a few years. Other species are obligatory nest-parasites in the stage of colony founding, that is, their queens intrude the nest of another ant species. Characteristic of the ant community at this stage is small-scale spatial variation which is not directly attributable to habitat characteristics but is related to interspecific aggressions.

Mature forests, in contrast, are dominated by a few mound-building species of the genus *Formica* which have mutually exclusive territories. The *Formica* colonies may take decades to build up, and the workers of the colonies defend efficiently their foraging areas that may cover up to a few hectares. A particularly important source of food for wood ants is the 'honeydew' produced by aphids living on trees, and several good aphid trees are included in each ant territory. A wood ant mound system may be very stable for decades, perhaps centuries, until the next forest fire burns down the stand and destroys the aphid trees.

[3] There is an interesting interaction between different time scales in the relation between vegetation and fauna in taiga succession. A slow scale, measured in decades, is constituted by the change in forest structure, and a fast scale, measured in years or even in months is constituted by reproductive cycles of short-lived animal populations. The slow change in forest structure brings forth a change in parameters influencing the dynamics of the fast system, the arthropod populations (Levandowsky and White, 1977). The dynamics of such a system are complex, especially where interspecific interactions play a role as well.

Overall, vegetation dynamics induce dynamics in animal populations – species of virgin taiga have had to cope successfully with forest fires. All phases of forest succession are equally 'natural', and relatively young phases may actually have dominated the landscape, as seems to be the case in eastern parts of North America. This brings us back to where we began: the taiga used to be a mosaic landscape, composed of stands of forest of varying ages, distributed randomly over the landscape, and statistical properties of the distribution of different successional stages in space were an important characteristic of the system.

Shugart (1984) called this a *quasi-equilibrium* landscape, which is 'composed of a sufficient number of mosaic elements so that the average behavior of the mosaic elements is predictable'. The mosaic view implies that the scale, measured in meters or years, is different for different organisms. In a taiga mosaic with a patch size of about 10–20 ha as in Finland, each mosaic element hosts *individual pairs* of breeding birds, but *local populations* of insects. Birds are influenced by local fires on the individual level, insects on the population level. Birds are efficient dispersers, and a single bird pair may easily colonize a new favorable site, while establishing a local population in a new area may be a problem for a beetle. This relates to a practical problem we shall discuss more thoroughly later on: to avoid irretrievable changes in the environment, we should be aware of the *natural dynamics* of the original ecological systems, and scale our own activities accordingly.

Changes in population size represent an important type of variation in ecological systems. When studying variation in population numbers, defining scales is important once again. We usually only observe variations on a local scale, but although variations are considerable locally they may add up to a pattern of regional stability over a number of localities. Distinguishing *local scale* from *regional scale* is critical but, unfortunately, extremely difficult. An analogous problem is met also in analysing variations in time: short-term fluctuations should be distinguished from long-term continuous increase or decline.

Small mammals are a group of animals showing spectacular population fluctuations in northwestern Europe. We show in Figure 2.3 some data on small mammal population fluctuations at Kilpisjärvi, another subarctic research station a few hundred kilometers from Kevo (from Laine and Henttonen, 1983, and unpublished data provided by Heikki Henttonen). Note particularly the almost perfect

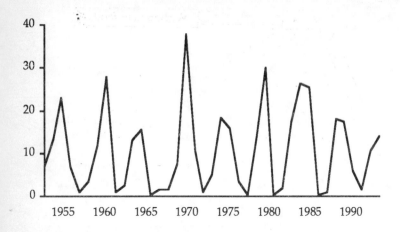

Figure 2.3
Variation from year to year in autumn catches of voles at Kilpisjärvi,
Finnish Lapland, 1953–91. Values on the y-axis indicate the number of
voles caught per 100 trap nights. This index includes four species of voles
of the genus *Microtus*, and the Norwegian lemming (*Lemmus lemmus*)

four-year cycles, and the great degree of between-species synchrony.
However, toward the south the fluctuations are far smaller, and in
southern Scandinavia they are entirely lacking (Hansson and
Henttonen, 1985). When explaining the cyclic fluctuations at Pal-
lasjärvi one ought to explain also the lack of cyclicity in southern
Fennoscandia.

The population cycles are influenced by a variety of factors; a
conceptual model putting them together is shown in Figure 2.4. The
main factor is predation by weasels. Following a population crash of
the voles, usually in wintertime, the weasels have originally a dense
population and predation on the voles over the following summer
is thus heavy, which reduces their already tiny populations still
more. Toward the following winter weasel populations crash as
well, and the vole populations begin to grow again.

Two additional factors are invoked in explaining the difference
between northern and southern Fennoscandia (Hansson and
Henttonen, 1988), namely, depth of snow cover and the number of
generalized, as opposed to specialized, predators preying upon the
voles. In the south there is no snow cover and generalized predators
abound (foxes, feral cats and hermelins). Generalized predators keep

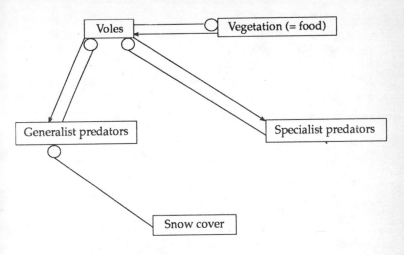

Figure 2.4
Relationships of major factors causing cyclic fluctuations in small
mammal populations in Fennoscandia. In the graph, → indicates positive
and —O negative effect. Snow cover causes critical asymmetry between
the efficiency of generalized versus specialist predators in consuming
voles and affecting their population size

an efficient check on vole populations all the time, and in times of vole
scarcity they can resort to alternative prey items which prevents
crashes in their own populations. In the north, in contrast, voles are
safe in the deep snow from other potential predators than weasels
which can intrude into their tunnels. On the other hand, weasels have
no alternative available prey to voles but die of hunger when voles
are scarce. Cyclicity is created.

Birds of prey are also greatly influenced by vole cycles and show
a variety of responses, called *reproductive strategies*, to the recurring
food shortage caused by fluctuations in prey abundance. Some
species are nomads, that is, they roam about and settle to breed in
areas where voles and lemmings are in good supply. The snowy owl
(*Nyctea scandiaca*), a tundra denizen, is the most spectacular representative of this group; the great grey owl (*Strix nebulosa*) is a nomad
in the northern taiga (Korpimäki, 1986a). Individuals of a migrant such
as the long-tailed skua (*Stercorarius parasiticus*) return to the same territories each year but during vole population lows the skuas leave
breeding grounds soon after arrival and move to the coast and open
sea (Andersson, 1976). Other taiga owls are sedentary through the year

and stay on their territories whatever the vole situation, but in years of small mammal lows they do not breed. The Tengmalm's owl (*Aegolius funereus*) is a nomad in northern Finland but sedentary a few hundred kilometers further south (Korpimäki, 1986b). There is good evidence that the Ural owl (*Strix uralensis*), a typical taiga bird, is able to assess vole populations in spring and modify its reproductive effort accordingly (Pietiäinen et al., 1986).

There are interacting time scales of different lengths in the system of voles, weasels and birds of prey. The population cycle of the mustelids is slower than that of the voles, which produces a time-lag in the response of weasels to vole abundance; this is an element enhancing instability in vole populations. Large birds of prey live on a time scale that is long enough to enable them to 'jump over' the bottleneck years of low vole abundance, and the total number of adult individuals is relatively stable from year to year although reproductive success varies greatly.

Human Intervention in Northern Nature

Often apparently minor infringements here become magnified and lead to irreversible basic changes in associations and landscapes.

Yuri Chernov[3]

The golden eagle fares better nowadays in Finland than only two decades ago, mainly because persecution at nest sites has almost discontinued, but in a global perspective change toward the better in the status of endangered species is, unfortunately, a rare exception: loss of species especially in the tropics is a major symptom of the ecological crisis.

The basic reason for extinctions is habitat loss: species adapted to a particular habitat cannot survive when the habitat is destroyed or reduced to tiny patches isolated from each other by human-managed environments. This conclusion has been drawn over and over again (Greenway, 1967; Myers, 1980). But there are clearly differences in susceptibility to extinction between species, and there seem to be differences also between biogeographic regions. This raises the question: what factors determine the extinction-proneness of species?

This question has no single answer but needs specifications as follows:

- What is the biogeographic zone considered and what kind of traits are expected in species adapted to that particular zone?
- What is the environment, and how does it change naturally?
- What kind of disturbance is threatening species living in this environment?

Let us explore these questions, using the golden eagle of northern Lapland as an example.

First, ecological communities in boreal and arctic zones are recent and have undergone dramatic environmental fluctuations on a time scale of 10 000 years. Thus, the species residing in the north are also adapted to great fluctuations of the environment. Although climatic stress and lack of organic nutrients make life precarious, northern species are relatively less sensitive to local changes in habitat than further south: they are good dispersers, having colonized the north in the recent past, and they are usually not specialized in habitat requirements. Large predators such as the golden eagle depend on the availability of prey, but predators usually eat many kinds of prey and hunt in many kinds of environments and are, consequently, quite adaptable to live in human-modified environments.

This generalization is not true of all northern predators however: a well-known exception is the spotted owl (*Strix occidentalis*) living in old coniferous forests on the west coast of North America. Each pair of the spotted owl utilizes about 3–7 km^2 of forest more than about 250 years old and below an elevation of roughly 1300 m, nesting in hollow trees and preying on small mammals, birds and insects; the bird is seriously threatened by logging (Forsman et al., 1984).

Second, northern taiga landscapes are dynamic habitat mosaics driven by wildfires. The natural fire rotation thus gives a standard against which human-induced changes should be compared. The golden eagle is not susceptible to forest fires by being able to move about, except when her nest is occasionally destroyed, and fires actually create open hunting-grounds with a good supply of prey such as hares. A comparison with the spotted owl is informative again: there is no natural fire cycle in the coniferous forests of western US – that is one reason why they grow so old and tall – and the owl is adapted to lead her life within this stable habitat.

Forestry is the main factor causing habitat change in the taiga and we need to ask: how do changes triggered by forest management differ from natural forest dynamics? There are differences of two main types: first, structural characteristics of the forest are changed because of removal of decaying wood and destruction of small-scale variation through the draining of bogs and peatlands, and second, area proportions of different types of stands are changed because clearances are vaster and more uniform than burns, and old forests are left only in small patches isolated from each other by managed expanses.

Many species are vulnerable to the second type of change. Among birds, species that stay over the winter in the north require large areas of natural forest to survive the snowy season, as documented by Raimo Virkkala (1990) on the ecology of the Siberian tit (*Parus cinctus*) in Finnish Lapland. Jorund Rolstad's work on the capercaillie (*Tetrao urogallus*) in southern Norway showed another type of threat caused by forestry (Rolstad and Wegge, 1987): the capercaillie mates communally in 'leks' similar to most other tetraonids, but in a fragmented forest landscape the number of birds participating in leks declines and mating success is also diminished, eventually leading to the disappearance of the birds.

Third, other threats faced by northern species include persecution and pollution. Persecution is generally diminishing but, unfortunately, environmental pollution is severe in northern Lapland from mining industries in the Kola Peninsula in the Soviet Union. Hundreds of square kilometers of forest tundra are completely destroyed in the vicinity of the industrial communities because of high sulphur emissions.

Seppo Neuvonen and Erkki Haukioja of the University of Turku have studied with their colleagues the direct effect of acidification on subarctic birch forests in Kevo by spraying experimental plots for three years with acidic water (pH 3 and 4), and comparing them with control plots (Neuvonen and Suomela, 1990). No dramatic effects were observed in the acidified plots in this period, the most significant changes occurring in the microflora of birch leaves and pine needles. Such changes may modify the interaction between trees and their pests. Some direct evidence pointing toward this conclusion was detected, namely, the European pine sawfly (*Neodiprion sertifer*), an important pest of pine, was less susceptible to virus disease in acidified than in control plots (Neuvonen et al., 1990).

However, the results of the experiment must be seen in perspective: environmental pollution from the Soviet metal industries covers vast areas and has already lasted half a century, whereas the experiment covered small plots in unpolluted surroundings and lasted only three years. A scaling problem, typical to ecological research, is met again. We simply do not know how to extrapolate results from experiments covering a few years and hectares to geographic regions.

Environmental stress is a generic concept often used for various types of long-term disturbance exerted by human activities on ecosystems (Calow and Berry, 1989). Acid rain is a prime example of a human-caused stress factor. Evaluating the consequences of any particular stress factor requires specifications as regards, first, the type of disturbance caused by the stress considered, and second, the susceptibility of a particular environment. Further, the ecological consequences of environmental stress should be evaluated on different levels of ecological hierarchy, namely, individuals, populations and communities (Underwood and Peterson, 1989): we come across the issue of appropriate scaling once again.

As to the vulnerability of particular environments to acid rain, the buffering capacity of the soils is of great importance. In the high north soils are mainly acidic, which makes northern ecosystems more susceptible to human-caused acidification than southern ecosystems on more favorable soils. One can also surmise that northern ecosystems are fragile because of the 'natural stress' of harsh environmental conditions (see Chernov, 1985), but a paradox, not very well understood, is inherent here: plants living in naturally harsh environments are stress-tolerant and it is possible that they also endure human-caused disturbances relatively better than plants of more benign environments (Grime, 1989). Because of environmental harshness one can be sure, however, that regeneration in heavily destroyed areas in the Arctic is very slow; thus, the damage caused by industries in the Kola Peninsula will be irreparable for centuries to come.

City Life

Northern forest landscapes are only moderately modified by human activities compared with numerous other environments. Let us turn our attention to the completely human-made environment of the city. Let us investigate Helsinki and accept a city dweller, the small black ant (*Lasius niger*) as our guide.

Small black ants are abundant everywhere in European cities. They differ from most other ants by being able to establish colonies in frequently disturbed, ephemeral habitats such as boulder shores and sandy river banks. In Helsinki they inhabit tiny cracks in downtown side-walks, and pure stone environments on the steps to the Dome and under the statue of Alexander II of Russia in the central square. The success of small black ants is facilitated by their broad food habits and by the short life-cycle of their colonies. They produce reproductive individuals in the next summer after the establishment of a colony, which is quite exceptional among ants. They are also excellent dispersers, and every summer on a few sunny July days winged males and females fly in the millions everywhere in the city searching for mates; a day or two later fertilized queens lose their wings and move on the ground looking for suitable sites to establish a new colony. Few of them succeed, however: they are consumed by every creature in the city interested in ant-sized food items from gulls, swifts and sparrows to other ant species as well as workers of already established conspecific colonies.

The combination of characteristics that make some species successful in colonizing human-created environments are generically called *preadaptations*. Nothing teleological is implied by the term. 'Preadapted' species were just lucky in having lived in natural environments which in some critical respects resemble new environments in cities. Other species preadapted to living in the inner city of Helsinki include a couple of birds that find nest sites in buildings (house sparrow, swift), a score of mainly annual plants that thrive on industrial wastelands and intensively managed lawns, insects of open, dry habitats, and a moth species living in larval stage on lichens on the roofs of tall apartment houses.

Synanthropy is a term often used for species that are entirely tied to human habitation. The domestic pigeon and house sparrow are synanthropic species; they get along only in towns and villages and were introduced by humans into the Finnish fauna. Swifts are a borderline case because they use buildings only as nest sites and feed in the air; furthermore, a completely natural population of swifts lives in forests where they nest in old woodpecker cavities. Most plant and animal inhabitants of Helsinki are not synanthropic but also get along in natural habitats.

According to Bernhard Klausnitzer (1988), genuinely synanthropic animals are preadapted to urban life owing to one or several of the following five factors:

- they utilize food provided by human habitation;
- they live in specific microhabitats in buildings, cellars, green-houses, etc.;
- they are favored by the warm and dry microclimate of cities;
- they are behaviorally flexible; and
- they have switched from natural biotopes to urban ones.

The degree of synanthropy of a particular species can be estimated as the proportion of local populations restricted to human-created environments. The degree of synanthropy of insects often increases toward the north, for instance, in the blowfly *Lucilia sericata* it is 33 per cent in Hungary but 98 per cent in Finland. The warm and dry microclimate of cities is more southern in character than the micro-climate in natural habitats in the surroundings. The synanthropic fauna of Helsinki is, however, impoverished compared with central European cities because of the winter: cellars and outhouses provide a habitat for a much more diverse fauna further south.

Small black ants have lots of available habitat in the inner city of Helsinki partly because frequent disturbances in the environment such as mowing of lawns preclude competitively superior ant species from colonizing the inner city. The only other ant occurring regularly in intensively managed parks in Helsinki is a yellow relative of the small black ant (*Lasius flavus*); they establish colonies underground and tend aphids on plant roots. Red wood ants with their elaborate mounds and colony cycles lasting up to decades can manage only in recreational forests in the suburbs.

According to ecological surveys conducted in Helsinki (Tonteri and Haila, 1990), the fauna and flora are ordered along a gradient from natural and seminatural environments in the surroundings of the city and in the suburbs to heavily disturbed and managed habitats such as industrial wastelands and downtown parks in the city center. Forest species decline in abundance toward the center, but commu-nities are surprisingly diverse very close to tightly built apartment areas, provided some free-growing vegetation is left among the houses. This means that a good principle for maintaining ecological diversity in urban environments would be *benign neglect*: a rich array of plant and animal species can colonize and establish local popula-tions in urban environments if they are not disturbed by too intensive management.

Why should it be important that ecological diversity is maintained in the artificial environment of the city? We can give two reasons: first, most people live in cities and it is in cities that they get their contacts with nature. Respect for plants and animals in cities is a bridge to respect for all wildlife everywhere. Second, it is critical for the long-term protection of ecological diversity on the earth that human-modified, economically utilized environments be as rich in plant and animal species as possible. Ecological diversity cannot be saved by merely establishing protected areas, as irreplaceable as they are for preserving particular environments. Urban environments are large-scale laboratories where the capability of plants and animals for living together with humans can be tested, and measures for improving this prospect can be put into practice.

Ecological Complexity

Roughly, by a complex system I mean one made up of a large number of parts that interact in a nonsimple way.

Herbert Simon[4]

Before the disaster of the spaceship Challenger, we often heard the question 'how is it that we can send a man to the moon but not ... ' The 'but not' was 'eliminate hunger' or 'establish peace' or 'protect the environment' or 'provide universal health care' or any one of a number of socially desirable goals. The question was rhetorical. The questioner did not expect an answer but was expressing exasperation at what was perceived as misplaced priorities. The implication was that the space program was surely as complex as the urgent problems that were proposed and yet was carried out to perfection while the pressing human problems were ignored.

Yet the question deserves serious consideration. A space program is certainly complex and yet manageable. How is the complexity of biosocial systems different?

First, the parts of a spaceship are clearly defined. They are manu-factured separately, tested in isolation, combined into subsystems that are themselves testable. In contrast, the 'parts' of ecological systems are not obvious or given. Should a plant be regarded as roots, stems and leaves or as photosynthesis, mineral uptake and transpiration, or as growth, reproduction and senescence? Should an ecosystem be seen as interacting species or independent species/environment relations, or as energy flow and mineral recycling or as succession, degradation and possible rehabilitation? In the end we are forced to recognize that the way we choose to identify the parts of a system depends very much on our purposes and tools.

Second, although the parts of a spaceship are chosen for their performance together, they are designed separately. And performance is unambiguous: a successful flight and return. Where ambiguity does enter, where criteria of profit or public relations schedules conflict with successful flight we have increased the likelihood of disasters. In ecosystems there is no one criterion of performance. The 'parts' evolve through the interactions of the component species each of which is evolving according to its own genetic makeup and ecology. Then these ecosystems recombine, conditions change, species which evolved in one set of conditions meet with those evolved in others, and the outcome is essentially indeterminate from the point of view of any of the species.

Third, the parts of a spaceship have well-specified behaviors that can be studied in isolation. But we cannot study all the processes of ecosystems in isolation without destroying the system. Therefore only some of the processes can be specified quantitatively while others can only be known qualitatively and others remain as unknowns that emerge to catch us by suprise.

Therefore it is not obvious how to understand or act on ecosystems. Several approaches have been developed by ecologists.

[1] The detailed study of pairwise species interactions, especially competition and predation. The hope is that the behavior of the whole will follow from the behavior of relatively few basic kinds of linkages in the system. Different equations for pairwise interactions may be proposed and studied in detail to see how these different assumptions affect the outcome.

[2] Statistical approaches attempt to avoid major theoretical commitments and to examine the data, numbers of individuals in populations, numbers of species at different levels in the food chain, concentrations of nutrients and some physical factors. The examination picks out correlations among variables or uses more sophisticated techniques of principal component analysis, cluster analysis and so on. The outcome is a statistical description of the system, not an interpretation, and predictions are made on the basis of assuming that things will behave the way they have behaved. Such models have

the advantage of not depending on many assumptions and have proven useful for predicting the behavior of the same system they were derived from, or similar ones. But they do not provide understanding of why a system behaves the way it does, do not help very much under changed circumstances or different systems, and do not tell us when things are different enough to matter.

[3] Search for controlling factors. Simplicity is sought in propositions such as: herbivore abundance controls plant abundancè, predators control herbivores, specialized predators are more important than generalists. Or particular species may be singled out as 'dominant'. Dominance implies not only greatest abundance but also some sort of control or determination of the other species present.

[4] Cybernetics or systems theory work with models that pick out the pattern of regulation in a system, the negative and positive feedback loops that determine how the system responds to external events and either approaches an equilibrium or returns to some pathway of development, or even breaks down. While cybernetic models stress information flow, what has come to be called systems models in ecology usually concentrates on energy flow and nutrient (mineral) cycling.

If the models are quantitative, equations are proposed for all of the interactions in the system. There are too many equations and these are too complicated to allow for pencil and paper solutions, but numerical methods can be used on computers. Then estimates have to be made of the various rate constants, life table parameters, etc. These are put into the equations and the computer simulates the supposed real process, giving us as output the values of the different variables (population numbers, biomass, etc.) at some hypothetical future time. These outputs are then compared to observations. Insofar as the observed values are close to the predicted ones, the assumptions of the model are supported. Where they differ more than an acceptable amount, either the estimates of the parameters are improved, or the measurements of the variables are reexamined for hidden sources of error, or the model itself may be modified to take into account new phenomena. The investigation proceeds as a cycling through measurements, simulation, comparison and modification until it does not seem worth while to continue.

Because of the large number of measurements needed to use these models, they are relatively expensive to set up and run. They are usually restricted to modelling a single object, one lake or forest tract or city, and are limited to variables which can be measured with some degree of accuracy.

Qualitative Models

'But it's theoretically impossible!'
'Maybe they use a different theory.'

Larry Niven[5]

Qualitative models avoid both exact equations and voluminous measurement and focus instead on the structure of the network of processes. By the structure of the network we mean first of all which components interact directly with which others, and what is the direction of their effects (that is, do they increase or decrease each other).

In building the model we exercise choices at each stage. First, what are the components of the system? This will depend on the problem, which usually specifies at least a few core components as being the objects of interest. Once we have these core elements, we ask, what affects them?

At this stage we have to unleash the imagination. Traditional scientific method usually attempts to reduce a problem to its smallest terms, with the fewest possible variables and the greatest possible isolation. This has usually meant that the variables chosen all belong to the same scientific discipline while those that fit under other disciplines are either ignored, accepted as given constraints, or treated as arbitrary external disturbances which are assumed to be independent of our core variables. Thus economic models of agricultural production link prices and yields but ignore the effects of these on erosion or pest problems that eventually alter yield. An engineering model of dam construction will consider irrigation, flood control and power generation but usually ignore the effects of the irrigation system on mosquitoes, on land holding, farmer debt or local climate.

After a period of free-wheeling brainstorming and widespread discussion, we arrive at a preliminary list of variables and their possible connections. Whereas the reductionist approach studies models that are too small to grasp the rich complexity of ecology, this first pass leaves us with an intimidating list of too many variables and relations, some of which are not at all clear.

The second stage in model building is one of reducing the number of variables whose changes have to be considered and resolving ambiguities in their relationships. We do not have to include everything we know in our models. Several guidelines have proven useful in deciding what to include or postpone or ignore.

First, components should be included as covariables in the same model only if they have direct or indirect reciprocal interactions. If the effects are only one way, the variables which are unaffected by the others can be removed to the outside and treated as external conditions or parameters of the system. Thus for example variation in the day length with the seasons impinges on the vegetation and animal life but is not affected by them and therefore is an external input, a parameter of the system rather than a covariable. But humidity is affected by the plants and therefore may be a covariable.

Note that 'external' here means dynamically external, not necessarily physically outside. For instance in studying the interactions between species we may consider a feeding preference to be fixed, genetically determined. This genetic influence is obviously located inside the cells of an individual but if it remains constant on the time scale of interest it can be treated as a parameter of the model. And if it changes as a result of evolution within a species we can treat it as an external input in tracing its consequences. But if genetic changes are responsive to demographic changes then the trait in question may have to be treated as a covariable. Similarly, something which is affected by the core variables of our preliminary system but does not affect them can be omitted from the network of covariables in the first analysis and treated as an outcome or output of the system. However, the question of whether there are or are not reciprocal interactions is not always obvious, and sometimes depends on the time scale of interest.

Second, components should be included as covariables with the core variables only if they change on comparable time scales. It has been proposed by many authors that variables which change much more slowly than the variables of primary interest can be treated at least provisionally as constants rather than variables, and that variables which change very much faster than the core variables can be assumed to be already at their steady state or equilibrium behaviors (Levins, 1973a).

Thus, while we examine population changes of nematodes in a forest we treat the proportions of tree species as constants and the bacterial flux as at a steady state because the bacteria change on a time scale of hours to days, the nematodes on a scale of days to months and the tree composition on a scale of decades to centuries. When we shift to the bacteria, they depend on the species composition of the litter which in turn depends on a constant tree species composition that produces the litter, and on the nematodes which on the scale of days can be considered constant. Finally, when we study the trees the rate of recycling of nutrients is important. This depends on the microorganisms present, which are taken to be in a steady state determined by the litter and nematodes.

It is not necessary for covariables to be similar physically. A model of a community of species may begin with the list of species and their feeding, reproductive and death rates. But the feeding rate may change with prey availability. And the reproductive rate may depend not on present food availability but on past food as represented by body weight. Then it may be convenient to recognize feeding preference and body weight as new covariables unless they change very rapidly and are completely determined by present prey abundance. If the metabolic rate is fast enough so that body weight is determined by present resources then the additional variable is not useful for the study of the dynamics. But if it is slow enough so that body weight is not at equilibrium with the resource level, then the whole system can fluctuate even when there is no fluctuating external condition to drive it.

Part of the power of the qualitative methods is that variables and parameters as different as pest abundance, feeding preferences of predators, bureaucratic reluctance, soil fertility and prices of farm commodities can be included in the same models without knowing the details of their inner workings but only the time scale and the direction of the influences.

Third, at this stage we often encounter ambiguities about the mutual effects of variables on each other. Sometimes the same pair of variables have different, opposing effects on each other. Trees of different species may jointly maintain the forest microclimate they all need, but compete for nutrients. Microorganisms may secrete vitamins that others need but also antibiotics that inhibit their growth.

Herbivores may consume their food plants but distribute their seeds. Or phosphorus may serve as a nutrient in small doses but be toxic at high concentrations.

Whenever these ambiguities arise, the model grows. The different effects have to be represented by different pathways by way of intervening variables. Thus we could represent the nutrients as a new variable. The trees no longer have negative, competitive links directly between them, but they are shown as consuming the same resource (and therefore having an indirect negative effect on each other) and having a direct positive interaction because of microclimate although microclimate is not represented as a variable. Or we could have chosen to represent microclimate suitability as a variable that they both enhance and benefit from, and show competition for nutrients as direct negative links. (Note that 'microclimate' cannot itself be a variable. A variable must be in principle quantifiable. Therefore we either use microclimate suitability and have positive interactions with the trees, or use microclimate harshness and show negative interactions.) Or we might have both microclimate suitability and nutrients as variables and no direct links between the trees.

There may be particular reasons for choosing one representation over the other. However, the important points are that two variables cannot be joined directly by more than a single link in each direction and that the distinction between direct and indirect interactions lies in the model, not in nature. We can always find some intermediate linking variables between any two variables. But their inclusion is only useful if they help resolve ambiguities, are observables that would help test the models, or have their own connections in another direction.

Fourth, the linkage of a variable to itself is usually the least obvious connection in the system and in many kinds of diagrams these are omitted, but they are important for analysing the process. Puccia and Levins (1985) give some formal mathematical ways of determining whether to include a pathway from a variable to itself. Here we note the following general guidelines:

[1] If a variable such as a population undergoes simple self reproduction, that is where the *rate* of reproduction does not depend on that variable, then there will be no link to itself. The rate of reproduction may be influenced by other variables in the system or by external conditions.

[2] If the rate of reproduction depends on the variable, there will be a link to itself. When this is negative, that is when growth slows down at high densities, this is referred to as density-dependent regulation, self-damping or autoinhibition. However, it is often the case that density dependence takes place through other variables such as food supply which have been omitted from the model. If these were included explicitly in the model, the direct density dependence would drop out. Thus the presence or absence of self-damping depends on the model.

[3] If a variable is produced by something else rather than by itself, such as nutrients being introduced into a stream or the resource for an insect being the sap of a plant, not the plant itself, then there is not simple self-reproduction and there is self-damping.

[4] If a local population is increased by immigration from other populations, this has the effect of self-damping. But if harvesters remove a fixed quantity of a population according to some predetermined plan regardless of the population level, this creates a positive feedback.

Fifth, when in doubt about the structure of a system, try the different alternatives. Examining models is cheap and easy.

It has been pointed out by O'Neill et al. (1986) that the time scales of change are often associated with the sizes of objects so that when we define a system in terms of similar objects they are often also changing on similar time scales, with the very small (molecules, cells) changing rapidly compared to populations and communities.

Once we have a preliminary model, a proposed description of the way a system is put together, we can use it to ask questions about what would happen if the model is a good one. We ask these questions for two reasons: to check the model by comparing its predictions to what we already know, and to predict new results. To the extent that models are consistent with what we already know, we can have more confidence in them with regard to what they predict about what we do not yet know. Different models will agree in some of their predictions and disagree in others. Where they agree, we have a robust result, that is a prediction which is not sensitive to the details of the model and therefore more likely to reflect what is going on in the world (Levins, 1966; Wimsatt, 1981). Therefore we can have more confidence in that prediction to the extent that the models are really different enough. Where the models disagree, we can use the disagreement to help us decide between models. The more diverse the various models are in their assumptions the more we learn once we have made the observations and decided among them.

System Dynamics

The more it snows, Tiddley pum,
The more it goes, Tiddley pum,
The more it goes, Tiddley pum,
On snowing.

A.A. Milne[6]

Now we have to consider what sort of questions the models can answer, what are the properties of complex systems that we want to know about. This depends on the problems we face in our dealings with nature and society. Although we might answer by saying we want to know everything about the system, in reality we cannot even say what 'everything' includes. Usually, we have in mind a particular class of questions such as, has this system been altered by human activity? Why does it fluctuate? What will happen if we do X? Is it stable? And we ask these questions not about the whole system but about particular aspects.

In agricultural ecosystems we do not really want to stabilize the abundance of all the species of insects that are present but rather to limit pest damage and increase yields. In protecting health we do not have to know all the fluctuations in the intestinal flora but only that certain bugs are kept within tolerable limits. In managing whole ecosystems we do not have to know what all the variables are doing, but are concerned with the question, do diversity and complexity confer stability. A major task of theory is to determine how much we can get away without knowing and still know what is important to us.

The major properties of systems we will consider are those concerned with stability and persistence, fluctuation and predictability, response of the variables of interest or of the stability pattern to changes of parameter or structure, what remains more or less constant in the face of all that fluctuation, what observations are most useful for monitoring the health of the system and deciding on interventions, and how to intervene to get desired results.

Although the analysis of such behaviors can involve rather complicated mathematics at least some of the results have simple meaning and are easily understood. We will proceed with a rather abstract discussion of 'systems'. A system can be any collection of variables (objects that undergo change) we choose to study. But in order to be interesting and worth studying, their interactions must be strong enough to have a detectable influence on each other. If most of what happens to these variables comes from outside the system, due to external factors, then system properties will not be interesting. Therefore we have to choose a system big enough so that most of what happens depends on the system itself with relatively few links to factors outside.

One possible outcome of processes in ecosystems is that after a while a steady state is achieved in which numbers remain the same. For instance the fixing of carbon dioxide and liberation of oxygen by plants may balance the consumption of oxygen and release of carbon dioxide by plants and animals together. This steady state will be perturbed by all sorts of events, changes in light intensity, temperature, available water and so on. But if the steady state is stable, then after a perturbation the system will return toward its equilibrium. If it is constantly being perturbed we may never see it at equilibrium but always in the process of returning toward it and being pushed away. Then the important questions are: how susceptible is it to perturbation (that is, how much of a response will it show to a given perturbation) and how quickly does it return, how quickly does it erase the traces of past perturbing events. These are the properties of *resistance* and *resilience*.

If a system has a stable equilibrium under constant conditions, then different starting points will lead toward similar results, and after a long enough time the circumstances of origin are no longer visible. The future of the system is predictable, but the past untraceable.

But a system may have more than one steady state outcome depending on the starting conditions. For instance, if enough vegetation and soils survive a flood or hurricane, a badly damaged forest may be restored after passing through a number of intermediate stages. But if too much is lost, erosion may accelerate to the point where it overwhelms any new soil formation and the vegetation pattern is permanently altered. In that case, we can visualize several steady states, and for each of them a range of conditions which will lead to that steady state. Then the history of the system is not completely erased: by knowing which steady state it is approaching, we know in what range it started, its basin of attraction.

The basin of attraction is an important characteristic of a system. It is the range of starting conditions which all move toward the same outcome. The basin of attraction may be very broad, in which case many initial conditions lead to that state, or narrow, in which case it may be stable if achieved but rarely achieved. Furthermore, if there are two steady states then there is also some condition which goes toward neither, which lies on the boundary of their basins of attraction. This will be an unstable steady state. Theoretically the system could remain there forever if not perturbed, but all real systems are perturbed sometimes. Then the outcome depends on the direction of the perturbation, and even a very small influence can have a big effect.

If a system does have a stable steady state and approaches that state after perturbation, it may approach smoothly, always getting closer, or through fluctuations that get smaller and smaller and finally cease. What its path is toward equilibrium depends both on the network of interactions among the variables and on where it starts. Following the pathway back toward equilibrium after a disturbance therefore tells us about the system. If the fluctuations diminish only very gradually, and by the time they do get smaller the system has been perturbed again, we may not be able to decide if it would have diminished fluctuating in the absence of disturbance.

The proportions of individuals of different ages in a population fluctuate although they tend toward a steady age structure that depends on the birth and death rates for each age. But if these rates themselves change, the population is no longer at a steady state and will move toward a new age structure, often by way of fluctuations. When this happens to insects with short generations we can look from the outside and see a pattern of fluctuations. When it happens to humans and we watch from the inside, we label the fluctuations 'baby boom', 'echo of baby boom' and so on.

A stable steady state is a simple outcome. But other outcomes are possible. A system may undergo permanent fluctuation even in the absence of perturbation. That fluctuation may be big or small and regular or irregular. It may be a simple cycle of abundance and decline, or a much more complicated pattern with no apparent regularity and can even mimic randomness.

The important point here is that if a system of variables fluctuates, this may be due either to some fluctuating outside influences, to its own autonomous fluctuations, or some combination of the two. Consider cyclic versus irregular epidemics. From the inside we can always give step-wise specific explanation. For instance, the epidemic declined this year because last year's outbreak left more people immune or there were fewer infected mosquitoes. Next year we may say that fewer infected mosquitoes meant fewer new cases, fewer people getting immune while last year's immune people lost their immunity so that there will be an increase. This level of explanation can be used for prediction of outbreaks from year to year, but something is missing: from the outside we might see that the relation between immunity and infection creates a cyclical dynamic. Both levels of analysis are necessary.

Qualitative analysis of the structures of systems can tell us when a system will have stable or unstable equilibria, when it will fluctuate (see Levins, 1974; Puccia and Levins, 1985).

Large-scale Ecological Theory

If you only pick up the physical appearances, you are likely to miss all the central social and economic questions, which is where ecological thinking and social thinking necessarily converge.

Raymond Williams[7]

Ecological theory is concerned with two fundamental questions of process and two practical problems dependent on these: Why are things the way they are instead of a little bit different? Why are things the way they are instead of very different? What do we want from and for the ecosystems of the earth? And how do we intervene in ecosystems to get desired results and avoid disasters?

The first is a question of the 'physiology' of a system, of how it maintains itself in the face of all the external and internal influences that act to change it. The persistence of ecological patterns is quite striking. In the course of the seasonal cycle, populations of mites on Cuban orange trees pass through some 50 generations during which their numbers may fluctuate by several hundred or thousand times. Yet over the course of ten years or so the pattern is reproduced and the numbers remain within very broad boundaries. Birds abandon and recolonize the Baltic islands every year, yet the numbers of species on islands remains more or less the same. Members of a species remain recognizably the same although environments change, natural selection buffets them about in different directions, and random mutations produce variants in every generation.

If there were no short-term fluctuations, we might have assumed that things remain the way they are because nothing is acting to change them. This would be a kind of inertial law – systems at rest remain at rest unless acted upon by an external force. Stability would then be taken as the 'normal' state of the world and only change would have to be explained. But this is clearly not the case. Ecological objects – populations and species and communities and geographic distributions – not only do change dramatically over short periods but are obviously acted upon by powerful influences for change, and yet they persist. This persistence is not absolute and should not be exaggerated into some universal law that protects us against disaster and denies evolution. But it is quite striking that the long-term trends are usually orders of magnitude slower than the short-term fluctuations.

Therefore the persistence of ecological systems must be sought not in the absence of change but in the restoring processes that keep the changes within bounds most of the time. Systems persist not in spite of but because of the changes they experience.

This is the problem of homeostasis or self-regulation. In a general way we can claim that the answer lies in the complex network of feedbacks within systems. But this abstract answer is clearly insufficient. We want to know what kinds of feedbacks operate in ecological systems. Do species reduce their reproduction when populations are high and increase it when low? Or are they regulated by their food supply, which is diminished when the consumers are abundant and increases when they are rare? Or does a population peak attract the predators of a species, thus reducing the numbers and therefore eventually reducing the predators as well? All of these are negative feedbacks: an initial change gives rise to chains of events that eventually feed back to offset the initial change.

But there are also positive feedbacks in most systems of any complexity. Well-fed predators are stronger and able to hunt more effectively, reinforcing their well-fed state. Excessive accumulation of organic matter at the bottom of a lake can kill the consumers of organic matter, increasing the accumulation. The 'bloom' of algal cyanobacteria in a lake increases the pH of water which increases the dissolution of phosphorus from bottom sediments to the water mass which increases the reproduction of cyanobacteria. The outcome of all these interactions may be to maintain stability, to destroy stability or to produce regular fluctuations which are themselves persistent.

The study of succession in forests may seem to be a different kind of problem. Here the object of interest, the species composition of a given area, changes as it develops from an initial clearing through primary colonization, growth of the colonizers, and their replacement by species belonging to later stages of succession. And indeed if we follow a single patch of forest the problem is one of change rather than persistence. But the trajectory of change is itself persistent. And the forest as a whole is a patchwork of areas in a 'quasi-equilibrium' state. We discussed above the succession of the taiga after wildfire, but a similar pattern holds true in a tropical forest in a hurricane zone.

The question why are things the way they are instead of a little bit different can be approached by experiments in which a system is perturbed from its natural state and we observe the course of restoration. Why do seeds of a particualr species germinate at a particular time of year? One possible explanation is that there are fewer consumers of those seedlings at that time. Another is that because of the seasonality of rainfall, that is when they have the best chance of having sufficient moisture. Or, other trees drop more leaves then, so they have more light. One way of approaching the question would be to collect seed, store them in the laboratory, germinate them artificially (this is no trivial problem, and may require special treatment), transplant them back into the forest and observe their survival in comparison to seedlings that are set out at the normal time.

Once we have some knowledge of the component processes in an ecosystem, we can explore their interactions theoretically to understand how the large number of components and their connections result in the observed dynamics.

The second question, why are things the way they are instead of very different, is a historical question, a question of biogeography and evolution. Why does Europe north of the Alps have fewer species than North America at similar latitudes in many groups of plants and animals? Why are there so many kinds of marsupials in Australia? Why are the plants of coastal lowlands very similar throughout the tropics whereas the rain forests include many species limited to particular regions? Why are there more species of plants and insects in the tropics than in the temperate zones? Why are there so few species in the Arctic? Why are there hundreds of thousands of species of beetles but only hundreds of mammals? Why, despite the enormous biochemical diversity of nature, are there so few kinds of chlorophyll? Why are proteins made up of some 20 or 30 kinds of amino acids instead of hundreds of kinds that we might imagine?

At first glance these two fundamental questions seem to be radically different. But on closer examination they deal with similar problems from different perspectives. For instance, we may discover that the narrow temperature tolerances among ant species of different local habitats contribute to the regional diversity of ants. But then we have to ask, why do the tropical species show more specialization than temperate ants? Or if we decide that the numbers of bird species colonizing the Baltic islands is the result of each species' colonizing suitable vegetation independently of the others, we have to ask the further evolutionary question, how did this fauna arise? Why is there not more visible competition among them for nesting sites or for food? And no matter what the historical answer we offer, we are thrown back again to a homeostatic question, what keeps the evolutionary processes from causing niche expansion of these birds and resulting in interactions that do not now take place?

In the last analysis every answer to the first question is an answer about the self-regulatory, restoring forces that are at work in a system. This then poses the historical question, how did they get that way? But every evolutionary answer which identifies the course of natural selection poses the homeostatic question, what keeps the evolutionary process on that track? And what allows radical changes in its direction?

Thus questions of equilibrium and questions of change presuppose each other.

The third general question is a question of societal goals, but goals constrained by what is ecologically possible. It is a much broader question than the immediate problem of preventing environmental deterioration and its consequences for production, health, climate and conservation. It also includes long-term questions of positive planning.

The difficulties in answering this general question arise from several sources. The first is, what is meant by 'we'? Environmental issues almost always confront us as controversies in which differences of opinion are linked to differences of interest. We never see the oil industry declaring, 'On second thought we don't want to continue off-shore drilling because it pollutes fishing grounds, makes the oceans ugly and is unsafe for production workers' against hordes of angry fisherman crying 'Drill! Drill!'

We suggest that there are three basic reasons for the pervasive destruction of the environment: greed, poverty and ignorance, and a particular ideological form of ignorance which we will describe as developmentalism.

By greed we do not mean the personal, irrational avarice of individuals seeking more consumption or acquisition at any cost. Rather we focus on the institutionalized greed of the capitalist economy in which not only profit but the greatest possible profit is not merely desired but is essential for survival of enterprises and entrepreneurs. This greed is rational once one accepts the system as a whole. Insofar as individual specialists propose goals that undercut profitability they would lose their credibility as experts. It is even rational, within the very special narrow rationality of business, to use up and destroy a resource completely and as quickly as possible and invest the profits in something entirely different provided the returns on such a procedure are greater than those from the long-term care and harvesting of the resource.

Of course, greed is not expressed directly as greed but using positive expressions.

The second major factor is poverty. Consideration of future and indirect consequences of a decision requires some reserves of resources and time to permit a transition from destructive to restorative uses of nature. Many farmers are aware of the harm caused by chemicalization of production but cannot afford the risks of switching to ecologically sound practices. Where there is a desperate need for food, governments which are committed to serving their population will provide pesticides, and countries with a desperate land shortage will clearcut forests. And it is even the case that the more committed an administrator is to 'serving the people' the more urgently he or she may promote destructive practices for short-term worthy goals unless the narrowness of a bureaucratic mission is offset by a vision of the whole.

The third factor is ignorance. There is first local ignorance. Sales representatives of chemical companies outnumber agricultural extension agents and are the major source of technical information for most farmers in capitalist countries. Government and public leaders are simply not aware of the ecological issues involved in agricultural development, environmental protection or public health, the urgency of addressing those problems or the availability of approaches different from the dominant destructive ones.

There is also the global ignorance. World science shows a very uneven pattern of knowledge and ignorance. The major way in which knowledge is put to use is through commodities, but the commoditization of knowledge strongly influences the kind of knowledge that is created; we elaborate this point further in Chapter 3. In the chapters on health and agriculture we will look more closely at alternative approaches to disease control and pest management.

But ignorance is not the passive absence of knowledge. It always has a particular content – ignorance about what? Knowledge or belief about what? It takes on a particular form in Third World countries: developmentalism. Developmentalism holds that there is only one kind of progress, the condition of the advanced industrial countries of Europe and North America. If this carries with it terrible costs, these are accepted as the 'cost of progress'. In our view this approach is seriously mistaken; we elaborate the criticism in Chapter 5.

Of course greed, poverty and ignorance are not independent factors. Large-scale institutionalized greed creates poverty and the arguments to justify it and reinforces ignorance; poverty imposes acquiescence to greed and perpetuates ignorance; ignorance recycles poverty and accepts the consequences of greed.

The fourth major theoretical problem facing ecology is how to intervene in nature. The starting point must be the understanding of the dynamics of complex ecosystems where ordinary common sense is often a poor guide to action. The physiological fact that DDT kills an insect pest does not justify the ecological claim that the use of DDT will therefore control that pest, or the economic claim that its use will make farming more productive, or the social claim that its widespread application is on the whole good for people. Each link in the argument requires analysis on a distinct level. The folklore of ecology is full of examples where common sense has suggested programs which are counterproductive – pesticides that increase pests, immunization campaigns that increase disease, crop improvement schemes that increase inequality and hunger, hydroelectric projects that destroy waterways and increase poverty. In all of these cases the direct linear inferences were more or less valid.

But there are two additional considerations when we study systems in which there is human intervention. First, once people intervene they become part of the system, not an external regulator. That is, the interventors' behavior depends on and acts on variables of the system and is therefore a covariable with the components of the system. As such they have their own operating characteristics. And second, there may be conflicting interests at work, each acting to alter the intervention in their own preferred direction. We will elaborate these points in Chapter 5.

In almost all large-scale policy issues related to the protection or management of the environment, conflicts arise not only of judgement but also of interest. Some of these conflicts of interest are secondary to common goals, as when ministries of health and agriculture work at cross purposes in insect control because they have different missions within a general common objective of improving the lives of people in a given region. But when the conflicts correspond to class interests the problem is especially difficult to resolve, and the solution usually corresponds to the relative political power of the contending parties rather than to any ecological or social rationality.

Our task as ecologists therefore includes the study of the dynamics of the combined human–natural system in which the rate of reproduction of fish is a co-parameter with the coefficient of bureaucratic inertia, and the variability of rainfall interacts with the variability of prices. Any recommendation for a regulatory scheme must take into account the responses not only of the natural system but also of the human participants with their own partly compatible and partly opposing goals.

Such an agenda clearly goes beyond the boundaries of ecology as a biological science. Our claim is not that ecology should expand to absorb these issues as its own preserve, but rather that it should set its own agenda in light of the pressing issues facing society, create the knowledge necessary to offer ecological perspectives on them, and ensure that ecological constraints and possibilities are taken into account as part of the larger political process.

3

Practicing Ecology

The question is: how, with a due sense of what the important problems are and a just weighing of evidence, do scientists move to the solution of problems in the forefront of their respective subdisciplines.

Marjorie Grene[1]

What are ecologists actually doing when they practice 'ecology'? What does what they are doing depend on? In this chapter we describe some of the problems we have been occupied with. But a mere description of somebody's investigations is not sufficient to give a picture of ecological research, because the practical work is conditioned by a variety of factors that are not manifest in the practice itself nor in the result. One of our motivations for giving this introduction is to scale ecological knowledge. What is known is often different from what ought to be known, and what ecologists actually do is often very different from what they would like to do.

Research is often viewed as a straightforward process of 'finding out the facts', and scientists imagined as open-minded heroes willing to examine everything. But this 'pure inquiry' myth of research clearly is not true. Scientists choose questions to investigate, and many factors enter that choice. Some are extraneous to science, and are presented to scientists by owners of science. Others are simply the hot questions of the moment that 'everyone' is examining and for which funding is available, while some are posed by the researchers because of practical implications or because they might help answer other, previously accepted problems.

We illustrate the 'pure inquiry' myth in Figure 3.1. All elements in this picture are false. Ecological research is imbedded in a set of social connections, and the actual work is done by a diffuse collective often called scientific community rather than isolated individuals.

64

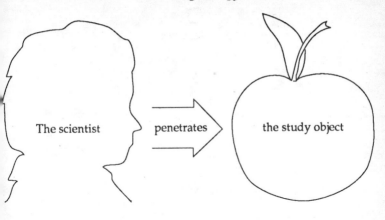

Figure 3.1
The myth of 'pure inquiry'

Research problems are constituted by previous research and social challenges, not found waiting out there. Options of research are restricted by constraints partly internal to intellectual work, partly forced by the society. The image of 'penetration' has nothing in common with this complex process.

We need to break the 'pure inquiry' caricature of science into parts. As a starting point we present in Figure 3.2 a scheme of six factors influencing ecological practice; they can be clarified as follows:

[1] Every specific ecological research endeavor in the field or in the laboratory comprises a diverse array of tasks integrated together by the research problem.

[2] The formulation of research problems is ultimately a theoretical task; theory is another field of research practice, and its fruitfulness is assessed on several grounds such as launching of new explanatory schemes, clarification of intuitive ideas, and derivation of testable predictions.

[3] A basic goal in ecological practice is a fruitful interaction between data and theory, but both data and theory have many faces, and assessing their mutual agreement is a multifaceted task, in which systematic criticism is a central element.

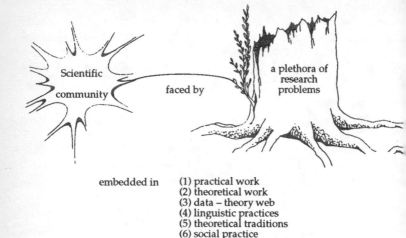

embedded in   (1) practical work
                (2) theoretical work
                (3) data – theory web
                (4) linguistic practices
                (5) theoretical traditions
                (6) social practice

Figure 3.2
The web of ecological practice

[4] Ecological practice is tied to language and linguistic communication.

[5] Ecological practice is tied to a web of accepted theories and ways of thinking that make those theories possible.

[6] Ecological practice is tied to social practice. The closer to environmental research one approaches, the more important this connection becomes.

In the following sections we elaborate upon these claims.

Research Practice: Working in the Field

An ancient Greek philosopher once remarked that there are two alternative ways of leading a human life: either to live, which is fine and nice, or to go to the sea. Similarly, there are two alternative ways of doing ecology: either to do ecology, which is fine and nice, or to go to the islands.

Leo Rybak[2]

Yrjö spent several years in the late 1970s studying the composition of land bird communities in the archipelago of Åland in the Baltic Sea, southwestern Finland. The archipelago consists of a main island of 1000 km^2 and 6000 islands and skerries of varying size in its surroundings, distances between the islands being short, seldom more than a few kilometers. The study area included 44 islands with an area range of 0.5 to 582 ha. In addition, reference censuses were made on the mainland of Åland.

In field research the actual work can be schematically divided into two phases: collection of data, and analysis of the data. In this particular study the field work comprised censuses of breeding birds on the islands in five summers. The breeding season in the north is compact, and the census work must be carried out during a few weeks from mid May through to late June. The censuses were made in early mornings, during 4–6 hours following the sunrise when the birds most actively sing. The results of the field work materialized in lists of estimated population sizes of all bird species on each island, the total population in the study area comprising in any single year about 7300 pairs of 65–70 species.

This technical description is obviously insufficient for characterizing the study. The element that is missing is the *research problem*, which would explain why the whole work was undertaken in the first place. The research problem was formulated as follows: which species of land birds are able to colonize small islands in the Åland archipelago, and what are ecological attributes of successful colonists? The archipelago can be viewed as a kind of 'natural experiment', where each small island is a unique combination of habitats distributed over larger areas on the mainland.

Formulating a research problem is a *theoretical task*, because empirical findings get their significance only in relation to previous theories. The separation between collecting data and analysing data breaks immediately down in a broader perspective. A theoretical grasp of the problem investigated is necessary *before* the empirical work is begun, and methods of collecting data and data analysis must be planned together; one also has to decide which information counts as 'data' relative to a particular problem.

The breeding land bird fauna of the main island of Åland comprises about 120 species, that is, the reference fauna is considerably richer than the breeding fauna of the small islands. One of the conclusions of the study was, however, that faunal impoverishment of the small islands is only apparent, being mainly due to the scarcity of a majority of the species in the mainland fauna. The reasoning was as follows: the pairs breeding yearly on the study islands number some 7200, whereas the bird fauna of the main island comprises some 330 000 pairs. Therefore some 2 per cent of the birds make it to the islands. If a species is represented by only 100 pairs on the mainland, and if each has an equal chance as any other species to settle on the islands, we would expect an average of 2 pairs on the islands but sometimes more and about one year in seven the species would be absent completely. The less common a species the more often it will be missing, so that if many of the 120 species are present in low numbers on the mainland, the islands would show fewer species at any one time.

Another main conclusion was that differences in the composition of bird communities on the islands were mainly determined by habitat differences: generalized species were everywhere, and species with specialized habitat requirements were lacking from islands that lack that particular habitat.

It seems that the colonization of islands by birds in the north can be characterized as 'sampling': the birds are mainly migratory, and the breeding community of a single island in a particular year can be viewed as a sample 'drawn' by the island from a species pool in the surrounding areas. The probability that a species is included in the community depends on its regional abundance and habitat preferences. An interesting corollary is that the composition of the community can be expected to change from year to year due to chance alone, analogously as in random sampling (Haila, 1983).

The Context of Field Work

The example could be multiplied. Ecologists are confronted by a plethora of practical research tasks, directed to various organisms and environments, and laboratory work is becoming increasingly common. However, we use this example to elaborate a few more general points concerning the empirical phase of field research.

[1] *The research problem* is an integrating category of field research. Censusing birds on small islands in the Åland archipelago is sensible scientific work once the underlying question is recognized as an interesting ecological problem. This is also true of purely descriptive work: recording and describing abundance and life-cycles of mites in the Antarctic, or reproductive behavior of the dwarf mongoose in

the Serengeti, or taxonomic relations among mosquitoes in central Asia, becomes a sensible scientific task once that particular phenomenon is recognized as an unknown that should be known.

Of course, descriptive work can be begun for whatever reasons, without any immediate connection with well-defined problems. Even in such studies, however, insight into relevant problems is needed when integrating the descriptive data into a larger body of knowledge.

[2] *Underlying theoretical ideas* influence greatly the defining of a research problem. The work on breeding bird communities on the Åland Islands was inspired by the theory of island biogeography, worked out in the 1960s (MacArthur and Wilson, 1967). The theory starts from an empirical regularity, documented in various archipelagoes over various taxa, that the number of species on an island tends to increase regularly with island area. The theory presents a hypothesis that explains this regularity as a result of a dynamic balance between immigration and extinction, viewed as functions of island area and isolation. The hypothesis predicts a particular equilibrium species number for each island (realized with stochastic variation, and with 'turnover' in species composition through time), which is larger, the larger and the closer the island is to the mainland. In addition, the theory includes considerations about factors influencing immigration and extinction rates, and about ecological and evolutionary processes on islands following colonizations. The latter aspects, however, are only loosely coupled with the equilibrium hypothesis; thus, a distinction can be made between equilibrium *model* and island biogeography *theory*: the 'model' refers to a particular explanatory scheme, the 'theory' to a set of generalizing considerations on the ecology of insular environments.

The theory of island biogeography had a revolutionary impact on ecological biogeography, for two main reasons. It emphasized the dynamic character of ecological communities on islands, viewed as a result of a long-term equilibrium between immigrations and extinctions of single populations. On the other hand, it assumed that the variation in species richness among islands can be ecologically understood by using just a few variables that are readily quantifiable, island area and isolation.

Geographic islands are more clearly identified than habitat 'islands', because terrestrial and aquatic environments are sharply distinct. Therefore islands put into sharp relief the situation which holds to some extent for all organisms: the environments of all living things are patchy, uneven, and discontinuous. A map of suitabilities would look like a topographic map, with contours of suitability 'elevations'. Therefore geographic islands were regarded as model systems for studying all of nature. In fact, MacArthur, Wilson and Levins had planned a sequel to *The Theory of Island Biogeography* on the theory of general biogeography. The idea of environmental patchiness was applied to the dynamics of single species populations by Levins (1969).

[3] Results of empirical studies often lead to modification of the underlying model and the theory. This is what happened during the Åland study: one conclusion was that the equilibrium model is actually inadequate for migratory birds in the north, because of their good dispersal ability (Haila, 1983, 1990). Island populations of migratory birds are not isolated as demanded by the theory, and interesting colonization patterns are not reflected strictly as presence and absence of species from islands, but rather as variation in population densities. The need is to investigate population sizes on different islands and compare them with the mainland, whereas the traditional equilibrium model is dealing only with qualitative, presence–absence data (Haila et al., 1983).

Once the equilibrium model became suspect in this particular context, the criticism led to further considerations. In a geographic sense 'an island' is a piece of land surrounded by water, but what is 'an island' in an ecological sense? In an ecological sense islands are pieces of land isolated from other pieces of land *relative to some relevant ecological process*. Defining appropriate criteria is an exercise in ecological scaling. For instance, small islands in the Åland archipelago are 'islands' for birds merely on the individual level, but for smaller organisms such as carabid beetles they are 'islands' on the level of population dynamics (Niemelä et al., 1988). Richard found similar variations when he studied some 140 islands in the eastern Caribbean in relation to the ant fauna. Some species can nest only in the ground and for them, mangrove cays made up of trees with their roots in shallow water were not islands at all. They were part of the space between islands. For tree nesting species, these cays were real habitats but coral sandbars were ecologically invisible. Finally those fortunate ants who could nest either in trees or in the ground faced a much denser archipelago and inhabited more islands of both types than the more exacting species.

This line of criticism thus leads to the conclusion that the different criteria of insularity need to be held separate in island ecology (Haila, 1990).

The criticism of the equilibrium theory also led to philosophical considerations about the role of theoretical models and their reification in ecological research. It began to seem that models have a 'semiotic dimension', that is, they are not only representations of ecological processes but also signs in the communication among ecologists (Haila, 1986). As a semiotic sign a model signifies a type of reasoning that is regarded as correct and acceptable.

[4] Any concrete ecological study involves a great variety of *methodological decisions* that are themselves genuine scientific problems. Collecting quantitative ecological data in nature is such a problem. A virtually new discipline has been born of bird census work alone, with international conferences held every two years. Censusing birds at northern latitudes is a relatively easy task, though, for several reasons: those birds are mainly monogamous, and singing or otherwise conspicuous males indicate each breeding territory. The breeding season is compact and occurs during the ecologists' vacation, which facilitates a concentrated census effort. Finally, the census work results in numbers that bear a reasonably explicit relationship to interesting ecological variables (the size of the reproducing population). For birds in, say, tropical rain forests, or for almost any other group of animals, the situation is not that fortunate.

Problems of methodology are fundamentally intertwined with theoretical issues. One must first decide which phenomena of nature to select for observation. One must then decide which details to record from the boundless flow of information potentially available to an observer. What one in principle has after a field work period is a table of data that stands for the phenomenon of interest (breeding bird communities on islands, for instance), and another table of data that stands for external conditions (characteristics of the islands where the birds were surveyed). These should be intelligently juxtaposed with each other. There is no way of doing this without a theoretical grasp of what the whole enterprise is about.

[5] Every specific research project has *implications for future research* and for *practical applications*. A continuation that grew from the work on the Åland Islands was to test whether the conclusions drawn on bird communities on these small islands, surrounded by water, also

hold true in 'habitat islands' such as fragments of old forests surrounded by clear-cuts and silvicultural areas. By and large, they do: bird communities are also assembled as 'samples' in forest fragments in the southern Finnish taiga (Haila et al., 1991). This fit between expectations and observations in forest 'islands' triggers another chain of theoretical questions and practical interpretations, for instance: can we somehow relate dynamics of bird communities in taiga 'islands' to dynamics of the taiga as an ecological formation? We can, as already discussed. Further, does this observation have implications for nature conservation in the taiga? It has, by emphasizing the space–time dynamics of the taiga as the appropriate framework for defining conservation needs instead of communities found at particular sites in a particular point in time.

[6] Our field work example also helps to undermine the myth that scientific results are achieved by individual practitioners. The competence needed in a single study ranges from theoretical understanding of the problem to particular methodological and data analytic skills, and it is clearly impossible that an individual ecologist command the whole spectrum. Consequently, it is also unrealistic to regard single research reports, drawn out of context, as important pathbreaking achievements. A variety of different tasks, appearing insignificant if taken in isolation, are integrated in the collective enterprise of practicing science.

An individual ecologist can contribute to this development in different ways. An element of 'relative independence' is involved here; good descriptive data have lasting value, whatever the theoretical interests of the ecologist who undertook the practical work, and the establishment of sound methodological procedures is of lasting value as well.

Theoretical Practice

Theory is not more one kind of thing than observation is.

Ian Hacking[3]

Theoretical work is carried out before, during and after the making of observations and carrying out of experiments. Before going into the field or laboratory, ecologists pose questions to be answered. We then have to ask, what observations or experiments will help answer the question? Often, the preliminary results pose new questions along the way. Then the results have to be analysed and interpreted.

Posing of Questions

What makes a theoretical problem seem exciting and worth exploring is itself a major question. Scientists are often unaware of the philosophical, esthetic and political considerations that influence the common culture of communities of scientists, particular fields of science, smaller groups or 'schools' of science and individuals. While some seek elegant simplicity, others enjoy the rich complexity of nature; while some emphasize the goal of precise prediction, others find the unexpected especially appealing; while some biologists see physics as a model to be emulated by biology, others regard 'physics envy' as retarding the development of ecology. While some enjoy the power of mathematical models to abstract general features from the tremendous complexity of nature, others are particularly sensitive to what is lost from the richness of the particular when theories are built. While some are consciously seeking results that can be applied, others regard practical work as second rate compared to 'pure' research guided apparently by caprice. Whether ecologists find stability or productivity or diversity or adaptability the interesting characteristic of ecosystems will certainly influence the course of their research, but the reasons for such choices, as distinct from arguments for them, are rarely examined.

Perhaps the sharpest controversies arise around the question of whether something is or is not a cause for concern. Are we significantly changing the climate of the earth or are recent droughts and heat waves simply part of the normal variability of nature? Are pesticides as a pest control strategy fundamentally flawed or is the solution more responsible design and testing of pesticides?

Sometimes the starting point for theoretical work is an observation: the earth seems to be getting warmer, scale insects on orange trees have an annual cycle of population growth and decline, gannets lay only one egg at a time, there are more species in the tropics than in the temperate zone and fewer on islands than on the mainland. The problem then is to explain the puzzling observation. Sometimes it happens that the general principle which explains the particular is not known, and has to be invented along with its application to the particular problem. Thus the relation of the general to the particular is not one way: new general principles are discovered, new concepts are put forth when the new observations do not fit previously recognized general principles.

A second way of choosing problems is to start with an answer and look for the problems it solves. Richard began research with the answer: environmental variability, and asked, what questions does this answer? That is, what is the significance for population genetics, ecology and evolution of the variability of environment in space and time? (Levins, 1968).

These questions seem to come directly from nature, but of course they do not. Concern for climate change is clearly related not only to its implications for human wellbeing in general but also to concern about what we are doing to the climate. Climate itself is an abstraction from the weather and from the experience of finding different places to be different. Population cycle is already a theoretical construct coming from counting insects at different times and organizing the numbers into patterns.

But other questions are obviously several steps away from nature: are niches broader in regions of environmental uncertainty? This presumes the notions of ecological niche, environment, uncertainty and at least some rudimentary way of measuring them. Do all species have the same rates of evolution? This presumes the general idea of rate of evolution as well as evolution itself. Is an ensemble of species at equilibrium? Here we take it for granted that the ensemble is a unit of some significance for us, and we either use 'equilibrium' in a loose common-sense way to mean the numbers aren't changing or in a more formal mathematical way that presumes a whole history of mathematics.

But all theoretical work is concerned with concepts which are several steps removed from direct experience. The objects of study are intellectual constructs – entities, classifications, concepts, equations and so on which have been invented in the course of scientific or pre-scientific practice in order to understand the world. Some have become so much a part of our common sense as to be immediately intelligible by everyone and to seem given by nature. Others are constructs invented for and by a particular field of science. Finally, some are new creations presented by a researcher along with the analysis of a problem. But in all cases what scientists study are intellectual constructs.

However, they are not completely arbitrary constructs. They have been constructed in order to understand something about the world and have been derived, however remotely, from the experience of interaction with and observation of nature. The important thing is to remember that they are constructs derived from experience. It is equally misleading to reject them because they are not simple 'objective' natural objects, or to imagine that they are, to reify them and allow our own creations to intimidate us.

Using Models as Tools

One common way to study a problem is through making a model and studying that model, as we already discussed in Chapter 2. There are many ways of representing the same kind of experience through models. They may correspond to different theoretical orientations or objectives, or evolve in the course of an investigation. We will examine now some of this process of model development in the case of population growth.

If we are concerned with population growth, we might start by saying, 'let N be the number of animals in a population' and ask how many will there be at some later time. Starting with 10 animals, we may then observe 20 a day later, then 40 on the following day, and then 80, then 130. The increases were first 10 and then 20, then 40, then 50 and as the population grows the successive increases are likely to grow bigger.

The arithmetic increase depends on how many there already are in the population, and therefore is not very informative. Another population starting with 30 and observed once a week is likely to give very different numbers, say, 30, 512, 8758, 17 067. It is not obvious how to compare them. But we believe that population increases come about by individual reproduction, and each individual (or pair or female) has a certain capacity to survive and reproduce. Depending on the situation we may decide to use total numbers, numbers of pairs or numbers of females for our calculations and redo the figures accordingly.

Next we can introduce an abstraction from these figures: a rate of increase. We divide the numbers present by the numbers present the previous time and obtain for the first population the numbers 2, 2, 2, and 1.6. These numbers are now much more uniform; we can say that the rate of increase was 2 for several days and then fell to 1.6. This way of looking at the problem gives a result quite different from the simple examining of the arithmetic increases. Whereas the first procedure tells us that the increases are themselves increasing, the second tells us that the *rate of increase* is slowing down. Further, we can now compare the populations. But since the first population was examined daily and the second weekly, in order for the results to be comparable we have to define the rate of increase as the ratio of population numbers on successive days. But we do not have such observations for the second population. Therefore we calculate the rate from weekly figures *as if* the rate per day was uniform during each week. This is done by saying, if the population is multiplied by R every day then in a week it is multiplied by R seven times, or R^7. Then R is the seventh root of the ratios of two consecutive weeks. The second population which was measured was multiplying by 1.5 per day for the first two weeks and then fell to 1.1 per day.

The theoretical work has allowed us to compare populations which were observed on different time scales and to show that the first population had faster growth rates than the second. We also discovered that although both populations were increasing, and the increases were themselves increasing, the *rates* of population growth were at first uniform and then decreased.

We have also created a new object of interest, the rate of growth per day, and can ask questions about it: how do these rates compare for different sizes of animals and plants? Is it different in the tropics from the temperate zone? Is it influenced by nutrition, temperature or population density? This type of question accepts the measure and asks about its pattern. L.B. Slobodkin (1953) gathered some of this data from the literature. Instead of using the ratio of populations in successive periods he used the more convenient form, the logarithm of that ratio.

A second line of work examines the measure itself more closely. This leads to new objects of interest: the rate of population change obviously depends on the birth and death rates. But since both death rates and the number of offspring change with age, we recognize the probability of survival to age x and the number of offspring produced at age x as objects of study. Further, we ask a new question: since the rate of growth will depend on the survival and reproduction of different age groups, how does the age composition of a population change as it grows? And what happens to the growth rate as a consequence?

Two different objects of study – the age distribution and the growth rate – have been brought together as mutually dependent under the same theoretical framework. The present convention is to study the numbers of females in a population, on the assumption that the ratio of males to females remains constant or that it doesn't matter, that there always are enough males to go around. Cases where this is not true are treated as special cases. Then the sex ratio becomes an object of interest.

We can now study the behavior of such a system – a table of age-specific survival and reproduction – independently of any real populations. We are asking 'what if' questions. If a population had this life table and these initial conditions, what would be the outcome. Several general conclusions have been reached from the study of these mathematical models of population growth.

First, under constant conditions (fixed birth and death rates) populations will reach a stable age distribution which is maintained·as the population grows or declines. (This will not happen if all reproduction is concentrated in a single age class.) Then, since all the ages occur in fixed proportions, we can trace the population growth by following only one age class or group of classes such as adults or larvae and calculating the others afterward.

Second, at the stable age distribution, the population is growing at a constant rate. If the population is increasing or remaining constant, then each age class is more numerous than any older age class. If some age classes are less common than their successors, this indicates either that the population is decreasing or that there have been non-uniform conditions in the past. In forests we frequently find cohorts of particular ages, corresponding to good years for reproduction, or missing age classes corresponding to disasterous years; this we observed in pine forests at Kevo (Chapter 2).

Third, while a population is approaching the stable age distribution its growth rate and even numbers may fluctuate. Fluctuations, if observed, lead to the following considerations:

[1] This is not evidence of a changing environment.

[2] The further the initial conditions are from the stable age distribution, the bigger the fluctuations.

[3] If the environment changes, the birth and death schedule (or l_x, m_x schedule where l_x is the probability of reaching age x, and m_x is the average number of offspring produced by individuals at age x) changes and therefore the stable age distribution also changes. The bigger the changes in the l_x, m_x table, and the more different the new stable age distribution, the bigger the fluctuations during transition.

Of course, for this claim to make sense we have to be able to define what we mean by a bigger difference in the table.

Further Directions of Theory

Now that we have a theoretical structure and some results that justify its use as interesting, research can take off in many directions. We could ask how the entries in the l_x, m_x schedule evolve, whether the population survives better when there are fewer offspring with higher survival probabilities or more offspring with lower survival per capita, what are the relative advantages of reproducing early under less favorable conditions or delaying reproduction until conditions get better, or of holding a territory through an unfavorable period with the risk of not surviving the stress. These questions lead to the notion of reproductive strategy we used when discussing taiga owls in Chapter 2.

The definition of r as $\log(N_{T+t}/N_T)/t$ allows us to write an equation for population growth:

(3.1) $dN/dt = rN$

This equation is formally correct. It becomes very misleading if we assume that because we have written the symbol r and called it a rate, it is therefore constant.

But we know that r is usually not constant. It may vary with the age distribution of the population as discussed above. It may change with the environment, either seasonally or erratically. One particularly interesting kind of environmental change is induced by the population itself, either attracting and feeding its predators or using up or stimulating the growth of its own resources. Or population growth could be affected directly by population density. The next step in theoretical research would examine, still as hypothetical questions on paper, what would the consequences be of any of these ways in which r is not constant? For instance, we might replace equation (3.1) by:

(3.2) $dN/dt = r_0 N(1 - N/K)$

Here we replaced r by $r_0(1 - N/K)$ so as to allow r to respond to population density. This is not the only way to allow density to enter the equation, but it is one that has been used frequently. If r_0 is positive, the population will grow from very small numbers upward toward K. As N approaches K, growth slows down and ceases. Therefore the original symbol r has been broken down into two: r_0 is the rate of increase when the population is negligibly small (sometimes called the intrinsic rate of increase), and K is the final carrying capacity of the environment for this population.

The use of this equation represents a step forward from (3.1) in that it allows growth to change with density and makes the distinction between initial rate of increase and final level. Populations can start growing very rapidly but then quickly reach a low limit, or grow slowly but for a long time and reach a high limit. Both r_0 and K are ecological characteristics of populations; they may vary from species to species or among populations of the same species, and may be subject to natural selection. Robert MacArthur introduced the notions of r and K selection to distinguish the directions of evolution for species in different ecological situations, and much work has gone into identifying the situations where one or the other might be expected to predominate. It has been claimed that under constant environmental conditions populations can approach their limit K, so that differences in K determine what happens. But if populations fluctuate due to random factors or if the species often colonizes new places (as small black ants colonize disturbed grounds in inner cities), then differences in K do not matter very much whereas differences in r_0 are the main cause of differences in growth rates.

But once again we confront the problem of reification, the treating of our own intellectual constructs as if they were natural objects and assuming that things given different symbols are therefore different.

While one direction of research works out the consequences of a theoretical approach, another is concerned with how to test the theory. Even the simple models of population growth make use of theoretical entities such as r and K, and abstractions such as populations. In order to test the theory or even to map the distribution of its objects we have to be able to measure or identify them. The more steps a theory is removed from direct experience, the more abstract its entities are, the more devious the pathway back to observation and experiment.

Suppose now that we have theoretical results indicating what might possibly happen. But do these theoretical conclusions have any relation to what really happens in nature? In order to test theory for relevance, we have to identify natural situations in which the assumptions of the theory are likely to be satisfied, and in which the process of interest will be strong enough to stand out among all the other influences so that it will be easily recognizable. For example, we have concluded above that the further a population is from its stable age distribution the bigger the fluctuations will be even under constant conditions. Where might we find such populations?

One possibility is during colonization. Usually colonization of a new area is carried out by one particular stage in the life cycle such as seeds, spores, winged aphids, salt water resistant dormant stages or young adults looking for territory. Small islands with their rapid turnover might be good places to look for colonization, build up, and fluctuations of populations. The species should have short life cycles so that we can observe several generations in a reasonable time or else be important enough for some practical reason so that they will be kept under observation for a long time. Plants are usually not suitable for this kind of study because generations are long and because as the plants grow they change their environments. Mouse populations do fluctuate widely, but the fluctuations are absent or at least much reduced on islands, and we suspect that their fluctuations are associated with predation rather than simple life table events. Further, the territorial structure of mouse populations violates the assumptions of the simple life table model.

Planktonic species might seem to be good choices. They are abundant and short-lived, but seem to be very much dominated by the seasonal changes affecting the whole community. Insects might be suitable choices; especially in cultivated fields where we have many replicates, the insects may invade at somewhat different times in different fields, and we could observe several generations per summer. There is, however, the difficulty that it is not easy to tell the age of an insect. We can certainly identify eggs, larvae, pupae and adults but not the ages of adults. Therefore the theory has to be modified to depend not on ages directly but on stages of development. In fish, size classes can be used instead of age. Caswell (1989) has worked out the life table model modified to distinguish stages instead of ages.

Mosquitoes might be a satisfactory choice. After the first rains following a drought, the eggs of species that breed in small bodies of water will hatch in large numbers almost simultaneously. These will develop, emerge and lay eggs in an almost synchronized pattern, giving a new burst of emerging mosquitoes several weeks later. But predators are important in their demography, and crowding of larvae in different bodies of water can affect development rates.

In the end it is a discouraging search: it is almost impossible to find situations in which life table phenomena can be observed in a pure form without the interference of environmental variability or density effects. We now have two choices: we could modify the model so as to take into account a variable environment or study the life table with density effects. Or we could create an artificial situation in which populations are grown in the laboratory under constant conditions and without crowding. If we make the second choice, the population is in a sense serving as a computer. It is no longer a natural situation and therefore avoids the question, do these life table phenomena play a significant role in nature. Therefore some ecologists argue that these experiments are a waste of time: if the assumptions of the model are satisfied the results have to follow, and we might as well do it on a computer. If the assumptions are not satisfied the experiment is irrelevant.

However, despite that plausible argument it doesn't turn out that way. No cage experiment really isolates a population from all processes other than those of interest. Under the controlled conditions, with quite precise expectations, deviations from the model are especially apparent. New, unexpected phenomena appear. In Thomas Park's (1962) studies of caged populations of flour beetles, there was always fluctuation. The population was too small to reach a real stable age distribution, and the random events of mortality and reproduction repeatedly worked to displace the age distribution further from its theoretical end point while the average processes approached it. Furthermore, although the departures from the stable age distribution were random events, the fluctuations showed regular periodicity that depended on the life table. That is, a combination of a life table that when acting alone would give an equilibrium population and random events which alone should give random fluctuations acting together gave periodic fluctuations. In addition, cannibalism was discovered as an unexpected density effect.

When Slobodkin (1961) studied competition between two species of hydra, he found that one of them contained symbiotic algae which carried out photosynthesis and shared in the product so that it did not depend on predation for all its food. In each case, the controlled conditions designed to isolate and magnify a particular phenomenon of interest in fact revealed new processes that would otherwise have remained hidden among the complexities of natural processes. The artificial communities now become systems for observing the effects of randomness in small populations, cannibalism or hybridization or competition modified by symbiosis.

The difficulty of isolating a simple life table process does not make the theoretical argument wrong. But it does require us to expand the theory, to ask questions such as how life table phenomena interact with density effects or competition or variable conditions. Therefore a major task of theoretical practice is to modify theory so as to make it testable and identify conditions under which predictions from the theory can be compared with empirical results.

It is often the case that different criteria for a good test of theory are contradictory. The better the control of conditions and the easier the setup for observation, the less natural is the situation. The more uniform the results the fewer replications we need, but the greatest uniformity usually occurs under optimal growing conditions so that the effects of environmental stress and variability are often lost. The simpler the setup, the more complete the isolation, the fewer the number of variables, the easier it is to observe and interpret the observations and the further it departs from the richness of nature.

Therefore ecologists are always juggling these contradictory demands on good research design. They are even divided into schools of thought based on sensitivity to the inadequacy of each others' approaches. But sometimes they recognize the need for a mixed strategy and move back and forth freely between easy observation or control and realism, between bottle or cage experiments and field observation. Then the controlled experiment is seen not as duplicating nature, but as amplifying certain aspects of nature for better observation, while distorting others in order to do this. And good theory not only understands the artificial experimental system but also how the processes revealed there will be changed or masked in other situations.

But testing a theory is not simply seeing whether its predictions correspond to observation. Any set of observations can usually fit several theories. The problem becomes one of choosing among alternative theories. The choice is influenced by a number of criteria.

First, is it plausible? That is, do the assumptions correspond to what we think we know? If the assumptions of a theory contradict our commonly accepted and strongly held ideas then we are likely to demand a much stronger preponderance of evidence before accepting the theory. This gives a conservatism to science, an intolerance of 'way out' ideas which makes it extremely difficult for new concepts to get a serious hearing. Examples of the resistance of establishment medicine to alternative approaches are classic, and are often cited as evidence that science is not open-minded or objective.

The plausibility criterion has been formalized in the statistical approach known as Bayesian inference. Bayesian inference starts out with the *a priori* probability of something being true before an observation is made, and the increment of probability due to the observation. As long as there is a common agreement about the *a priori*, the procedures lead to results that people could agree to. But where differences in interests, philosophies and experience divide the participants in a dispute there is no procedure which can eliminate the differences in judgements about the *a priori* probabilities, and the biases easily become bigotries. The decisions among theories are strongly influenced by prior beliefs. We are better off accepting this reality and investigating what those beliefs are and where they come from in the process of criticism and self-criticism.

Theories are not proven. At best they can be shown to be consistent with observation and previous accepted theory, and to be better than alternative theories. By better we usually mean covers more situations, predicts more accurately, is more testable, opens up new and exciting questions and is less offensive to our beliefs. The question of whether it is better depends very much on what alternative theories are used for comparison. Then theoretical practice must determine what are reasonable alternative theories, what the competing theories predict, where their predictions coincide and where they are different, seek out as many predictions as possible in which they differ, and design experiments or observations which make it easier to determine which predictions hold.

With the increase in computing capacity and data banks of all sorts, literature search has become a common research method. For example, to test a hypothesis about the relation between island area and the number of species of ants or birds that live there, we could look up the results of expeditions to these islands and surveys of distributions of particular birds or ants. This kind of literature search is not the preamble to research, the kind of review of the literature which aims at finding previous opinion on the topic of interest, but is itself the research.

However, the use of data collected for different purposes and at different times has its own problems. The numbers of species reported will be related to the number that were there but also to the thoroughness of the search, the techniques used at the time and the status of the taxonomy when the reports were made.

Sometimes the preferences of the researcher have a strong influence on the outcome. For example the numbers of orchid species reported from Martinique and Guadaloupe are quite a bit higher than those from Dominica, which lies between the two and has comparable habitats. The difference is that Martinique and Guadaloupe were French possessions and were surveyed by H. Stehle, who had a special fondness for orchids and a tendency to recognize small differences with distinct names. Dominica, although near by, was not directly accessible from the French possessions but had to be reached indirectly by way of Antigua. Surveys of the British possessions were carried out by Beard, whose interests focused more on trees and who was more inclined to combine slightly different specimens of orchids under the same species name.

Data and Theory

If you do not know what you are measuring, take the more accurate measurements.[4]

In the preceding pages we have elaborated on different aspects of collecting data in the field, and juxtaposing the data with theory. Ecological research aims at solving problems, and a basic prerequisite for success is that one understands what the problems are all about. Another prerequisite is a satisfactory agreement between data and theory. In this section we elaborate further this relationship. Our starting point, presented in Figure 3.3, is that theory is not a fixed 'body' but rather consists of multifaceted activities which seek congruence with different types of data.

Theoretical work can be divided into three parts: *speculation, calculation* and *experimentation* (following Hacking, 1983). 'Speculation' means trying to make sense of the phenomena under study and making loose, verbal models of what that piece of the world might be like. Speculation is not idle, nor blind guesswork, but an integral part of scientific activity which draws upon various types of knowledge, intuition and aesthetic preferences.

The most elementary type of data corresponding to speculation is *existential generalization* – growing awareness that a particular phenomenon of nature is interesting and deserves explanation. Existential generalizations are arrived at by induction. Induction gives no 'proofs' but is a perfectly legitimate (and, in a historical perspective,

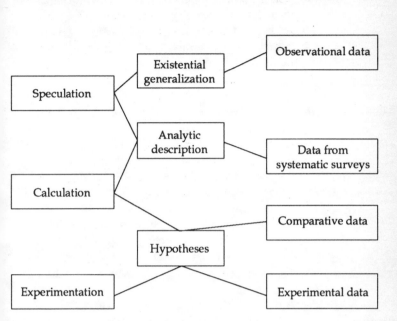

Figure 3.3
Interactions among different types of data and theory in ecological research

the only possible) starting point for theoretical reasoning. (Recall Aristotle: 'As we cannot know the reason for a fact before we know the fact, we cannot know *what* a thing is before knowing *that* it is' (1964).)

'Calculation' is the derivation from a speculation such consequences that are testable – that is, we know both *what* to test and *how* to conduct the test. Calculation is used to derive explicit logical consequences from an idea arrived at by speculation, and thus brings the idea into closer resonance with the world. Calculation should ideally result in formulation of specific explanatory hypotheses. Calculation can be pursued as an entirely theoretical activity, but formal theorizing should be indirectly related to data through the following two elements.

The first of them we call *analytic description* which is situated halfway between speculation and calculation. Analytic description is systematic data collecting such that the data are continuously reflected against theoretical ideas and intuitions. A theoretically conscious analytic description provides a first test whether constructs 'speculated' about in a particular field make sense at all. On the other hand, a systematic description can give novel starting-points for 'calculating' such specific predictions that are realistic enough to be worth experimental testing.

The second element is *experimentation*, which means conducting controlled tests of particular hypotheses. The need for experiments is widely acknowledged among ecologists today, but experiments have in several ways a different role in ecology from that in classical laboratory sciences. In some fields of ecology, for instance, biogeography or morphological adaptation, manipulations are impossible and intelligent comparisons are as close to experimentation as one can get, just as in astronomy or geology. To this corresponds a particular type of data, collated with a comparison as a purpose. Comparisons must be based on criteria that are theoretically justified.

Another problem is that ecological experimental systems have a non-trivial history, as we discussed in the previous section. This means that experiments that are 'purified' of such effects are, in a very strong sense *constructed*, and it is very difficult to appreciate the relevance of experimental data to what is going on in nature. The nature of the data extracted by experiments is strictly determined by the experimental setting and by the hypothesis being tested.

The structure of theory–data interactions depicted in Figure 3.3 does not represent logical or chronological primacy. All the elements of the scheme are continuously necessary in research although they, of course, get varying primacy in different research projects.

Criticism in Research

Mutually contradictory views are held on the most fundamental issues of ecology. Systematic criticism is the way to evaluate different views, test their credibility. Thus, criticism is both a negative and a constructive activity. It is doubt, but it is also a means to find out what is valuable and worth upholding in various views and beliefs, for the time being.

Karl Popper (1935) introduced criticism into the analytic tradition of the philosophy of science as a methodological procedure known as *hypothetico-deductivism*; the idea was anticipated by many nineteenth century thinkers, most explicitly by Charles Peirce. The key element in hypothetico-deductivism is the realization, based on classical logic, that it is impossible to prove universal statements true, it is only possible to falsify them. Hence Popper's term *falsification*. Popper reacted against logical positivists of the 1930s who used *verification* as their methodological slogan: positivists held that scientific statements ought to be unambiguously verified by empirical observations, but this is logically impossible.

Popper's argument is based on a logical rule often called *modus tollens*: when considering a hypothetical material implication ('if p then q'), which is the logical form of a causal hypothesis, an observed 'q' does not allow accepting the implication, but an observed 'non-q' is a sufficient condition for rejecting the implication. In other words, the relationship between evidence supporting a causal hypothesis and evidence contradicting it is asymmetric: a positive observation cannot prove a particular causal explanation, because some factor other than the one postulated in the explanation may be the real cause. In contrast, if a negative observation is made, then the assumed causal mechanism predicting a positive outcome cannot possibly be correct.

This is the methodological doctrine of *hypothesis testing*. Predictions are deduced from the hypothesis that is tested, and these predictions are compared with observations (or, preferably, experiments). If predictions and data are in disagreement, the hypothesis is rejected. If they are in agreement, the hypothesis gets support.

The domain of hypothesis testing must be qualified for several reasons. It is sobering to notice that the basis of Popperian hypothetico-deductivism is open-ended. This is because refutation of a hypothesis is based on a *positive* decision to accept an observation contradicting predictions of the hypothesis. But observations are theory-laden: what is observed depends on what is expected to be worth observing, and an idea is needed about how to formulate reliable basic statements. *Induction*, that is, generalization based on recurring observations, is the process of arriving at basic statements held true for the time being. The ambiguous relation between statements held provisionally true and theories criticized on the basis of these statements demonstrates that observations and the theoretical context develop together, and criticism relates to this whole.

By implication, it is rational to be interested in where the tested theoretical ideas come from. This is denied by Popper who assumes a very sharp distinction between the basic statement, which is not to be questioned, and the hypothesis which is tentative. He then assigns a very specific and limited role to contradiction in the scientific process. When some observations make a hypothesis incompatible with the basic statement the hypothesis must go. This is indeed the situation in many kinds of research: if an animal gains weight during the winter, we would reject the hypothesis that it does not eat at all during winter rather than reject the physical principle of the conservation of matter.

But when we move to more interesting and general questions the issue is less clear. Then Popper's formulation hides the role of contradiction in scientific research and the context within which two statements may become contradictory. Consider for instance the following propositions: first, elephants are tropical species, second, Siberia has a tundra habitat. There is nothing contradictory about these statements.

But now let somebody find elephant bones in Siberia and we face a contradiction. It may be resolved in several ways. First, the bones were not after all those of elephants but rather elephant-like creatures which did not have the same habitat restriction. Then both original statements may still hold, but they are no longer contradictory. Second, they were indeed elephant bones, but Siberia used to be tropical. The proposition 'Siberia is a tundra' has to be modified (not abandoned) to recognize that climate is not a permanent characteristic of a region. Third, elephants are not inherently tropical but just happen to be restricted to the tropics now. Then we investigate what determines the range of a species. Fourth, the bones were indeed elephant bones, and the habitat indeed a tundra, but the bones were transported to the tundra long after the death of the elephants, perhaps as trade goods of ancient hunters. One major theme among paleontologists is the study of deposition remains and ways of determining whether they were found at the site of death or transported afterwards. The assumption that bones are found where the animal dies must be questioned.

Each of these alternative questions leads to different research. During a prolonged period of time, the contradiction remains alive and dispute continues, with different sub-sciences, schools of thought or individuals giving greater or lesser weight to each statement depending on the way in which it is congenial or disturbing to their broader outlook. The presence of contradiction in science, unlike in formal logic, does not bring down the whole edifice. It can even be tolerated for an extended time without causing too much discomfort. This is especially true if the means for resolving the apparent contradiction do not yet exist.

The promotion of hypothesis testing as the only sound method of ecological research is misplaced: ecologists get too dogmatic a conception of how ecological research should be conducted. Hypothesis testing becomes the dominating mode of work, irrespective of whether the hypotheses to be tested make sense in the first place, and pushes aside other types of research. In particular, a dogmatic emphasis of hypothesis testing means that *good descriptive work is underrated*. It is a completely legitimate procedure to begin with good descriptive data and move 'backwards' to hypotheses about causes, and it is perfectly reasonable to be concerned with how this might be most effectively achieved. It is both an interesting and important problem how a particular (hypothetical) explanation is derived; whether it is plausible in the light of underlying data, methods applied and the reasoning used. Specific hypotheses are indeed specific; if a work is designed from the beginning to test a specific hypothesis, the data collected are likely to be worthless for any other purpose. This is a particular issue in fields of ecology where most of the hypotheses around are unrealistic. Devastating attacks against unrealistic hypotheses may promote an ecologist's academic career, but they do not increase our substantive knowledge of nature.

Herbert Simon (1977) mused about the following paradox: imagine that a scientist has found unexpected features in a data set A_1, and comes up with a plausible explanation. Then another, independent but equally relevant data set A_2 is found in the literature, and the explanation E is congruent with the new data. Compare this to the situation that the data set A_2 had been collected in a formal test of the hypothesis E. Simon notes that, purely logically, the evidence in favor of E is equally strong in both cases, but scientists oriented to hypothesis testing tend to regard the second case as more supportive than the first one.

Hypothesis Testing Versus Blind Empiricism

A strong argument in favor of hypothesis testing is that it entails: first, identifying potential causal mechanisms for the phenomena of interest; second, deriving implications of these assumed mechanisms; and third, constructing (or trying to find in nature) situations where the implications may possibly be empirically registered. Hypothetico-deductivism helps to make theoretical thinking explicit and rigorous, in contrast to intuitive and muddled, and conteracts blind empiricism.

Empiricism is running wild for instance in the applied fields of agriculture, forestry and fisheries (Levins, 1973b; Cox and Atkins, 1975; Larkin, 1978). It is enhanced by the apparently atheoretical and narrowly 'practical' nature of problems in those fields. Consider the following problem: how does adding artificial fertilizer influence the growth of forest? A standard way of studying such a problem is to establish so many experimental plots that are treated with fertilizers in various ways and wait to see what happens. Possibly one gets, after 5, 10 or 20 years, a set of numbers indicating differences in forest growth that correlate with treatment, for instance, the amount of fertilizer per hectare.

The most immediate, and usually devastating enough, problem with such a research setting is that during a period of a decade or two the experiment most probably becomes 'confounded', that is, the experimental plots are influenced in a systematic fashion by uncontrolled factors. Suppose a winter occurs with unusually heavy snowing, with consequent damage to trees. It may turn out that fertilized trees are damaged more badly than unfertilized, in which case the experiment is nullified.

However, even if a plausible general correlation is achieved, the result leaves us in the dark concerning what actually has happened. This may be significant for the practical question the study was supposed to address. Artificial fertilizing may, for instance, induce trees to grow more rapidly but with the tissues becoming softer than they used to be. The resulting timber may be economically worth less than timber of the old type. As a matter of fact, this seems to happen to Finnish pine-trees (*Pinus sylvestris*) under artificial fertilizing.

In addition, if one just records 'what happens' without theoretical hypotheses about relevant processes one may notice afterwards that an entirely wrong type of data was collected. Suppose the experiment described above was supplemented with a study of the effect of fertilizing on soil fauna. Average numbers per m^2 of various soil-living arthropods such as springtails, mites, spiders and worms were monitored in the study plots from year to year and it was found that the numbers of different animals vary in correlation with the amount of fertilizer added.

However, this is not sufficient to answer, *why* did the composition of the fauna change? Other measurements than mere mean numbers should have been made – but identifying necessary measurements requires that hypotheses be formulated about causal pathways. Neither do the data tell, *how* did the changes observed actually take place? To answer this question we would need data, for instance, on spatial distribution and age structure of the populations.

Designing and conducting experiments is a much more demanding task than is usually acknowledged in applied research. When criticizing dogmatic hypothetico-deductivism we are not propagating blind empiricism but urging that experiments and hypothesis testing be conducted with full consciousness of the conceptual issues involved.

Language and Reification

> *Obviously, subject is what is said, style is how. A little less obviously,*
> *this formula is full of faults.*   Nelson Goodman[5]

Science is tied to language: the interpretation of theories, models, mathematical equations, concepts and terms boil down into sentential statements. This claim is not likely to raise much opposition, but its implications need elaboration; an excellent introduction is Hacking (1975). In this section we pursue the question, what complications does language create in ecological practice?

How do Theories Refer to the World?

An elementary problem concerning the role of language in science is the following: we are inclined to think that terms and concepts used in science are transparent and refer directly to external objects and states-of-affairs, but such a view is untenable. Gottlob Frege (1892) drew a distinction between two dimensions of the 'meaning' of words, namely, *extension* and *intension*. 'Extension' (often called 'reference') is the object designated by the word, and 'intension' (often called 'sense') is the meaning of the word within the linguistic context where it is used. The distinction is clarified by the example Frege used himself: the terms 'Morning star' and 'Evening star' have identical extension, the planet Venus, but their intensions differ.

But if the distinction between extension and intension is relevant concerning terms as straightforward as Morning star and Evening star, how can we figure out the significance of the distinction concerning theoretical constructions used in ecology such as growth rate, r, or carrying capacity, K? In other words, when we use theoretical terms in ecological writing, do we 'mean' their *extensions* and the relations among them, or *intensions* and the relations among them? Does the distinction matter?

Our sensibility in this matter is confused by the heritage of positivism, discussed more thoroughly later. Logical positivists of the 1920s and 1930s overlooked completely Frege's distinction and tried, instead, to construct an ideal language of science that would be purely extensional. The ideal language was supposed to be mediated to external objects by 'sense data', linguistically expressed by 'observation terms', and structured by rules of elementary logic.

Thus, the intuition of most scientists is that entities spoken about by terms in scientific theories are found out there in the world, and that is all. A fortifying factor is that elementary logic and set theory, which give formal tools for model building in science, are, by definition, extensional; this is a purely formal characteristic of classical logic.

Let us clarify the significance of the distinction. The crux of the matter is the extensionality versus intensionality of theoretical terms. The use of nouns that refer to individual objects usually presents no problems in ecological practice. We can take single observation terms for granted provided we can take for granted our ability to make the observation needed and to recognize the object observed, as we normally do. For instance, when we see a chaffinch singing in a tree and say so, we can skip over semantic subtleties and regard the chaffinch as the extension of the statement. (But, of course, the noun 'chaffinch' is theoretical to the extent that you need to tell chaffinches apart from willow warblers and bramblings.)

However, if we say: (S_1) 'here is a Chaffinch advertising his territory by singing in a tree', the question of extension versus intension arises with a new force. We are now making an *interpretation* of the behavior of the bird, instead of merely stating it, with the help of a theoretical term, 'territory'. What is the status of terms such as 'territory'?

One possibility would be to think that the term 'territory' has a straightforward extension but this would lead to serious difficulties, as medieval nominalists realized: one should resort to a Platonic doctrine that ideal entities exist independently of the mind, that somewhere would be a 'territory in general' as an extension of a statement about the territory of a particular chaffinch. On the other hand, when using the term 'territory' relative to a particular chaffinch, we want to express something general, something more than observed in this particular situation. It thus seems we must consider a theoretical term intensional: the 'meaning' of the term territory is a generalization from single cases.

The solution to this puzzle is that it is misleading to take theoretical terms as single words. Theoretical terms are defined by, and thus get their 'meaning' from, a whole network of linguistic usage.

W.V. Quine has pursued this idea further by arguing that meaningful entities in language are not individual words, nor individual sentences, but bundles of sentences. That single words appear meaningful to us is because we are used to meeting them as elements in complete sentences, but it is a fallacy to take single words as 'refering to' well-defined objects.

An important clarification of the conceptual structure of science follows. Quine (1961: 42) characterized the totality of our knowledge as a man-made fabric which impinges on experience only along the edges. The fabric includes statements with alternative roles in the totality. Some of them are directly related to experience regarding particular objects and events, others have a systemic role in twining the threads together. Sentences and terms of the latter type cannot be directly extensional; when we talk of their 'meaning' we talk of their intension.

Quine's metaphor serves to emphasize the social reality of science as a domain of human activity as against the naive notion of science being 'out there'. He argues that science is created, not found. But like all metaphors it is also misleading and can seem to justify the viewpoint that science is completely capricious. If science is indeed a human-made fabric, the threads none the less come from nature, as passed through previous human experience. Cotton, linen, wool or polyester all give different final fabrics. In our view no aspects of science are free of social or natural aspects, and it would be futile to attempt to isolate or assign relative weights to the one or the other.

To elaborate the point further, let us look at our statement about the chaffinch and its territory (S_1). The theoretical notion of 'territory' is an integral part of the intension of the sentence. The bundle of sentences from which the term 'territory' derives its meaning comes from how 'territories' have been talked about in the past. The notion of territory in ecology dates back to the early twentieth century, and it is in very popular use today as a common-sense interpretation of how various animal species, particularly birds, use space: they acquire, occupy and defend a territory against their conspecifics in order to monopolize some scarce resource such as food, safe nest site or mate. Bird males commonly announce their territory by singing; this is supposed to deter conspecific males from entering the territory. In recent decades territorial behavior has also been the object of formal models that investigate, for instance, the economy of territorial defense.

Even taking this popular view of territoriality for granted, the relationship of an observation of a singing bird and territoriality is, of course, oblique. The bird may be a migrant that continues his journey further north a few minutes later, or he may be a 'floater' that has not acquired a nesting site at all but is merely roaming about, temporarily singing here and there.

But even if the chaffinch actually were singing close to a nest where his mate is brooding, and even if it were firmly established that singing equals deterring neighboring males, this observation is ambiguous concerning the nature of territoriality. The observation implies no idea about what is the point of deterring other males in the first place. What is defended against conspecific males is hardly 'space' *per se* (another abstraction), rather something that is in space and is important for the birds. Resources? Nest site? The mate?

We push further this example because of some surprising empirical results recently obtained in a study on chaffinch territoriality in Finland (Hanski and Haila, 1988). Movements of individual chaffinch males in the breeding season were tracked using radio-telemetry, and the result produced the surprise: although singing was localized within an area of 1–2 ha, which might be labelled 'singing territory', the males spent up to 50 per cent of the total time observed outside their singing territories (often more than 1 km away), moving around apparently foraging. In other words, territoriality and foraging movements are largely uncoupled in the chaffinch, which implies that the common sense notion of territory, emphasizing the importance of food resources, is inadequate. So are formal models that elaborate territorial behavior from the defensibility of resources; chaffinch males do not seem to defend resources.

To sum up, the 'extension' of (S_1) is the situation in which the observation interpreted by (S_1) was made, including our reasons to believe that the observation was adequate. The 'intension', on the other hand, depends on the theoretical perspective adopted in interpreting the term 'territory'.

Language in Scientific Communication

The role of language is not merely that of referring to the external world. Using language is essentially communication. A purely semantical view of language is thus restrictive. Medieval logicians already realized that the study of language can be divided into three fields, namely, *syntax* dealing with the rules of constructing meaningful sentences, *semantics* dealing with the meaning of sentences, and *pragmatics* dealing with the practical use of sentences.

We can formulate the significance of 'pragmatics' as follows: in order to be meaningful to its users, language must be interpreted, and interpretation takes place within a communicative context. The interpretation of a linguistic expression builds upon *presuppositions*, which are assumptions needed in order that the statement be understandable at all. Such presuppositions are of different types. Some are logical and depend on the form of the expression (an example being the famous question, 'Have you discontinued beating your husband?'). Others are more directly related to substantive claims about the world; this we discussed in the section on theoretical practice. The point to remember is that communication is always based on a shared background of beliefs. In interpreting single statements most of what is said is taken for granted in order that it be possible to assign the statement any meaning at all.

This is the 'hermeneutic circle' of interpretation: language used in communication consists of words and expressions, but words and expressions get their meaning only in the context of the whole communication. Disturbingly enough, this is true of the language of the sciences as well.

It is possible to approach this problem area by asking first, how is a linguistic context created? Ludwig Wittgenstein (1953) used the notion of *language-game* to describe a particular language as well as the specific communicative context in which it is used; here we take up the interpretation of 'language-games' of Hintikka and Hintikka. In their view the traditional way of comprehending language-games as purely 'horizontal', that is, as dealing merely with the role linguistic expressions have in a community of speakers, has been misplaced. Instead, they related language-games to the relationships between words and the world. In this view language-games are 'vertical' and constitute 'the mode of existence of the basic semantical relations between language and the world' (1986: 213).

A community of speakers is not related to the material world only by means of words, neither is the language used in the community dissociated from extralinguistic practices. Hintikka and Hintikka included in a language-game both linguistic expressions and extralinguistic activities resorted to when comparing those expressions with reality. Underlying was an assumption that language is related to how people make a living, and living is made in a material world. Thus, the whole set of practices connected with making a living constitutes a 'language-game', and different subactivities constitute more specific language-games. This is what makes the notion of language-game relevant for understanding science: science is an activity based on a variety of practices, and science results in linguistic expressions carried further in scientific communities that have partly their own vocabularies, related to their own practices and traditions.

The view that science is a 'language-game' allows two alternative interpretations about the relationships of scientific language and the world. A 'pessimistic' alternative would be to regard language as a closed prison-house in which the terms used are internally defined and from which it is impossible to contact the world. In contrast, the view of language-games promulgated by Hintikka and Hintikka is 'optimistic' in the sense of seeing the specific practices of scientific communities constituting their language-games as a material bridge between words and the world. Which one of these views is more plausible depends on the character of scientific practice itself, in other words, on our ability to incorporate into scientific practice procedures that help us avoid falling prey to closed linguistic structures.

Scientists are traditionally 'optimistic' about the truth of scientific theories and accept the simple assumption that the sciences have an ultimate, transcendental justification. Such grounds are defunct; the traditional epistemological justification of science that stems from Descartes – and ancient Greece – and views science as a 'mirror of nature' in the head of a conscious observer, was shown untenable by Richard Rorty (1980). We have no transcendental, epistemological bridges to material reality available, all we have are various developing practices within historical contexts. This underlines the conclusion that it is necessary to investigate science not as a theoretical structure but as *practical activity* which is anchored to the world through systematic, material interventions.

Origins of Reification

What we have discussed thus far makes understandable *reifications* in science, that is, that abstractions used in theoretical models are often taken as representations of reality. The logical basis of reification is in disregarding the distinction between extension and intension, in assuming that scientific terms are simply extensional. An elementary form of reification is to assume that parameters used in an analytic model – such as growth rate, r, or carrying capacity, K – actually do have straightforward, material references in nature. They do not; they are intensional constructs we make use of in order to generalize about the growth of populations, and about the maximum size populations can reach.

In addition, there is a communicative dimension to reification, namely, the possibility that some particular type of using abstractions in scientific communication turns into a 'sign' and takes up a significance on this ground. This idea draws upon *semiotics*, defined by Charles Peirce as a study of the laws by which one sign gives birth to another and one idea gives birth to another, in a scientific intellect. That a particular 'sign' inspires ideas may be completely disassociated from the 'meaning' of that sign except as a symbol of a specific way of approaching a problem. These ideas can shed light on some recent problems in appropriating ecological models; Haila (1986) originally applied the idea to the equilibrium model of island biogeography. A model may turn into a sign and begin to lead its own life within the community of ecologists as a signifier of 'interesting ecology' by purely formal criteria.

This is reification of a whole model, which also implies a presupposed way of viewing the object the model is thought to stand for. Sharon Kingsland (1985, 1986) recorded illuminating examples of controversies around analytic models in ecology.

The logical and communicative basis of reification does not alone, however, explain its pervasiveness in interpretations of ecology. Reification is the more likely, the more 'obvious' reference a particular term has in our every-day experience. But every-day experience is of course interpreted in the same linguistic context as scientific experience.

The notion of territory provides a good example. As we saw, it is in popular use in connection with the occupation of space in a whole variety of animal species ranging from mammals and birds to insects, but the phenomenon of 'territory' has a great number of different facets in different species and circumstances. The general notion of 'territoriality' skips over this variation and, taken literally, implies that animals have a general 'territorial instinct'. This instinct can then be transferred to humans as a 'territorial imperative'. The territorial imperative helps to 'explain' such features of human behavior as having a home, fencing in a pasture or feeling emotional ties to one's place of birth. The next step is to use the 'territorial imperative' in interpreting the behavior of animals ('of course animals defend their territories similarly as we humans do'). The 'territorial imperative' of the poor animals then feeds back to the human society once more – and so on, indefinitely. Being firmly embedded in the social psychology of capitalism, the 'territorial imperative' has the force of Aunt Jabisco's theorem, 'It is a fact the whole world knows.'

The Burden of Traditions

Since theories are not wholly determined by empirical data, they must share to some extent the norms, presuppositions and prejudices of their own culture. Mary Hesse[6]

In the previous section we introduced the concept of presupposition in a logical and linguistic context. However, the most important presuppositions of scientific claims originate from theories, beliefs and ways of thought by which every single statement is backed. On this level it is also true that to say anything at all, a whole network of presuppositions must be assumed. Young though ecology is, its development is based on traditions and ideals of scientific reasoning, and tracing the roots of our prevailing scientific ideals helps to clarify the conceptual issues ecology is struggling with.

The Newtonian Background

The post-Renaissance scientific revolution reached its culmination in Newton's theory. Thanks to its success, Newtonism became a model for modern science. But the Newtonian physics is based on a Newtonian metaphysics. Newton's work was based on an assumption – which was by no means invented by Newton but was rather part of the corpuscular philosophy of the seventeenth century – that matter can be reduced to mass-points, and material interactions to one-to-one forces between material bodies. These metaphysics and the mechanistic explanatory model were incorporated into biological disciplines (Koyré, 1965; Jacob, 1982; Prigogine and Stenghers, 1984).

Although the Newtonian approach works in mechanical systems that have a fairly small number of components and where forces can be reduced to pairwise interactions between the component parts, it is inadequate in systems with a more complex structure. Vitalism was a historical reaction against mechanicalism, but traditional vitalism is just the other side of the Newtonian coin: if a mechanical world-view is the only one justifiable on the basis of science, then phenomena that transgress classical mechanics (living organisms) must transgress scientific explanation as well, and one must resort to a mystical spirit of life.

An important heritage of Newtonian science is the way it has been philosophically justified. Newton and British empiricism had a relationship of mutual inspiration but, somewhat paradoxically, it was left to Kant, the major critic of empiricism, to push justifying empirical knowledge as far as it can be pushed on purely philosophical grounds. Kant himself called his achievement against the empiricists 'Copernican revolution'. Kant's Copernican revolution culminates in the idea that we do not extract knowledge from nature as passive observers through our senses but rather actively construct knowledge out of our experience; 'Our intellect does not draw its laws from nature, but imposes its laws upon nature' (*Prolegomena*, Sect. 37 (1953)).

How does our intellect achieve such a feat? Kant's solution was to adopt a set of *a priori* principles that make human knowledge possible. The Kantian *a priori* is closely similar to the Newtonian metaphysics as regards concepts such as space, time and causality. In his *Prolegomena* Kant wrote ('Appendix: On what can be done to make Metaphysics as a Science real') that

> space and time and everything that they contain, are not things or properties in themselves, but merely belong to appearances of them … space (and likewise time) with all its determinations can be known by us a priori because it, as well as time, is present in us before any perception or experience as pure form of our sensibility... For us space and time (in conjunction with the pure concepts of the understanding) prescribe their law a priori to all possible experience …   (Kant, 1953)

This is a philosophical (transcendental) justification of empirical science, but it also includes an answer to the problem, how to comprehend space and time? Through Kant the Newtonian basic postulates that time and space comprise a uniform stage on which processes of nature take place, and causality equals a one-to-one relationship between events, were turned into inevitable attributes of thinking. This is another great paradox concerning Kant: a philosophical critic of reason *par excellance* nailing down substantive dogmas.

Kant's influence was overwhelming on the philosophy and epistemology of science far into the twentieth century. As a rule, scientists occupied by epistemological problems in the nineteenth century – Herz, von Helmholz, Bolzmann, Mach – were followers of Kant one way or another (Mandelbaum, 1971). In physics it was Ernst Mach who seriously began to doubt Newtonian assumptions of absolute space and time, and his writings later stimulated Albert Einstein. But space and time figure in biology as well. In traditional biological thinking space and time are unproblematic Newtonian concepts and form together a uniform whole 'in which' biological processes occur. This view is not adequate. Problems in comprehending space and time are reflected in problems of scaling in ecology, as we discussed in Chapter 2. In a uniform, Newtonian space scaling does not matter because in the last analysis processes take place in the 'same' space. But if space is not Newtonian, then adequate scaling of time and space becomes a fundamental issue.

Reductionism

Another burden imposed on us by the traditions of modern science is reductionism, the doctrine that all phenomena of nature or human existence can be properly explained only in terms of the behavior of elementary units. Complex wholes have no existence but they can be reduced to their parts either ontologically (only parts exist), epistemologically (parts are the basis of our knowledge), or methodologically (research must begin from parts).

The line of descent of reductionism, particularly concerning biology, can be traced back to Descartes (Rose et al., 1984). However, as an explicit doctrine reductionism is of a more recent origin. According to Foucault (1970), in the seventeeth and eighteenth centuries knowledge was founded on a metaphysical idea of order in the world and the possibility of an immediate representation of this order in human language. 'Reductionism', as we understand it today, was not an issue. There is no point in distinguishing 'wholes' and 'parts' from each other if they all belong to the same order. The question whether wholes or parts should be given priority arises only when a preordained order is substituted with something that changes in time, with an idea of evolution – evolution of both nature, thinking subject, and thinking itself. This is a nineteenth century idea.

The basic doctrine of the nineteenth century in our scientific heritage was classical positivism (Mandelbaum, 1971). The term was coined by August Comte and refers to the ideal of positive knowledge obtained using proper scientific methods, modelled after the most advanced sciences of the time, that is, Newtonian physics. Positive knowledge had freed itself from metaphysical preconceptions and consisted instead of empirically discovered reliable correlations with experience. Immanent forces or transcendental entities were rejected from explanation: 'to explain a phenomenon is to be able to subsume it under one or more laws of which it is an instance. A law, in its turn, is simply a well-authenticated general statement of uniformities which have been observed to occur in the past' (Mandelbaum, 1971: 11).

In the context of positivism the modern reductionistic program makes sense. While laws used in explanation are stated in terms of abstract attributes, the role of these abstractions is to lay bare functional relationships within the phenomena explained. ('Paradoxical as it may sound, it is precisely because a functional law is abstractive and is not directly concerned with actual cases, that it can serve to explain such cases' (Mandelbaum, 1971: 123).) What we have then is elements and their functional relationships that obey causal laws, and all complex entities can be reduced to their elementary parts. *Unity of science*, built upon the disciplines dealing with the most elementary particles of matter, was a resulting ideal. It is reductionism.

The logical positivists of our own century shared this conviction albeit on partly different grounds. Their view was based on a purely logical idea of an empiricist language of science, and promulgated reductionism on these grounds. We take Rudolf Carnap's programatic article 'Logical foundations of the unity of science' (1938) to represent this view. Carnap defended unity of science not ontologically or epistemologically as classical positivists did but 'as a question of logic, concerning the logical relationships between the terms and the laws of the various branches of science'. He formulated the condition of reducibility as follows: 'If now a certain term x is such that the conditions for its application (as used in the language of science) can be formulated with the help of the terms y, z, etc., we call such a formulation a *reduction* for x in terms of y, z, etc., and we call x *reducible* to y, z, etc.' (emphasis in the original). The realization of this condition would be achieved by first constructing a *thing-language* used in speaking about the properties of the inorganic things surrounding us; by then constructing a *physical language* that describes general physical properties of things and is reducible to the thing-language; and by then reducing statements about biology (using a *physiological approach*) and psychology (using a *behavioristic approach*) to the physical language (the emphasized terms are Carnap's).

This later became a standard definition of reductionism popularized for example by Ernst Nagel (1961). The same view, including Nagel as a central authority, is still alive in recent 'common sense' defenses of reductionism in ecology and evolutionary biology (for example Schoener, 1986; Caplan, 1988).

The problem with this view is not that it was not logically coherent as it stands but that it is irrelevant. It is irrelevant on three grounds.

The first reason for the irrelevance of classical reductionism we already touched upon when discussing the role of language in science. The program of logical positivism to construct an ideal language of science is obsolete. It follows that the program of building a unified science based on this ideal language is obsolete as well.

The second reason why classical reductionism is irrelevant becomes clear when we pursue further Carnap's conception of the unity of science. In the early part of his article he framed this goal as a purely logical one, but it actually gets a much more powerful status by the following addition: 'Since it [the unity of science] belongs to the *logic of science*, the question concerns scientists and logicians alike' (emphasis added). What is this thing called 'logic of science'? It is a reflection of a strong metaphysical belief in the ability of science to construct a 'true' picture of reality. Unity of science is thus ultimately not merely a question of logic, it is a question of truth. A strong metaphysical foundationalism was a basic drive of logical positivists, as was noticed by contemporary critics such as Edmund Husserl and Max Horkheimer and as has been demonstrated by post-positivistic critics such as Jürgen Habermas and Richard Rorty.

What Carnap and others called 'logic of science' is a vestige of the Kantian *a priori*, and so is 'unity of science'. From the point of a post-Kantian, non-foundationalist understanding of science, *disunity of science* is a far more plausible attitude (Hacking, 1983). This means that there is no point in trying to 'reduce' one discipline to another. Different disciplines are about different issues.

Our third reason for regarding the reductionistic doctrine as irrelevant is directly related to substantive ecological arguments. Ecological problems are addressed on different levels of organization of nature, and the question whether 'wholes' or 'parts' are ultimately more important is misplaced because both the whole and the parts are integral elements in the research setting. One is certainly well-advised to avoid invoking transcendental essences in explaining what happens in an ecological system and to identify instead causal mechanisms that are at work within the system. This is a division-line to mystical holism that pervaded the 'superorganistic' school of ecological thinking in the first half of this century.

However, an explanation in terms of internal mechanisms of the system does not mean that the system would 'vanish' – the characteristics of the system are in-built in the mechanisms extracted from the system. Mechanisms and the context of their working cannot be isolated from each other. That a particular mechanism actually functions in a particular way in a particular system is a feature of the whole system. Relevant features of the system must be explained on another level.

It is important to distinguish *reduction* as a research tactic from *reductionism* as a philosophy. The former is a perfectly good method, and has proven very successful in the history of science. The latter makes the sweeping claim that lower levels are more 'real' or 'fundamental', that all phenomena can be reduced to the lowest level and are best understood in that way, and that higher level phenomena are the foam on the surface of the truly important events.

The Theoretical Heritage

Not only grand philosophical schemes but also substantive theories set constraints on research practice. A basic unifying framework for the biological sciences is provided by the theory of evolution, Darwinism; remember Theodosius Dobzhansky's aphorism, 'nothing in biology makes sense except in the light of evolution'. Every biological process takes place in time, and there is no difference between past and present tense in the 'why?' and the 'how?'.

As is well known, Darwinism was primarily a conceptual revolution. Most of the facts Darwin based his work upon were known to contemporary scholars, but his theory of evolution gave a new context for interpreting the facts. The real novelty in Darwin's theory was his view of natural selection as the mechanism of evolution.

The core of Darwinism from the point of ecology was characterized by Ernst Mayr (1963) as 'population thinking'. The term refers to the idea that species in nature are not 'pure types' but they consist of individuals with varying characteristics, and every type (such as a type-specimen of a particular species, held in a museum) is only one member of a population. This variation is an essential raw material for natural selection to act upon, that is, for evolutionary change.

There is a philosophical dimension to this methodological point of Mayr's. We use the history of physics as an analogue: Renate Wahsner (1981) studied the role of atomistic philosophies in the development of physics. She concluded that the Democritean notion of 'atom' was not empirical, but rather a *mode of thinking* (our translation for the term *Denkprinzip*), that is, a conceptual construct that enabled Democritos to grasp movement of bodies. Atomism, as 'corpuscular philosophy', had a similar important role for Descartes and his followers in the early phases of modern physics in the sixteenth and seventeenth centuries by providing a general framework for grasping movement of bodies (Kuhn, 1977). In an analogous fashion, the Cartesian mechanistic model of life was applied to organisms as a *mode of thinking* ('In the seventeenth century, the theory of animal-machines was imposed, therefore, by the very nature of knowledge.' (Jacob, 1982: 35))

Similarly, 'population thinking' is a *mode of thinking* facilitating the understanding of evolutionary change in living nature, the transition of one species to another. Population thinking makes it both necessary and possible to view the research problems of ecology in a new way. Observations pertaining to adaptedness of organisms to their environment were the same for the theologians of the early nineteenth century and for Darwin, as they are for modern creationists and Ernst Mayr. However, the observations are grasped in contradictory ways if they are viewed in a 'typological' framework as opposed to a 'population' framework. The former presents adaptedness as a basic feature of organisms that ultimately evades explanation or is used to exemplify the benevolence of the creator. It allows for the notion of 'perfectly adapted', and where adaptation seems less than perfect this is attributed to our ignorance of deeper purpose. The latter offers a mechanism that not only suggests how we can attempt to explain adaptations in each individual case. It also allows us to explain non-adaptedness as an equally significant aspect of evolution and rejects the notion of perfection.

While adaptation shows us the ecology of a species as an evolutionary force, non-adaptedness emphasizes history. Organisms reflect not only their ecology but also their past history as imposing the constraints of time and rates of change, structural correlations among parts and genetic systems on the adaptive processes. When pre-Darwinian attitudes infiltrate evolutionary thinking, adaptation is often reified, organisms are assumed to be optimally adapted, traits are treated as unitary objects of selection, and fanciful 'Just so' stories are invented to demonstrate that things are just as they should be.

It takes time to adopt a new mode of thinking. It was only in the 1960s that evolutionary population biology as a research field consolidated, and it is still easy to find university departments of zoology or botany where ignorance reigns as regards populations. A mode of thinking is not primarily empirical – it is a way of organizing thoughts and concepts within a research branch using some basic theoretical construct ('population') as a starting point. A mode of thinking thus establishes a general frame of reference for more specific hypotheses and paradigms within individual research fields. This also implies that modes of thinking can become constraints on solving new problems.

But 'modes of thinking' are naturally embedded in larger contexts of theoretical thought. *Paradigm* is the term made popular by Thomas Kuhn's *The Structure of Scientific Revolutions* (1962). A paradigm specifies the domain of concern, the objects of interest, the problems about objects that are worthy of attention and the types of solutions that would be acceptable. For instance, for classical astronomy the domain was the visible sky, the objects of interest were the stars and planets, and abstracted from these their orbits, masses and velocities. An acceptable solution would be expressed in terms of laws of motion and their application to particular heavenly bodies. Questions of what these bodies were made of or how they got to be where they are or how they were formed were simply not on the agenda of the early astronomers.

Modern dialectical thinking was developed by Hegel and later by Marx and Engels as an alternative to the Cartesian, reductionist, mechanistic and atomistic Newtonian mode and to the rigidities of formal logic. Although much of the original motivation came from the study of society, its domain of application has been extended to natural science, the arts and politics as well. The dialectic mode of thought emphasizes processes over things, the interpenetration rather than mutual exclusion of opposites, context and complexity, historicity both of the objects of study and of the ideas about them, the relative autonomy and mutual determination of levels of analysis. Both co-authors of this book were educated as scientists in the Newtonian mode but consciously adopted the dialectical mode. Our work therefore reflects both influences.

Social Practice

While our sensitivity to the influence of social and political forces has certainly grown, our understanding of their actual impact on the production of scientific theory has not.   Evelyn Fox Keller[7]

In this section we explore the last layer constraining ecological research depicted in Figure 3.2, namely, social practice. Science is a social activity and tied to a complex web of partly institutionalized structures that have control over funding, allocation of research facilities, education and recruitment, and also effectively determine how research problems are defined. Social structures are seldom visible to individuals subjected to them. Instead individuals find themselves working in, and their work constrained by, a nebulous network of social and societal relations. Relations are to a certain extent flexible and can be manipulated. Practicing ecologists must, for instance, establish relations to foundations and governmental bodies to secure funding for their research. Such apparent manipulation, however, takes place within the framework of the underlying structures and, as a matter of fact, local networks contribute to the reproduction of the structures they depend upon.

The relationship of social practice and ecological practice is not only a matter of obstructing or facilitating particular research endeavors but is rooted in the general rules and values underlying decision making in the society. This assertion opens up a whole area of theoretical inquiry into the relationship of ecology and social rationality; we elaborate these aspects below. At the end of this section we discuss the profile of environmental science.

Science as Work

A traditional Marxist view of science emphasizes science as a social phenomenon, social activity. In a passage in *Das Kapital* Marx characterized scientific work as 'generalized work'. 'Universal labour is all scientific work, all discovery and invention. It is brought about partly by the cooperation of men now living, but partly also by building on earlier work' (*Capital*, Vol. 3, 1981). Peter Ruben (1980) took this passage as a starting point for elaborating a general Marxist view of science. Two particular points were incorporated into his view. First, 'work' immediately implies 'society'. This point relates to the genesis of science in connection with the development of productive facilities. The close interaction between productive needs and the origin and development of science was pursued by J.D. Bernal in his *Science in History* (1954), and it is recognized by most historians of science today. Basic impulses behind the origin of modern ecology were such practical activities as agriculture, forestry, fisheries, and life expectancy calculations necessary for insurance business.

Second, science as work is a form of human activity. According to Ruben, a central category of science as an activity is *measurement*. Measurement potentially constitutes a bridge between human beings and nature. But measurement is a conscious human act. When deciding which objects and which characteristics to measure, the human scientist defines the object of cognition, constitutes nature as an object of research. Experiment is an extension of measurement: by experiment the human scientist tries to control the conditions under which measurements are made.

These ideas connect with what we have previously discussed: decisions about measurement and procedures of carrying measurements through establish practical traditions within different disciplines, and thus lie at the foundations of the 'language-games' of the disciplines. But such decisions are also conditioned by existing traditions and theoretical presuppositions about the processes studied and thus reproduce underlying, implicit assumptions that perhaps ought to be challenged.

The Marxist view of science also incorporates a class position. This has two dimensions. The first one is an analysis of the role of science in social reproduction. A dramatic change has happened in this respect in the twentieth century, particularly after the Second World War – science is an absolute requirement for modern industrial production, and the capitalist state has taken over the task of providing the necessary infrastructure.

Science is also increasingly a commodity, bought and sold on the market. When we refer to the commoditization of science we mean that like other commodities it has a dual nature.

Each product of research is unique and has some irreplaceable utility of its own even if within a narrow community. But it is also produced for sale. It has a market value which is only accidentally related to any intrinsic worth or usefulness. As such, it is interchangeable with all other commodities on the single scale of value. A company can calculate the costs of production of scientific research, for example per new pesticide, estimate its market potential, and decide on research priorities accordingly. A research company has the research report (for example an environment impact statement) as its only product. It must then balance the opposing needs to keep costs competitive, to do a complete enough job to win at the hearing, and not raise troublesome points. Satisfaction of the client becomes the measure of quality.

In universities, the commoditization of scholarship is less complete. But dramatic, publishable results contribute to the university's ability to raise money through the intermediate variable 'prestige'. Research grants, instead of being the means for doing research, become the purpose of research and the measure of a scientist's worth. Scientific fraud then becomes a rational business choice.

The commoditization of science also fortifies the international division of labor in science. High-technology research is almost entirely restricted to the industrialized countries. In the Third World, science is itself impoverished. Not only is the science budget a much smaller proportion of the national income, but the cost of supporting a scientist requires the labor of more non-scientists. Therefore most of the world's scientific research, publications and patents continue to be concentrated in a few industrial countries. Under these circumstances it is very appealing for Third World governments to think in terms of adopting the results of world science more than creating scientific knowledge in accordance with their own agendas.

A class-based approach toward science recognizes secondly that the internal hierarchies and working mechanisms of scientific institutions are an indistinguishable part of the class structure of the society. The means of scientific production are owned by somebody who invests in science for some reason. The enterprise is directed on behalf of the owners. Other people do the work, are recruited, educated and rewarded in particular ways depending on whether they are research directors, laboratory assistants or repair and cleaning staffs. Somebody controls the product.

Public and private institutions differ from each other to a variable extent depending on the country, but we may ask about both institutions and the individuals within them the following questions: how do they relate to the specific content of science and to scientific production as commodity production? What systems of belief do they bring to the enterprise? How do their interests converge toward or clash with those of the other participants? And how does this structure and dynamics of science affect the rest of society and its relations with nature, again differentiated by class, gender, race and ethnicity?

A class-view of science motivates the further question, are the effects of class-bias merely in the 'externalities' of science or is there a deeper, 'internal' connection? Asking this question is not fashionable today, partly because of the unfortunate legacy of the 'proletarian science' of the Lysenko era, partly because it is the deepest belief of established science that in spite of occasional distortions, science is ultimately sound and 'objective' and aims at nothing but the truth.

But the question needs to be asked. Feminist critics of science have most consistently pursued it in the last decades. Feminist criticism of science started from the realization that science has traditionally been fully involved in the ideological distortions of male-biased societies. This became obvious in investigations and criticisms of what science has said and says about sex and gender. Biology was from the very beginning an important discipline, as it has often provided a 'scientific' justification for gender oppression (Hubbard et al., 1982; Bleier, 1984).

This criticism raised the question, is the problem only 'bad science', or is there something wrong with Western scientific traditions? Most feminist critics of science do not accept the 'bad science' thesis but demand a thoroughgoing revision of scientific thinking. Several lines of thought are currently followed:

[1] Questioning dualisms that lie at the background of Western scientific traditions and imprison our thinking. Culture/nature, male/female, mind/body, self/other have been persistent in Euro-North-American traditions and are systemic to the logics and practices of domination (Haraway, 1985; Harding, 1986).

[2] Seeking for alternative ways of conceptualizing the research object, of 'naming nature' in Evelyn Fox Keller's (1985) phrase.

[3] Seeking for a basis for an alternative epistemology, more firmly rooted in practical activities and experience than modern 'objectivist' science which looks at the world from a distance (Rose, 1983).

[4] Analysing the significance of language in scientific discourses in shaping preconceptions about research problems and objects.

The class and feminist analysis of science raises questions as to how we may want to change the structure and direction of science so that it better serves the interests of the majority of our species. An emancipatory perspective must include changes in the ownership, agenda, leadership, composition and organization of the scientific enterprise. In particular, those who are supposed to do the job must have real influence on how the job is defined.

This imperative is particularly clear in environmental research which studies problems subjected to strong vested interests. When Rachel Carson prepared her *Silent Spring* (1962), pesticide manufacturing companies threatened the publisher of the book with a lawsuit and magazines and journals printing favorable reviews of the book with withdrawal of advertising. Rachel Carson was able to complete her project because she had a relatively independent position in the scientific labor market, thanks to royalties from her previous books and a teaching position in a local college (Schnaiberg, 1980); she was able to organize support for her work from social resources independently of established institutions that were submissive to pressure from the pesticide corporations.

Substantive Versus Instrumental Rationality?

Social practice can be divided into two spheres, the specific 'techniques' adopted in particular social activities, and the totality of societal practices, or *Praxis*. The former aspect of social practice appears relatively straightforward, but how to characterize 'societal praxis'?

Max Weber adopted the concept of *rationality* to analyse the transformations that took place in the basic tenets of decision making in Western societies in the period of transition from feudalism to capitalism. 'Rationality' was a historically new phenomenon and brought about secularization and rationalization in how social issues were reasoned about. An increasing proportion of social activities became subject to decisions evaluated by independent criteria. 'Rationality' as a guiding principle contrasts with trust on divine providence or compliance with earthly authorities, which were guiding principles earlier. This transformation took place simultaneously and interdependently with the birth of modern science and scientific rationality.

A concomitant transformation occurred in the conception of 'human nature'. Human beings became gradually viewed as autonomous individuals who deliberate their decisions primarily on economic grounds.

Weber suggested that the birth of modern, capitalist society also brought about a change in the structure of the whole culture, which became divided into three autonomous spheres: science, morality and art. The spheres came to be differentiated because the unified world-views of religion and metaphysics broke down. The spheres were aimed toward three different goals: knowledge, justice and taste, and they were judged by three different sets of standards: truth, normative rightness, and authenticity and beauty (Habermas, 1970).

But Weber's important specification to the perspective of secularization and rationalization was that the very concept of rationality got divided into two parts, namely, rationality about goals to be pursued (*Wertrationalität*), and rationality of matching means to ends economically and effectively without asking where the ends come from (*Zweckrationalität*); substantive rationality versus instrumental rationality. Moreover, Weber concluded that instrumental rationality tends to dominate the capitalist world, particularly economic and bureaucratic institutions. He saw a close connection between capitalism, rationality and domination as follows: the specifically Western idea of reason realizes itself in a system of material and intellectual culture (economy, technology, 'conduct of life', science, art) that develops to the full in industrial capitalism, and this system tends toward a specific type of domination in the contemporary period: total bureaucracy. The comprehensive and basic concept is the idea of reason as Western rationality (this presentation follows Herbert Marcuse's essay 'Industrialization and capitalism in the work of Max Weber', in Marcuse, 1988).

Changes in culture are intimately related to changes in the way people live. Daily experience either reinforces or contradicts and alters the prevailing models of the world which tell how things are, and usually also by implication how they must be. The separation of the two kinds of rationality was forcified by the division of labor and the spread of wage-labor in capitalist society. Instrumental rationality is the only rationality allowed on the job for most people; the selling of labor power makes work time sharply differentiated from the rest of life.

The development of science and technology was historically closely tied to the process of rationalization; indeed, science and technology provide basic models for Weberian instrumental rationality. This gives the background for the pessimistic view often expressed that modern science and technology are just another means of domination over nature and humans. Marcuse summarized the pessimistic view, implicit in Max Weber as well, as follows:

> The very concept of technical reason is perhaps ideological. Not only the application of technology but technology itself is domination (of nature and men) – methodical, scientific, calculated, calculating control. Specific purposes and interests of domination are not foisted upon technology 'subsequently' and from the outside; they enter the very construction of the technical apparatus. Technology is always a historical–social project: in it is projected what a society and its ruling interests intend to do with men and things. Such a 'purpose' of domination is 'substantive' and to this extent belongs to the very form of technical reason.
>
> (Marcuse, 1988: 223–4)

However, this ultimate pessimism can and must be challenged on several different levels: first, the philosophical background from which Marcuse drew his pessimistic view can be questioned. This is one strain in the work of Jürgen Habermas whose thesis is that all subject–object relationships are both historically and logically preceded by communicative relationships between social subjects. Relations of domination are not logically primary relations, but they are imbedded in a larger context of what Habermas calls communicative rationality. It is, however, beyond the scope of this work to pursue the point further.

Second, we need to question the neat division of social practice into 'techniques' and 'Praxis', adopted in the beginning of this section. An alternative is to distinguish several 'social practices', organized around different fields of social activity (MacIntyre, 1985). Then the problem whether social practices are ultimately permeated by relations of domination or whether alternative ways of organizing social practices can be envisaged also becomes a concrete, historical issue. We investigate the character of scientific rationality in specific social practices in Chapters 4 and 5 using two examples, health and agriculture. Our claim is that ecological knowledge can be incorporated into particular practices in such a way that exploitative domination is not a necessary outcome.

Third, the issue of nature domination is intertwined with historical dynamics of the culture–nature relationship. Economic and cultural history and the ways of life of people shape the conceptions of nature and the particular relations to nature adopted in any given society. The culture–nature dualism characteristic of modern Euro-North-American society is not a historical constant but, on the contrary, a fairly recent invention (MacCormack and Strathern, 1980). There is no reason why domination should be a universal principle in people's practical relationships with nature. We adopt this historical perspective in Chapter 6.

Environmental Science

'Environment' is a social category because 'environment' does not exist without somebody defining it as an 'environment' of something. If the defining subject disappears, the environment disappears. Only social human beings are capable of such definitions. Consequently, environmental research is intrinsically laden with social considerations, and criteria used in assessing the quality of environment are based on some point of view.

Schnaiberg (1980) extracted from the literature two mutually complementary notions of the environment, namely, environment as a home for mankind, and environment as a sustenance base for society. These alternative views also give alternative criteria for defining environmental problems: those related to 'fouling the nest', and those related to destruction of the productive potential of nature.

What kind of observations entitle ecologists to conclude that 'the environment' is being destroyed? This depends on the criteria adopted. A great number of relevant observations relate to facts that connect with ecology indirectly. Such as, for instance, change in the gas composition of the atmosphere which influences ecosystems through climate change. Pollution is usually related to ecology indirectly through questions such as, how does DDT accumulating in the tissues of eagles affect eagle populations? Is the growth of trees impeded if soil acidity increases from pH 6 to pH 4? How do plants close to mining pits, or mussels close to coastal industries cope with increasing heavy metal burden? Answering such questions requires knowledge about the ecological processes involved and is often complicated because of scaling problems. DDT accumulating in eagles affects entire populations and is a direct threat to their survival. Heavy metal concentrations close to mining pits, in contrast, are localized and significant primarily as local laboratories of plant adaptability.

Some issues are directly related to the productive potential of ecosystems, and ecologists should then understand how to protect the potential, and how to restore ecosystems already destroyed. How intensively can we exploit a fish community and still avoid population crashes? What proportion of a habitat should be preserved in order that species dependent on that habitat could be protected?

Different criteria are usually mingled together. Although the distinction between 'fouling the nest' and 'destroying the productive basis' is useful, it usually breaks down in relation to particular issues. Furthermore, the criteria used in any particular case change through time. Assessing the significance of a particular case of environmental destruction is always a matter of struggle, with ecological research as one participant. The following course of events could, for instance, occur after it becomes known that a textile factory discharges sewage into a river. The first stage is documenting what happened. What were the chemicals leaking into the water? What concentrations? How many fish were killed? Is the skin irritation experienced by swimmers related to the discharge?

The next stage is evaluating the significance of these observations from different perspectives. Are the chemicals in the recorded concentrations dangerous or harmless? Do the chemicals break up rapidly in natural conditions or, in contrast, accumulate in the food web of the ecosystem? Although the chemicals are indeed highly poisonous, does it matter when they get rapidly diluted and only a minor part of the river is affected? Was the latest fish kill a temporary event readily compensated by reproduction of the remaining population and immigration from above the factory, or an indication of the vulnerability of the whole population? Does it matter if the skin of sensitive individuals is irritated after a swim, why not take a shower?

The significance of the conclusions reached is assessed on the basis of value judgements. A stretch of the river is damaged, but does it matter when there are lots of rivers in other parts of the country? Trout are indeed sensitive to the discharge but minnows manage quite well at moderate distances from the factory and may even increase; who eats trout anyway? There are several forest lakes excellent for swimming at a driving distance from the community; why swim in the river?

Finally, the question of compensation is raised. The river is indeed biologically dead, but a sausage factory and indoor swimming facilities will be established in the community.

It is not possible to understand the recent development of environmental science without seeing it as a domain of conflicting interests.

Those industries which use resources, release their products or dump their residues into 'the environment' want to maximize their profits without interference. This usually means denying that they have caused any harm, then minimizing the damage, counterposing it to claimed benefits, and by presenting themselves as environmentalists.

Industries contract research to serve these needs. The proliferation of environmental consulting firms, originally mostly out of sanitary engineering backgrounds, is a response to this new market. Their agenda is determined by the conflicting goals of lucrative contracts, competition for costs, the need to satisfy the client and to be thorough enough to win at hearings but not so thorough as to raise new problems or cost too much.

The scientific staffs of these businesses may adopt completely the outlook of their employers and devote their creativity to belittling environmental problems. But they are also members of the scientific community, may expect to return to academic research or training some day, and want to retain their professional respectability. Some even join these firms in order to work for environmental protection.

A minor but growing party to environmental issues is the group of new industries and businesses developed around environmental protection and alternative technologies.

Other participants are the employees of the industry. They suffer the impacts of harmful substances as part of their normal exposure in the workplace, when 'unexpected' disasters occur, and at home as residents of the industrial communities. Health issues have become increasingly important in collective bargaining, and the whole sphere of occupational health has grown up around the allocation of responsibility for health impairments. But the workers are also worried about their jobs. This makes them uneasy about strict regulations which might affect profits and encourage the industry to move to a more favorable 'climate'. Therefore the labor movement has so far had an inconsistent relation to environmental protection, and local communities are often divided according to dependence on the industry.

As an illustration of how conflicting interests penetrate environmental research and permeate conclusions drawn from research results, we use a detailed case study by Brian Martin (1979) on how scientists evaluated the hazards of supersonic airplanes in the early

1970s. Brian Martin found out that two research groups, drawing upon basically identical data bases and similar technical arguments, reached nevertheless contrasting conclusions about the hazards. He analysed the argumentation of both sides and concluded that the contrast was due to a mechanism he dubbed *pushing the argument*, comprising the following steps:

[1] Technical assumptions made at the outset were selective, and they were not neutral concerning the conclusions reached.

[2] Evidence was used selectively. All evidence distantly relevant for the issue investigated cannot be assimilated anyway; in particular, uncertainties behind the evidence were under- versus overrated depending on presuppositions concerning their relevance.

[3] Both groups used their own results selectively in drawing conclusions. In the research papers this was reflected as a difference, even contrast, between 'results' of the study and the summary of those results in the 'abstract'.

[4] Arguments challenging one's own conclusions were discussed in a pejoratory style and thus made to appear as simple blunders, instead of plausible alternatives.

A basic issue in the argument was, where is the burden of proof supposed to lie? Is it necessary to prove that supersonic transport is (probably) hazardous *before stopping* the project, or is it necessary to prove that supersonic transport is harmless *before starting* the project. The groups differed in this perspective, which led to the contrast in results. One group was British, and Britain was committed to the joint development of the Concord supersonic airplane; the other group worked in the US, where policy opposed that development.

4

Health as Part of the Ecosystem

Researchers at the Genespec institute have reported the isolation of a cluster of proteins from the stomachs of wellfed people which are absent from the starving. It is expected that this discovery will lead to the identification of the gene for hunger, the molecular basis for world malnutrition. Although it has long been known that hunger has a genetic basis, this is the first time that its molecular structure has been approached. American and French research groups are applying to patent the gene for the international market. The Nabi-Rybak Confidential Health Newsletter[1]

Whereas infection or calcification of a joint or chronic exhaustion may be biological facts, health is a social category. We propose a preliminary definition of health as the capacity to carry out those activities which a given society considers necessary. But immediately we run into difficulties: which society? Who does the considering and about whom?

During the period of slavery in the Americas the health of a slave was judged by the owner as the capacity to work; good nutrition therefore meant sufficient calories. As long as the price of slaves was relatively low, a low working life expectancy was acceptable. Ailments which did not obviously prevent working were not taken seriously by physicians and were often regarded as malingering. The owners of course judged their own health differently. And the slaves had their own ideas about what was a legitimate ailment, so that two health care systems existed side by side: that of official medicine and the network of healers and herbalists derived from African and Native American traditions that attended to the health needs which were ignored by the physicians.

Throughout the world-wide colonial and neocolonial period, which has not yet come to an end, public health efforts reflected the perceived needs of the rulers. Diseases that affected the armies of

117

occupation and the colonial administrators motivated the establishment of colonial (usually military) medicine. If the disease vector was highly mobile, such as the mosquitoes that transmit malaria or yellow fever, it was difficult to protect the rulers without working also to protect the ruled. But malnutrition or intestinal parasites could be ignored safely. At a later stage, when the sources of cheap labor were less plentiful, the survival and the physical energy of the workforce became a matter of concern and the scope of medicine correspondingly broadened. In the 1950s and 1960s the panic about population growth in Asia, Africa and Latin America erupted in Europe and North America, making reproductive matters major issues of health. Finally, in the period of colonial revolutions, general health service became an arm of pacification and counterinsurgency. Each major change in the economic and social relations brought with it a different list of recognized health problems.

With the development of scientific medicine, conditions which do not produce any impairment but which predict future disease were themselves seen as disease, so that high blood pressure or sugar in the urine became indicators of health problems even before any impairment.

Thus the definition of health and disease is the result of social processes of economic development, conflicting interests and ideological change as well as the technical development of medicine, which is itself in part a result of these processes.

In the discussion that follows, we will use a method of successive approximations. First we ignore health and discuss infectious disease, treating it as if each disease were a separate entity. Then we examine non-infectious and chronic diseases as distinct from infectious disease. From there we examine health more generally, seeing the organism as responding to the conditions of its own existence in ways that partly preserve and partly undermine its capacity to continue doing so.

Infectious Disease

The dose needed to kill a man is only a few times greater than that needed to disinfect him.   J.B.S. Haldane[2]

We define infectious disease as a disease in which the presence of a parasite is a necessary ingredient for its development. We prefer this to a definition in which the parasite is the cause of the disease because the discomfort or death which may occur depend on a whole context of factors in which the parasite is only one. The great advances of microbiology starting in the last century have established the necessary participation of bacteria, protozoa, fungi, worms and more recently viruses in disease but have often led to identification of disease with the parasite and have diverted attention from the factors which determine the outcome of our encounter with particular infectious agents.

In infectious disease a parasite enters the human body where it uses available resources to grow, develop and reproduce. It may have little or no effect on the wellbeing of its host, or may produce severe symptoms and even death. The harmful effects come about if the parasite diverts nutrients to its own needs, secretes toxins which either break down tissues to make them more available or help overcome resistance, disrupt the normal control and feedback systems, and cause mechanical destruction of body structures. In addition, the body's defense system becomes activated, sometimes in ways that themselves produce harmful effects such as fevers.

Therefore in order to understand the role of infectious disease in human welfare we have to step back and examine the general phenomenon of parasitism in nature.

Almost all living things except green plants themselves obtain their energy and their organic nutrients directly or indirectly by consuming green plants. Parasites are similar to predators in that they acquire their nutrition by consuming another organism, their prey or host. In distinction from predators, parasites live in or on their host and consume it gradually. Intermediate between predators and parasites are the insect parasitoids, mostly wasps and flies.

According to Peter Price (1980), most organisms are parasites, especially of plants. The parasite–host relation covers a very wide range of intensities from situations in which the parasite visits its host briefly like mosquitoes, or remains on the surface of the host taking only small amounts of nutrition (ticks, fleas) to those that penetrate superficial tissues (ringworm, wart-causing viruses), deep tissues of all kinds, cell nuclei and even chromosomes. The parasites may be relatively innocuous and merge gradually with the commensal organisms which live in their hosts without doing any harm and mutualists whose presence is actually beneficial. For instance the bacteria of the digestive tract of animals are mostly harmless; some aid digestion even to the extent of being necessary as in the cellulose-digesting bacteria in termites and the rumen bacteria in cattle. Others are beneficial in maintaining the internal environment and controlling pathogens. Along another dimension, parasites overlap with decomposers that feed only on already dead tissues. The intermediate types can infest the dying or weakened organisms or the dying tissues of live organisms.

There are perhaps several hundred species that live in or on the human body. Some are more or less permanent inhabitants, mainly in the digestive tract, while others are sporadic invaders. Some can cause diseases, and of these perhaps 100–200 are shared with other animals.

From the parasite's point of view, a parasitic way of life has both advantages and disadvantages. It provides an escape from the competition of other organisms in the free-living habitats of soil and water. The host provides an environment protected from the stresses of desiccation and temperature and extremes of acidity. The host provides a wide range of nutrients maintained by the host's own homeostasis within tolerable limits.

But it is a specialized environment, with very particular conditions to be coped with. The parasite must be able to reach its host in some way, recognize that it has found a host, overcome the barriers to invasion, find its way to its preferred or necessary habitat within the host, complete its life cycle there, and its offspring must find a way out of their safe refuge to another host individual. It is usually the case that the more intimate the relation between parasite and host, the more the parasite penetrates the host organism, orients itself there and synchronizes its own development with the life processes of the host. A mosquito can usually bite a wide range of blood donors but a hookworm has to penetrate the skin of its host, migrate through the circulation to the lung, move out of the lung into the throat and finally reach the digestive tract, recognize that it has arrived and latch on before it can start feeding. Therefore hookworms tend to be rather specific in their hosts. One species of hookworms parasitizing dogs will sometimes penetrate human skin but then gets lost, cannot enter the circulation, and after wandering around in the skin for a while where it causes 'swimmers' itch', eventually dies.

The precarious nature of the parasitic way of life is seen in their very high reproductive rates. Since populations of most species more or less maintain themselves, each individual leaves an average of one offspring, or in sexually reproducing species each female leaves an average of one female offspring. Therefore if she lays n eggs during a lifetime, the chances of survival of an egg through a complete life cycle to egg laying are about $2/n$, since half the eggs produce females. These are of course only long-term averages. Populations may increase and decrease rapidly in the course of an annual cycle, invade new territories or new hosts. Even so, we can distinguish between large mammals and birds who produce single or double digit numbers of young in their lifetime, and tapeworms that may produce 300 000 to 1 000 000 eggs *per day*.

It is sometimes the case that parasites are capable of completing their life cycles in alien hosts, but not sufficiently often to maintain themselves as infections of that host alone. Reproduction in that host may be too low, or the chances of transmission to another host insufficient. The encephalitis diseases are of this type. These are mosquito transmitted infections that do not maintain themselves as human diseases but rather infect other species of vertebrates. Every once in a while they spill over into human populations, and we have usually small epidemics with perhaps dozens of cases. The circumstances that favor such spillover seem to be associated with the weather in particular habitats.

Let us consider the sequence of events which must take place before such an infection is transmitted. Assume first that a female mosquito lays two batches of eggs in her lifetime. Each batch of eggs requires that she have a blood meal obtained by biting at least one host. (Adult male mosquitoes do not bite. They accumulated all the protein they need for a lifetime as larvae, and subsist as adults on carbohydrates obtained from nectar.) For convenience we will assume that she gets the meal from a single host. The probability that the first host is carrying the parasite is the proportion of infected individuals in the host population, or slightly less since a recently infected host is not infective immediately.

If the mosquito bites an infective host, there is a certain probability of picking up the infection. This depends on how many parasites are in the blood and therefore the degree of infection, and also on how long the mosquito can continue sucking blood. The mosquito must then survive long enough to develop and lay her eggs and go out in search of another host for a new egg batch. This depends on the dangers to her during this period, which is related to the numbers of predators and the presence of mosquito diseases in the sites where she rests and refuels with nectar.

If she survives to bite again, the probability that she bites a human host depends on how far she has to fly from her natural habitat, and the influences which may send her searching in such places. When she gets there a human must be available and located. This depends on how many people are around and how they spend their time during the warm humid periods when mosquitoes are most active. If she does bite a person, there is a certain probability of transmitting the parasite. This depends on her feeding behavior. Transmission usually takes place when the mosquito is injecting an anti-coagulant into the host to facilitate feeding. The behavior of the person is important here. The whining of some mosquito species, the pain of the initial puncture and the itch associated with the anti-coagulant alert the host to her presence, so that feeding may be interrupted and if many mosquitoes are present people may take protective action. Finally if the mosquito succeeds in injecting the parasite into the blood stream of its victim, there is the probability of the parasite escaping the body's defenses and reproducing sufficiently to cause symptoms.

The probability of all of these events taking place is found by multiplying the probabilities of each of them occurring. Since this calculation was done on a per-mosquito basis, the number of times this transmission occurs is the calculated probability times the number of female mosquitoes.

We can now see how an outbreak occurs. Most of the time, the probabilities are so low that even when multiplied by the vast numbers of mosquitoes we are left with fewer than one complete infective event. But none of these probabilities are fixed permanently. The use of pesticides may affect the numbers of predators. The clearing of vegetation may make the mosquitoes less comfortable where they usually are and cause them to fly further when looking for resting places. Housing developments may bring people nearer. If people take up gardening after work they may stay outdoors during the twilight hours when humidity is most favorable for mosquitoes. Large numbers of other kinds of non-infective but annoying mosquitoes or blackflies may drive them indoors or encourage them to use repellants or protective clothing. Awareness of the first reported cases of disease may make them more careful. Their own state of health may influence the fate of the parasite after it enters their blood stream. Regional development projects and recent weather may change the numbers of mosquitoes.

The final result is that any changes in natural and social conditions may affect the probabilities of infection and disease caused by parasites that do not normally come in contact with people. Short-term changes can produce sporadic outbreaks while long-term changes may change animal infection into an occasional or regular human disease.

Defense

Whether or not an invading parasite succeeds in establishing itself and causing harm to its host also depends on the state of the host. This 'state of the host' has many components of resistance to invasion, containment of the parasite, elimination of the invading parasite, reduction of symptoms or tolerance of the invader.

Disease resistance often entails the creation of environmental conditions within the host that are unfavorable to the parasite. But both host and parasite are living creatures with environmental requirements that overlap. The problem for the defense system is how to create conditions unfavorable for the invader without also harming itself. For instance, when plants block their vascular tubules in order to prevent the spread of a wilt fungus they also block their own distribution of nutrients. Therefore part of the plants' defenses is the growth of new xylem vessels that bypass the blocked ones. If the formation of the bypass vessels is inhibited, the plant may wilt. This wilting is not caused directly by the invader but by the plant's own response to the invader.

The fever which makes conditions too warm for some bacteria that invade mammals can also inhibit vital processes in the host and increase the burning up of the host's energy reserves. Further, the higher metabolic rate in fever requires more oxygen supplied to the tissues, and therefore may increase the heart rate. The increased heart rate increases the demand for oxygen to the heart muscle itself. If this is not available because of blockage of the coronary arteries, these muscle cells may die and we have the common heart attack.

Effective disease resistance requires an intricate coordination of the host's responses which create unusual, partly unfavorable conditions for the life of the host which are even more unfavorable for the parasite, and then mechanisms that compensate for these unfavorable conditions. Many of the symptoms of disease are caused directly by the defensive responses of the host even when these are working the way they are supposed to. But it may also happen that the defenses are disrupted and the self-regulatory systems themselves become a threat to life.

A parasite invading the organism successfully must first of all be able to thwart the body's defenses. It can do this in several ways.

It may reproduce more rapidly than the defenses can be mobilized. This is most likely if there is a massive invasion so that the parasite starts out ahead. The very rapid development of cholera after infection is an example of this strategy.

The parasite can concentrate in places such as the skin or gut or the interiors of cells where the circulation is sparse and the blood-born immune system cannot reach. This is the strategy of wart-causing viruses and inhabitants of the gut.

The parasite can change its own surface so that the immune system will not recognize it as an invader. The trypanosomes are a group of protozoans that follow this strategy. They are the active parasites involved in sleeping sickness. The flu virus mutates frequently, so that the course of the disease often shows cycles of recovery and relapse.

The parasite can weaken the defense system either in a non-specific way (undermining nutrition, as in the diarrheas) or by attacking the immune system directly as in AIDS. In the case of diarrhea, malnutrition increases the severity of the symptoms, while the diarrhea undermines nutrition by reducing appetite, reducing absorption of nutrients, and if accompanied by fever, by increasing the metabolic consumption of nutrients.

Since the success or failure of an invasion depends on the opposing processes of host defenses and parasite evasion or destruction of these defenses, the prior condition of the host and external conditions may determine the outcome. It is often the case that a parasite is successful only if the host is already weakened by some kind of stress. But since that stress may also affect the invader, the relation between the environment and disease can be rather unpredictable. For example, the root fungus of tobacco *Thielaviopsis basicola* has a temperature optimum in the range 28.5–30.5°C. But this is also the optimum range for the host plant, and under these conditions the vigorous growth of the plant resists the disease. The disease develops maximally in the range 17.5–23.5°C, which is not so good for the growth of the parasite but is the situation where the *relative* growth of the parasite compared to the host is maximal.

The presence of one kind of infection is often a precondition for the successful invasion of another. A classic example of opportunistic infection is the frequent infectious diseases that accompany AIDS once the immune system has been undermined. However, it also happens sometimes that one infection evokes the defense responses against another. This is especially the case in plants, where defenses are less specific than in animals. It is well known that a *Verticillium* infection increases the resistance of tomatoes to *Fusarium*.

The immune system of mammals is sensitive to stress. It has been found that after an emotional trauma the level of immunoglobulins in the blood decreases for several weeks and the frequency of streptococcal infection increases. It is generally true that poor countries and the poorest people of affluent countries suffer from the worst health. This is a combination of increased exposure to pathogens, lower resistance and less available therapeutic care.

In addition to evading or overwhelming the host's defenses, the parasite has to obtain the nutrients it needs. Sometimes this can be done innocuously. Intestinal roundworms take their share of the food consumed by their hosts without doing much harm as long as the host is well nourished and there are not too many worms. But the blood sucking ticks act to increase the circulation in the skin so as to obtain their meal, producing the rash that indicates their presence. The nematode *Neoaplectana* injects a culture of bacteria into its insect host. The bacteria grows in the insect, breaking down its tissues, and the nematode feeds on the bacterial culture.

Finally the parasite must get to a new host. This may require migrating to different tissues from the ones in which it reproduces best. It may also be facilitated by producing special symptoms that increase transmission, such as sneezing or coughing for respiratory infections, the migration of liver flukes (*Schistosoma*) into the intestine, or the aggressive behavior of rabid animals.

Thus the severity and outcome of infectious disease depends on the size of the invasion, the environmental conditions, the prior state of the host, and the care received. The symptoms depend on the mutual responses of parasite and host as the former acts to reach favorable locations, overcome resistance, obtain nourishment, and escape to a new host, while the host acts to isolate or eliminate the parasite, neutralize its toxins, or compensate for its damage. With the development of medicine and plant pathology, drugs and antibiotics produced industrially rather than in the host's body are added to the defense systems.

Coevolution of Host and Parasite

It has been observed that when diseases are introduced into populations which have not been exposed to them previously, the disease is much more severe. The native populations of the Americas,

Australia and Oceania were devastated by European diseases such as smallpox and plague. This has given rise to the hypothesis that diseases are most severe when new, and then evolve toward a milder form both because the host develops resistance and because it is supposedly to the advantage of the parasite not to kill its host. Richard Johnson (1986) has reviewed the evidence and the argument. He has concluded that hosts do indeed develop resistance, but that the evolution of the parasite is less clear cut. The one striking example which has been used in support of this hypothesis is that of the myxomatosis virus in Australia. When first introduced to control rabbits in 1950, it caused a mortality of 99.8 per cent, but this rate decreased to 40–60 per cent during the third outbreak, coinciding with the activity of mosquitoes, and at present the virus has little effect on the rabbits. In this particular case it is in fact to the advantage of the virus not to kill the rabbit in order to permit transmission. However, in other cases severity of symptoms and even death facilitate transmission.

In order to evaluate the direction of natural selection on the symptoms of disease, we have to determine the significance of the symptom-causing events for the life of the parasite and the host. The pain of a mosquito bite starts with the puncture of the skin. However, the pain is a disadvantage to the mosquito since it may cause the victim to react immediately and interrupt feeding or even kill the mosquito while she is stuck to the host. The after itch alerts the host too late to do anything about that mosquito bite, but after several bites the victim may take protective measures which make feeding more difficult for other mosquitoes. Therefore there would be an advantage to the mosquito to evolve a less annoying bite, provided that this is compatible with obtaining sufficient food.

From the point of view of the person bitten, the amount of blood taken by a mosquito is negligible and the discomfort, no matter how annoying, does not threaten either survival or reproduction in any obvious way. Therefore, unless the itch is so severe that we scratch to the point of bleeding and open up entry for infection, there will be no natural selection to alleviate the discomfort of mosquito bites. Sometimes insect bites or jellyfish stings cause allergic reactions that are quite serious and even fatal. Here selection would act to reduce the severity of the reaction at least to the point of removing threats to life. Or, if the mosquito carries disease, then heightened sensitivity to the bite may be an advantage as a signal to do something.

The important point is that there is not an evolutionary confrontation in which mosquitoes evolve to become nastier and people evolve to become less sensitive.

The widespread use of antibiotics against bacterial infections has confronted bacteria with new environmental stresses that threaten their survival. If an antibiotic is 100 per cent effective, the bacteria are killed and their species is not altered by the loss of that local population. But the destruction is rarely so complete. Among the vast numbers of bacterial cells in a single infection, some will carry mutations that result in changes in the chemistry of the bacteria. This altered chemistry may reduce the penetration of the antibiotic, combine it with some other molecule to render it harmless, denature the active parts of the molecule, replace enzymes that are inactivated by the antibiotic with enzymes that are less sensitive to it, speed up some metabolic processes to compensate for the damage done by the antibiotic or in some other way change the interaction of the bacteria and antibiotic so that the bacteria survives better. All of these mechanisms are lumped under the general description of *resistance*, and the genes involved in the altered metabolism are referred to as genes 'for' resistance. The offspring of these bacteria will usually also carry the resistance.

The more widespread the use of an antibiotic, the more likely it is that resistance will appear. Not only are more bacteria exposed to it, but also under more varied conditions. The concentration of the antibiotic is not uniform. At low concentrations even a small improvement in resistance will help its carriers survive, so that resistance can be acquired stepwise.

The defenses a bacterium has against antibiotics sometimes require the expenditure of energy or other resources. Therefore when the antibiotic is not present cells with these traits may be at a disadvantage compared to their more sensitive relatives. The population may undergo fluctuations, alternately acquiring and losing resistance as they experience exposure and isolation from antibiotics. This fact is used in planning antibiotic use. On the one hand, an individual course of treatment should be complete so as to eliminate those cells which have partial resistance before they can contribute their new talent to the general population. On the other hand, antibiotics should be rotated so that resistances become useless and even disadvantageous to the bacteria. When faced with many kinds of antibiotics, the bacterial cell is loaded with many, possibly conflicting demands on its capacity to confront alien molecules without the opportunity to acquire and retain resistance to all of them.

Bacteria have ways to confront this strategy. First, resistance to different antibiotics may be based on the same mechanisms of horizontal resistance. The fact that two molecules have different structures and names does not mean that they are different enough to require different mechanisms for resistance. The use of different kinds of antibiotics has created a selective advantage for those mutations which confer less specialized types of resistance.

Furthermore, bacteria may acquire inducible resistance in which the molecules needed for defense are produced only when the antibiotic is present. Inducible resistance gives all the advantages of resistance when the antibiotic is present, but avoids the costs in its absence. There are two disadvantages to this defense: time is lost between first exposure to the antibiotic and the operation of the resistant mechanisms, and the capacity to be induced is represented in the cell by some molecules that are waiting on standby until needed. Nevertheless, inducible responses are an effective adaptation to changing conditions.

A final wrinkle in the bacterial defense system is that although bacteria reproduce asexually, they can exchange genes. Virus-like particles can carry genes from one cell to another, even of a different species, so that bacteria can pool their defensive resources.

All of these defense mechanisms make the medical strategy based on antibiotics and bacteriocidal drugs a self-limiting one. As long as each species of bacteria has to develop its own new defenses against each synthetic, research can keep up with mutation. But the appearance of horizontal defenses conferring cross-resistance to several antibiotics, and the exchange of resistances among bacteria suggest that the golden age of chemical defenses in clinical medicine as in agricultural pest control may be running its course after a mere half century, and that a more complex strategy in which antibiotica and drugs are only a part will have to be adopted.

One element in such a strategy may be commensalization. Commensals are organisms which inhabit a host without doing any harm. Most bacteria in our digestive tract are harmless, some even beneficial, in which case they are called mutualists. In a few cases they are necessary, and the host has evolved along with its intestinal flora.

It does not seem to be true that all parasites necessarily evolve into milder infections, commensals and then mutualists. But the fact that they can do so offers us a possible approach. Instead of confronting bacteria head-on with threats to their survival that channel their evolution into ways to overcome our efforts, we might work to domesticate them by creating an internal environment in which they do not produce symptoms. This strategy can also be proposed for agricultural pest management, and will be discussed in more detail in Chapter 5.

Infectious Disease in Populations

Epidemiology is concerned with the occurrence of diseases in populations. The capacity of a parasite to invade an individual of a species and reproduce there is not sufficient to determine whether that disease will be able to persist in a population. Zadoks (in Horsfall and Cowling, 1977) in discussing plant disease states,

> That the pathogen is the cause of a disease is readily accepted, but what about the pathogen as the cause of an epidemic? If we take the pathogen for granted, we might as well call the weather the cause of the epidemic if the weather was exceptionally favorable to the pathogen. In a way the eighteenth century scientists up to Unger were right.
>
> In the present day terminology, the fungus is considered to be the only cause, and the weather is ranked among the constraints, the limiting conditions that allow or inhibit the cause to exert its effect. This way of looking at causality is a matter of convention, be it an appropriate one among plant pathologists, a convention resulting from the victory of the pathogeneticists. Other conventions are possible, and indeed the convention used in dynamic simulation is decidedly different from the elementary cause-and-effect type of thinking discussed here.
>
> (Horsfall and Cowling, 1977)

An infection may be a permanent part of a population, maintained at a more or less constant level, or it may undergo fluctuations with some regularity, or may usually be absent but break out occasionally as a spill over from some other species. It may be universal as the common cold, widespread in some climatic range like malaria, or local such as Lyme disease. Finally, the prevalence of the infection may be associated with either severe or mild symptoms.

The prevalence of a disease depends on the rates at which new cases appear and old cases disappear through recovery or death. New cases depend on contagion, which in turn depends on the frequency of contact between infective and susceptible people, the probability of transmission of the parasite if there is contact, and the probability of the parasite invading successfully if there is transmission. The disappearance of cases depends on the death rate and the recovery rate. If there is no mortality or immunity so that there is only contagion and recovery, and if the process is fast enough (such as with colds) so that we do not have to consider births of new susceptibles, and if a person is infective as soon as she or he is infected, then we could represent the process mathematically as follows.

Suppose that the fraction p of the population is infected and infective, and $1-p$ is not infected but susceptible. Then the number of new cases in a given time period is $2cp(1-p)$ where c contains the probabilities that two people are in contact, that if they are in contact there is transmission, and if there is transmission the parasite succeeds in establishing itself. But only those contacts in which one person is infective and the other susceptible result in transmission. The term $2p(1-p)$ is the fraction of all pairs of people in which one is infective and the other susceptible. The number of infectives that recover depends on how many are infected and the recovery rate and is therefore equal to rp.

If the infection reaches some equilibrium level in the population there must be a balance of new cases and recoveries so that

(4.1) $cp(1-p) = rp$.

We can solve this equation to find p, the equilibrium level. There are two solutions for this equation. The first solution is $p = 0$. Then the disease is absent from the population. The other solution is

(4.2) $p = 1-r/c$

Since p is a fraction of the population infected it cannot be less than zero or greater than one. If r is greater than c, p would be negative so that this solution has no real meaning and the only equilibrium is $p = 0$, no infection. This means that if a few infected people are introduced into the population the disease might be around for a while but will disappear eventually: it has no non-zero equilibrium.

The contagion and recovery rates determine not only the equilibrium values of p but also how quickly changes occur. The range of values of c and r in nature are enormous, and they determine the rates of development of epidemics. In plants of agricultural importance, epidemics develop most rapidly in vegetatively propagated crops, next in self-pollinated crops, and most slowly in cross-pollinated crops where genetic heterogeneity acts as a brake on contagion. In woody plants viral and fungus diseases spread very slowly. In the *Tristeza* disease of citrus, some 35 000 aphids moving from an infected tree per year result on average in 2 new cases. In citrus canker, the removal of non-infected trees within 125 m of an infected one is considered a sufficient quarantine procedure. But in annuals the parasite has little time to reproduce and spread, and epidemics advance rapidly over a scale of weeks.

In humans, we have the very rapid spread of highly contagious influenza but also the extremely slow spread of diseases like leprosy with low contagion but long survival. Now that we are aware of slow viruses, attention is focusing on conditions such as multiple sclerosis which may involve a slow virus, yet rarely spreads within a family.

The model presented above is very naive and can be criticized on many grounds, but it already grasps a few essentials of epidemiology.

First of all, a disease can be eliminated from a population if $c < r$. It does not require that c be zero but only that it is less than the recovery rate.

Second, we can see how sensitive the equilibrium level is to changes in c or r brought about by natural events, social changes or deliberate interventions. If a disease is rare in a population, say only 2 per cent of the people have it, then $1-r/c = 0.02$ and $r/c = 0.98$. Now increase r/c by about 1 per cent to 0.99. Then the level of infection is reduced by half, to 1 per cent. But if almost everybody is infected, say $p = 0.9$, $r/c = 0.1$ and a doubling of r/c to 0.2 reduces the prevalence of the disease to 0.8 or by only about 11 per cent. Therefore the same amount of change in any of the factors that affect r and c has a much bigger effect when a disease at equilibrium level is rare than when it is common.

Third, c and r themselves are complex and can be unpacked. Let us begin with c. It depends on the frequency of 'contact'. But the meaning of contact is different for different diseases. For a respiratory infection such as the flu, contact means sharing the same air mass. In the case of AIDS, contact means either sexual relations or sharing syringes for addictive or medical reasons, or exchanging blood through transfusion. For the intestinal pinworm (*Enterobius vermicularis*) contact usually means sharing a bed since the worms leave the anus at night and wander about a bit. It is common among children in large impoverished families. For hookworm, contact means walking barefoot over the same ground where someone else has defecated within the time period that hookworm larvae survive in the soil. For other worm infections, contact may mean sharing a common water or latrine system. For mosquito borne infections, contact means being bitten by the same mosquito.

Contact can be modified by any change in social activity whether or not it is aimed at disease control. It may vary seasonally, as behavior and parasite survival vary. When people are aware of being sick they may remove themselves from contact either to avoid infecting others or because they don't feel well. But the option of staying home in bed when sick is not equally available to all people. Among wage laborers it may mean loss of a job or at least loss of income. People may take pride in working when feeling awful and even consider that feeling awful is a natural part of existence unworthy of any special attention.

The distinction between contact and transmission is somewhat arbitrary. Usually we restrict contact to mean the opportunity for transmission. For example, fungal spores may land on the surface of a leaf. They are then in contact. But unless there follows a period of at least several hours of high humidity, the spore will not be able to germinate, produce a mycelium and penetrate into the plant tissues. Therefore the use of different irrigation techniques will influence transmission if there is contact. Once a parasite is transmitted to a host, there is the probability of successful establishment. This will be influenced by the complex factors of resistance and the parasite's mechanisms to evade the host's defenses. The number of parasites introduced in a single transmission will be important.

But perhaps the critical factor at this point is the state of health of the host. We already noted that disease resistance may be of two types: generalized 'horizontal' resistance, relevant to all infections, or highly specific 'vertical' resistance to a single disease. In mammals, vertical resistance is represented most commonly by specific immunities, usually as a result of previous exposure. But there are other cases where particular physiological conditions affect vulnerability to particular diseases, such as high blood sugar as in diabetes increasing the susceptibility to gangrene, or exposure to coal dust (black lung disease) or textile dust (brown lung) creating openings in the lung for opportunistic respiratory infections. Here obviously poor health in one regard reduces resistance to other threats to health.

Horizontal resistance is in humans associated with the obvious indicators of general health such as nutritional status and responsiveness of the immune system. We will discuss aspects of this system below. For the purposes of our simple model, all of these factors are included in the parameter c, the contagion rate, and therefore can be objects of social policy aimed at reducing the prevalence of parasite infections.

The other parameter in this system is the recovery rate. It too is related to general health of the host, but particularly to the state of general health as affected by the specific disease. Some diseases such as the diarrheas weaken nutrition, while others such as AIDS attack the immune system directly. Recovery is also influenced by therapeutic efforts in some cases.

Equation (4.1) allowed us to find the equilibrium level for an infection which is transmitted from person to person. If instead the disease passes from animals to people, the number of new cases could be c(1-p) where c includes the number of animals that are infected. Then equilibrium occurs at:

$$(4.3) \quad p = c/(c+r) = 1-r/(c+r)$$

Since r/(c+r) is always less than 1, such a disease will always persist. Such a disease can only be eliminated by reducing c all the way to zero.

It would be possible to examine the equations further to follow the time course of an outbreak when a new disease enters a population or when c or r change. However, after a while such pursuits become misleading because of the many ways in which the equations are inadequate. For example, these equations imply that if r and c remain constant the proportion of people who are infected would either increase or decrease toward an equilibrium level and remain there. The model represented by the equations does not allow for fluctuating rates of infection unless we allow c or r to fluctuate. More sophisticated models are needed to get representations realistic enough to show the time course of epidemics, how populations with different rates of contagion or recovery affect each other, the role of immunity, mortality, births, immigration and emigration, the spatial pattern of disease, and how health interventions affect the course of the epidemic.

For example, the contagion rate will be lowered if people are aware of the disease and take precautions. Suppose that the precautions increase when p is greater. For instance, let c be replaced by c/(1+ap) so that as p increases contagion declines. We introduced the new parameter a to represent the sensitivity of behavior to the current prevalence of the disease. Then equilibrium would be reached at:

(4.4) $p = (c-r)/(c+ar)$

Other modifications would introduce new variables such as the level of concern by health authorities, which may be induced by the level of the disease or by its rate of increase.

It is possible for epidemiologists to become fascinated by the models and forget that these are intellectual constructs designed to help us understand the dynamics of an epidemic. Since the model focuses on the variable p, the numbers who are infected, we may forget to ask the question, but how sick are they? In studies on malaria it has been found that when there is a high level of partial natural immunity in a population, we may have situations in which there is a high prevalence of infection but with mild symptoms. A massive innoculation campaign could reduce the prevalence of infection so that fewer people carry the parasites but they are very sick.

It is clear that even though particular infectious diseases have been controlled and in a few cases such as smallpox apparently eliminated, infectious disease as such is a permanent problem facing humanity. Each change in the environment and in the organization of social life changes the values of the parameters c and r and the other parameters of more realistic models, making it possible for new parasites to become significant diseases.

The prevailing strategy for control of disease has been a combination of reducing contagion and chemical therapy. The reduction of contagion among people has included such classic measures as the pasteurization of milk, introduction of latrines, purification of water, drainage of swamps, and quarantine of infected persons. Since the decline of the big killers of the early industrial revolution has taken place in the era of development of immunization, it is easy to attribute their decline to the immunizations. However even in the classic case of smallpox (McKeown, 1976) it can be shown that the decline preceded the widespread use of vaccination. It is more likely that the general improvement in living conditions in Europe was the major determinant of the decline.

The dominant strategy in dealing with the other side of the equation, the recovery rate, has been chemical therapy based on antiseptics and antibiotics, but this is problematic because of the evolution of resistance as we have seen. But there is another problem here: substances which attack many fundamental life processes in the pest or parasite are also more likely to be toxic to the host.

How then can we face the problem of infectious diseases? One way to begin exploring this question is by asking, how do plants and animals survive in nature? Why are crops so vulnerable when weeds do so well?

It is quite striking that 'In natural plant ecosystems devastating diseases do not develop though occasional flare-ups may take place on a limited scale. Epidemics are curtailed by the balanced interaction of the host–parasite system adapted to the environment.' (Segal et al., in Horsfall and Cowling, 1977). These populations usually do not possess absolute immunity or single resistant genotypes. They depend on:

[1] Escape from infection. Populations may be sparse, mixed with non-susceptible species; their development may be timed so that the most vulnerable stages occur under conditions least favorable to the infection; and they may pass through the vulnerable stages rapidly.

[2] Heterogeneity. A diversity of biological types within a species, differing in their physiology in ways that affect infection, reduces the possibilities of spread of disease. On the other hand, monocultures of single genotypes selected for yield are especially vulnerable.

[3] Tolerance, 'the ability of a cell, plant, or field to perform acceptably while providing the habitat necessary for the growth and reproduction of pathogens of that cell, plant, or field' (Henry Mussell, in Horsfall and Cowling, 1977).

[4] Resistance, itself composed of many different mechanisms that block the entry, migration within the host, or growth and development of the parasite.

It is the combination of many different ways of confronting disease that allows populations to survive without causing the parasite to evolve ways around those protections. These would include the classical methods of prevention, an increased emphasis on general health components of resistance and tolerance, and a strategy of domesticating the parasite, reducing the harmful effects and making it evolve toward being just one more benign inhabitant of the body, perhaps even a beneficial member of our internal microbial community.

Non-infectious Disease

Now listen, Mr. Philosopher, I can understand an aggregate, a tissue of tiny sensitive bodies, but an animal! ... A whole, a system that is a unit, an individual conscious of its own unity! I can't see it, no, I can't see it.
Denis Diderot[3]

Most of the patients coming to emergency rooms, clinics and hospitals of the industrial countries do not come with infectious diseases. They are not feeling well, are exhausted, have aches, pains and allergies, suffer from impairments of one or another body system, or have fresh injuries suffered at work or play, are depressed or anxious. In many cases people do not even seek medical attention because the condition seems just natural, part of life or a consequence of ageing.

In order to develop some approach to these issues, we have to make use of some general ideas of how the body functions.

First, a multicellular organism is a complex system whose survival and reproduction depends on the exchange of material and energy with its surroundings. Unlike non-living materials and artifacts which are preserved by isolation from the environment, organisms have to be open to the outside. Food, water, air and information are taken in; the waste products of metabolism pass to the outside along with carrier materials that allow them to get out, such as water; heat moves in both directions depending on the situation. Under extreme conditions it is possible for a living system to almost shut down and be isolated. Spores of fungi and bacteria can survive inside their thick outer coats with almost no interchange; seeds can remain in the ground for years in the 'seedbank'; insects can become dormant during the cold or dry seasons; mammals hibernate, and people can become inactive on smoggy or very hot days or under conditions of starvation. But all of these mechanisms in a sense postpone living. The completion of the life cycle requires active interchange with the environment.

Nutrients are useful because they can be used, that is, they are either turned into part of the living organism or consumed as fuel or assist in the absorption of materials that can be used in those ways. Proteins are broken down into amino acids which can then be recombined into new proteins; complex carbohydrates are broken into simpler sugars, combined with phosphorus and then oxidized to release energy leaving a residue of carbon dioxide and water or, if oxidized less completely, a residue of lactic acid. Or they may be put back together into glycogen and stored in the liver until the glycogen is broken down again into sugar. Or they may be broken down partway and used to make fats or other substances. Whatever their eventual fate, they are turned into something else. There are very few cases of something being absorbed and incorporated without change into the living structure. Water is perhaps the outstanding exception. Water is the medium in which life takes place, substances dissolve or float in suspension, move from one part to another, wastes and heat are removed.

The transformation of food into body substance or fuel makes the production of waste inevitable. Parts of molecules are removed to make new things. Food comes not as separate nutrients but in packages as plants or animals are eaten. Even if a predator eats a prey with more or less the same body composition as itself, there will be waste because different components turn over at different rates. For instance if protein is used in body structure and lasts ten times as long as fats consumed for energy, then eating enough prey to provide sufficient fat for a day will result in getting ten times the protein that is required for that day's replacement of structures. Furthermore, with changing external conditions the organism's needs change so that there is no perfect all-purpose diet with ideal proportions of ingredients.

To some extent, this problem of waste can be alleviated by using the leftover bits and pieces for other purposes. The cell or body is not like a factory in which each final product has its own inputs and wastes. Rather each item of resource can end up in any of a rather large number of places depending on the circumstances; metabolism is 'tinkering' rather than 'manufacturing'. Proteins can be burned for energy, leaving a surplus of nitrogen. Surplus carbohydrates can be used to make fats, iron can be incorporated into the hemoglobin of the blood or the myoglobin in muscles, in bile salts and in certain enzymes. And the end products of one process can be the starting point of another.

But this creates another kind of problem. The living material is certainly quite complex and diverse, but far less diverse than it might be. There are thousands or tens of thousands of different chemical substances in the body, but not millions. They are all based on relatively few basic structures and types of chemical bonds. The development of industrial chemistry and the synthetics industries reveals how simple our bodies are in some ways. Industry now synthesizes some 70 000 different substances which are more diverse in their chemistry than the protoplasm of cells.

The similarity of chemical structures in the components of organisms reflects their evolution. In some ways it increases the organism's efficiency since the same molecule may be used for several different purposes. But the involvement of important substances in multiple uses and their capacity to react with many kinds of molecules in potentially harmful ways makes the problems of their coordination enormous. If some enzyme is able to break the carbon–nitrogen bond of an amino acid in some protein, what is to prevent it from breaking those same bonds in other proteins? What keeps the enzymes from breaking each other down? If hydrochloric acid in the stomach helps digest protein, why doesn't it digest the stomach as well? If some processes require an acid medium and others a more basic environment, how can the organism do both? How much bile should be produced to digest fat when bile acid residues can also contribute to cancer? If a particular substance is produced to cope with some emergency situation, what is to prevent it from also getting in the way of many necessary processes?

Much of the organization of living material is concerned with the coordination of processes under changing circumstances with contradictory needs.

Self-regulation

The coordination of biological processes is different from the regulatory systems of engineers. In electronic/mechanical systems we can identify the processes to be controlled and those that do the controlling. The controlled processes involve moving or transforming relatively large amounts of material while the control structures are much smaller, involve distinct sensors that monitor the state of the system and carry out their control through the use of minimum signals, usually electrical. The control system can even be far away from the system that is controlled.

In the living organism the distinction between controller and controlled is less sharp. What we identify as organs or substances of the control system are themselves part of the same living system, are produced by it, are subject to the same sorts of stresses, and have similar requirements for their production and functioning: *the controllers must themselves be controlled.*

The heart, as an organ of circulation, maintains the oxygen supply to the tissues. But it itself needs oxygen and even has its own circulation. The kidney plays a major role in regulating blood pressure, but it also does other things with its own requirements and its own cells are sensitive to that blood pressure. The brain, which is involved in all corners of the body, is especially sensitive to its sugar and oxygen supplies. It is therefore more apparent in biological systems that we are dealing with *self-regulation*, while in engineering systems it seems as if there is a clear separation of regulators and regulated. It is only when we move on to social analysis of production that we see the engineering system as part of a larger whole which shows more of the properties of self-regulation.

Early models of the organism stressed its similarity to machines: the heart is a pump, the blood vessels are like plumbing pipes that can become corroded, the bones are the mechanical support understandable as columns and levers, spinal disks are like felt cushions between vertebrae, fat is insulation, ageing is wear and tear of machinery, sugar is fuel, etc. These models have proven very useful in the early stages of understanding. But beyond those early stages they are increasingly misleading. The major errors consisted of taking these mechanistic models too literally and ignoring that body parts are living material in interchange with other parts.

Bones do not simply wear away. There is a constant flux of material in bone, with calcium being deposited and removed in response to conditions in the rest of the body. Therefore the loss of calcium from the bones is not a unidirectional erosion but a shift in the balance of opposing processes. Fat does indeed insulate, but it is not a mere overcoat. We are increasingly aware of its metabolic role in the production of steroids and other materials, and have had to make finer distinctions between different kinds of fat. Nerves indeed transmit signals but unlike telephone wires they can regenerate when cut, their connections form and reform with use, and their insulation is far from perfect. Muscles do pull the bones around in motion, and can indeed be overstretched or torn. They also regenerate, but this regeneration depends on how they are used, which in turn involves conscious as well as non-conscious choices. And they are also the locus of emotional tension. Plaque does accumulate in arteries, but unlike corrosion in pipes it is an active two-way process which is actually reversible at low enough cholesterol levels. At each stage in the development of medical physiology we find new insights that reveal the body parts as more alive and connected than the mechanical models assume.

In the case of the nervous system, mechanistic ideas lead to a separation of the 'higher centers' from the autonomic nervous systems. The cerebral cortex has a relatively recent evolutionary history and is one of the ways in which humans are most different from our closest relatives. It was assumed to be concerned with consciousness, the interpretation of sensory information, decisions about movement and the finer ideas. The autonomic nervous system, divided into the inhibitory and excitatory divisions (sympathetic and parasympathetic) is more ancient in its evolutionary history, it was supposed to function automatically, inaccessible to conscious control, to be less changeable and in some ways more basic. Consciousness was therefore seen as a superficial varnish over deeper, darker, ancient and powerful forces, the reptilian brain.

Now we recognize that the separation is not that complete. The performance of the autonomic nervous system is sensitive to the cerebral cortex. Emotional experiences can affect its behavior and through it the state of the organism as a whole. It is well known, for example, that heartrate and breathing, which are under mostly autonomic control, are also responsive to judgements about external situations and interpretations of the state of the body.

This physiological impact of consciousness is often a factor in disease. More recently it has been increasingly utilized as a factor in health. Studies of 'biofeedback' have shown that it is possible to learn a certain conscious control over body temperature and its distribution, heart rate, blood pressure and other physiological processes that were assumed to be out of reach of consciousness. In the higher animals the younger parts of the brain provide the linkage between ever more complex aspects of the surroundings and the older structures, make them responsive to entirely new kinds of situations. In humans, society becomes a physiological force through the cerebral cortex as well as through the physical environment it creates.

Some Design Principles for Self-regulation

The systems of self-regulation have some general features worth examining:

[1] The state of the system is preserved through the interaction of opposing processes rather than by its isolation from all influences perturbing it. Thus maintenance is not like the inertia of physical systems. The nerves do not generally lie about, waiting for some stimulus, rather, each neuron can receive both excitatory and inhibitory impulses from other neurons. Therefore activation may come about either by increased excitation or by reduced inhibition. Since inhibition comes from other neurons, these must themselves have been inhibited, perhaps by the excitation of their inhibitors reacting to the original neuron. Hormonal activity also responds both to stimulation and inhibition. Control systems can be seen as networks of enhancing and reducing processes.

[2] Regulation depends on the networks of positive and negative feedbacks and feed forwards in the organism.

A negative feedback is a pathway by which an initial change in some part of the organism spreads through some other components and returns to reduce the original change. Thus, for example, an increase in blood sugar can stimulate the release of insulin from the pancreas and thus reduce the blood sugar. Or the sound of a baby crying can induce the caretaker to remove the source of crying, and thus reduce the crying.

A positive feedback is a pathway by which an original change gives rise to events which enhance the original change. The eating of some desired food can stimulate the appetite and thus increase the desire for it and its consumption. Or the sound of a baby crying may anger the caretaker, who hits the child and increases the crying. In real systems of any complexity, there are both negative and positive feedback pathways. What happens depends on their interactions.

It is usually stated carelessly that negative feedback stabilizes and positive feedback destabilizes. This is often but not always true. Strong negative feedbacks, especially if associated with time delays or which take place through long indirect pathways can throw a system into oscillation. For instance, a delay in the release of insulin can result in rising blood sugar after a meal, intense stimulation of the pancreas, the release of greater quantities of insulin, and a big crash in blood sugar levels. This is the situation in one kind of reactive hypoglycemia. When excessive lagged negative feedbacks can destabilize a system, this can actually be offset by positive feedbacks.

Feed forwards are responses which anticipate a condition of the organism. Thus for example hunger, the depletion of nutrients in the body, can increase food consumption. But people do not continue eating until nutrient levels are restored. Digestion is too slow for that to be an effective control system. The sensation of a full stomach is often the signal to stop eating. It anticipates that after digestion the nutrient level will rise. Feed forwards are important because some of the processes are too slow for the final outcome to be an effective control signal.

The control systems that coordinate all this complexity are themselves structured at multiple levels. Some control is very local. For instance an isolated heart, if provided with nutrients, can continue beating more or less regularly. But there is also system-wide control. The heart rate responds to signals entering through the circulation and the nervous system. We can see the adaptive significance both of local autonomy and central control. Local autonomy prevents a disruption of the center from destroying the organism completely, but also impedes coordination of parts. Central control gives better coordination when it works properly but if it is disrupted the results are more disastrous. In the course of evolution, these opposing design criteria have been combined in multilevel control systems.

Regulation also proceeds on different time scales. Consider for example the response to lowered oxygen availability due to altitude. The first, immediate response is to breathe harder and to lower the level of activity. Over the course of a few hours, the red cell count increases as red blood cells are released from the reserves in the spleen into the general circulation. Over a period of weeks, the production of red blood cells increases in the bone marrow, and the cells are released more quickly, when not yet fully mature. Over a longer period, the myoglobin concentration in the muscles increases. On an evolutionary time scale, body build and other characteristics are altered so that populations living at high altitude are physically better able to cope with these conditions than recent immigrants to the mountains.

Adaptations at different time scales are geared to different time scales of environmental changes. The rapid responses are readily reversible, are effective in the short run but can be harmful or simply too draining if prolonged. The slower responses are unable to keep up with rapidly changing conditions and by themselves would lag hopelessly behind. One form of misadaptation is always being in the right state to meet the previous circumstances.

Under extreme conditions and in some diseases, the opposing demands on the physiology may become increasingly incompatible, so that mechanisms which cope well with some problems cause harm in other ways. For instance, during starvation animals reduce thyroid activity, which lowers the metabolic rate and therefore saves energy. But this also produces a lethargy and increased sensitivity to temperature which may interfere with getting food. In the cold, mammals remove circulation from the body surface and concentrate it in the inner organs. This preserves heat but makes the skin and appendages more susceptible to infection because they receive less blood and are therefore less accessible to the immune system. And we are now aware, especially through the work of Hans Selye (1989), that the responses to stress which mobilize the body's resources for brief emergencies (release of adrenalin, increased heart rate, increased blood pressure) when prolonged have harmful long-range effects, threatening heart disease and strokes. Thus one kind of pathology results from circumstances which increase the incompatibility of physiological requirements.

[3] The development and maintenance of the body depends on continued functioning. Starvation weakens the digestive system, inactivity not only leads to consumption of muscles but also the loss of calcium from the bones. Sensory deprivation causes sensory loss and can induce hallucination. Weightlessness removes the load on the heart and can lead to cardiac degeneration.

[4] The regulatory mechanisms work more or less adequately under normal conditions. But there are always worst case circumstances under which the normal functioning of regulation produces harmful results. This may happen when a demand on the system is prolonged beyond the capacity of the regulating processes. For instance, an increased body temperature which creates unsuitable conditions for the bacteria in an infection, implies more rapid depletion of energy reserves. Mechanical injuries to the body often result in changes of posture which themselves eventually produce new stresses and discomfort. Thus the systems of self-regulation are not perfect but only adequate, and can even become mechanisms of disease when subject to circumstances they had not evolved to meet. Conditions in which

the positive feedbacks are cut free from their inhibiting negative feedbacks are especially important.

[5] Since the regulatory system is part of the living organism, it too can be damaged. A damaged regulatory system responds to misread signals, or responds too little or excessively, or takes too long to respond or to shut off. Therefore damage to the regulatory mechanisms are especially important in disease. Damage to the immune system can result in the autoimmune diseases in which the body attacks its own tissues as alien or fails to respond to invasion. Damage to the kidney can misregulate blood pressure, doing more damage to the kidney.

Damage to the regulatory systems can arise in the same way as damage to any other aspect of the organism since it is not really an isolated structure but part of what it regulates. There are several ways in which damage occurs:

(a) The direct impact of external influences: injuries and poisonings. Some of these are reparable, some not. But if repair is slow compared to the rate of acquisition of new insults, the effects will be cumulative and we attribute the outcome to 'ageing'.

(b) Exhaustion of the regulatory mechanisms from excessive use. This is especially important in stress-related conditions.

(c) Indirect effects from other parts of the organism in their responses to external events. For instance emotional stresses suppress the immune system.

(d) Genetic alterations in regulatory components. Genes are part of the developing and regulatory apparatus. They act to produce particular proteins or to regulate the rate or timing of production of those proteins. Therefore they appear in the regulatory system as rate differences, and these affect the effectiveness of regulation. From the point of view of the rest of the body, the genes are responsible for accumulations, deficiencies and distributions of substances and therefore are part of the environment that the body responds to. The replacement of one gene by another has especially strong effects when some substance normally present is not produced at all, and a link in the regulatory network may be totally absent with devastating consequences. But most genetic differences are small and can be compensated for by other pathways in the physiological network.

The pathway by which a genetic difference results in a different body state can be quite indirect and is not wholly contained within the body of the person with that gene. Once a detectable alteration is produced, it can become a signal to other individuals which affects their behavior and feeds back on the carrier. An altered tyrosine metabolism in people can influence the deposition of melanin in the skin, by itself a trivial trait. But under conditions of racism this darker color places a person in a different social and therefore physical environment. Through economic impact nutrition is altered. Through inferior housing, body temperature is stressed more often. Through inferior schooling learning is impeded. And the whole conspires to reduce life expectancy. In a technical sense then there is a genetic basis for higher mortality, lower academic achievement, increased respiratory disease, etc. Statistical analysis would really show the expected correlations between the offending gene and all sorts of social consequences, and verify that relatives are more likely to have similar social characteristics than unrelated people chosen at random in the population. Therefore claims would be made of the inheritance of all sorts of complex behavioral differences.

Because of the absurdity of the above example it might be dismissed as a misuse of the ideas of heredity. But it is not at all inappropriate. All genetic differences operate by changing some physiological processes which place other processes in new circumstances. The longer the chain of events required to produce a given outcome, and the more open to other influences, the more the trait will be seen as modifiable and the heredity aspects may be pushed into the background and disappear. But all genetic differences affect their carriers through a series of intermediate links that are imbedded in whole systems and are in principle vulnerable to modification. The genetic make up of an individual is better thought of not as 'traits' but as a norm of reaction, a pattern of response to an environment which it also chooses, modifies and defines. The norm of reaction itself changes as a result of responding (Levins and Lewontin, 1985).

A living organism is necessarily in active interchange with its surroundings. But once the doors are open there is the possibility, even the inevitability, of harmful materials, energy or information entering the body or useful resources leaving. The extent to which this happens depends on the environment as well as the state of the organism.

[6] The response system extends beyond the internal organs and includes behaviors of many kinds. The organism responds to all

sorts of sensory signals coming from inside or outside. Some of these responses are conscious, others take place without awareness. People usually react to physical stress in such a way as to remove themselves from that stress. We can respond to cold by going to a warmer place, increasing clothing, putting another log on the fire, warm our hands by rubbing them together or holding them in front of our exhaled breath, or generating more heat internally by vigorous muscular activity. We could also drink alcohol, which produces a sensation of warmth by relaxing the blood vessels near the body surface, allowing warm blood from the deeper organs of the body to return to the surface. Therefore more heat is lost, and during prolonged exposure to the cold alcohol is counterproductive. The Saint Bernard dogs save lives by leading people to safety, not by getting them drunk.

People respond not only to physical stresses but also to experiences of a more social nature. There are both physiological and social responses to events that threaten or enhance our safety, security, comfort or self-esteem, to surroundings that are ugly or appeal to our sense of beauty, to events that affront our sense of justice, etc. Through modern communication impinging on the cerebral cortex, news from across the world can become part of our environment. The behavioral and social responses are learned, and a product of our whole development. They may or may not be beneficial.

A Biosocial Model of Individual Health

I wandered lonely as a cloud
Of sulphurous hydrocarbon fume
And not of water vaporized
As poets carelessly assume,
My eyes atear, my craft all gone
And mute the music of my lyres
'Til my olfaction came upon
A mound, a mount of smould'ring tires
Beside the lake, where grew no trees
In pools of aging PCB's.
Below, an irridescent spring
Did bubble from the sequined sod,
It glowed in every spectral shade
And colours quite unknown to God!

While quite unseen by eyes like mine
A billion molecules peruse
A billion ways to recombine
Unthought of since the Cambrian ooze.
How could I not be touched that day
In heart. And lung. And DNA.

Isadore Nabi[4]

Let us begin by visualizing the individual organism as a network of physiological pathways familiar to medicine. These pathways will be pretty much the same qualitatively for all individuals although differing in quantities and intensities. We add to this network the psychological pathways that interpenetrate with it: for example, anxiety can be caused by a release of epinephrin whether this is due to some social event or a decline in blood sugar, and may be reduced by offsetting social events or by an increase in blood sugar. Similarly blood pressure, muscle tone, heart rate, release of digestive juices, etc. are responsive both to internal physiological changes and to psychological events.

People have social/behavioral responses that can cope with changes in the network. They can eat when hungry, rest when tired, breathe deeply or beat up their kids when anxious, etc. Therefore behaviors should be included in the network, reacting on and responding to physiological processes. (At some level, psychological states are physiological in that they correspond to states of the nervous system. But they are nervous system states which are organized in particular ways with a coherence that makes them recognizable at the level of psychology.)

The repertoire of behaviors that are available to a person will differ very much from person to person both because of their immediate surroundings at work, in their communities and in the larger society. But they will also depend on the system of ideas and feelings the person uses, how they have learned to perceive themselves and their circumstances and define acceptable options.

An event which arises internally or externally will percolate through the network, diminishing along some pathways and being amplified along others. The outcome then depends on the available pathways and the time scales on which they operate. Consider for example the network shown in Figure 4.1. The core of it is common to all people: there is a positive feedback between the level of anxiety and epinephrin in the blood, with anxiety drawing out epinephrin

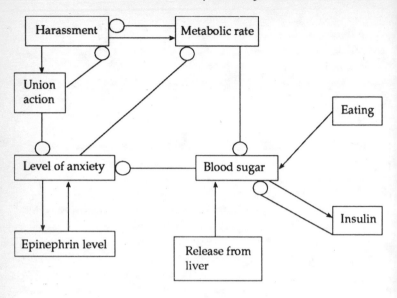

Figure 4.1

The feedback network between physiology and anxiety, mediated by workplace conditions. In the graph → indicates positive and —o negative effect

and epinephrin causing symptoms of anxiety. Blood sugar enters either by eating or by release from the liver. Since a lack of sugar often produces the anxiety symptoms of hypoglycemia, we represent this in the diagram by sugar reducing anxiety. The sugar also brings out insulin from the pancreas, and the insulin speeds up the removal of sugar from the circulation into the cells that use it. We have omitted other components of the physiology such as glucogon and cortisol for purposes of exposition.

Now consider that a person with this network works in a factory and expends energy at work. The greater the work effort the higher the metabolic rate. The metabolic rate determines the rate at which blood sugar is consumed. Now suppose that blood sugar falls with exertion, and the person experiences the hypoglycemic response including anxiety. This can lead to release of epinephrin, followed by sugar and insulin. But there may be a behavioral option: take a break, eat a snack, slow down. If this option is available, the blood sugar level may be restored. Therefore we have drawn a negative link from anxiety to metabolic rate.

But it is not always an available action. Suppose now that the person can reduce their metabolic rate. In some work situations, the surveillance by the supervisor is such that when a worker stops to rest or eat there is immediate harassment by the foreman. This appears in our diagram as a negative link from metabolic rate to harassment (the more work, the less harassment). The harassment increases anxiety immediately and if effective also increases metabolic rate. Finally, this shop may have a strong and militant union which is able to observe the harassment by the foreman and intervene with support for the harassed worker. This can reduce anxiety immediately and also perhaps more slowly, reduce the harassment.

Each of the behaviors by the worker, the foreman or the union is a possibility which gives rise to a different network and therefore influences the physiological outcome of the initial event. The same network can show us what would happen if harassment is initiated by the foreman not in response to reduced work effort but as part of an effort to extract more labor from the workers, or if the anxiety is the primary event coming from outside the work situation, or if the union gets stronger or weaker. All of these pathways form part of the health system for the person, and may be what physicians should be characterizing.

Some researchers in occupational health have been examining the relationship among stress, personal autonomy and the health outcomes of workers. Karasek (1989) has found that the degree of autonomy that workers have over their own activity is a major determinant of how stress is handled and therefore of the frequency of stress-related diseases.

But 'stress' and autonomy have to be described in terms of their time scales of operation. In general, assembly line workers have the least autonomy, their second to second or minute to minute movements being controlled by the speed of the line and the decisions of management. Most office workers typically have minute to minute control of their bodily movements but not hour to hour control: they can lean forward or back, get water or go to the bathroom but have to finish tasks usually on a scale of hours. Housework usually allows an autonomy over minutes to hours, but with episodes of emergencies that allow no autonomy. Those skilled crafts that are recognized as semiprofessional usually allow hour to hour autonomy and maybe even day to day but not week to week.

These socially determined autonomies must then be matched to the reaction rates of the physiology. The flux of epinephrin takes place on a scale of seconds and minutes, blood sugar and insulin on minutes to hours, the immune system on a scale of days or weeks, vitamin nutrition over days to weeks, body weight fluctuates over weeks to months, and so on.

The proper analysis of somebody's health situation requires the understanding of the networks of physiological and social responses on the various time scales, recognizing that the networks are different for each person according to their location in society and production.

When we stand back from the details of the physiology, we can still see the importance of the network pattern as shown in Figure 4.1. Let us abstract from the kinds of diseases and recognize that there is such a thing as 'resistance' to disease, R, which depends on many different factors, some of which may be specific for particular diseases and others constituting more generalized good health. This resistance is not a permanent characteristic but must be maintained actively; any resistance-promoting condition such as immune globulins or vitamins breaks down at a characteristic rate and must be restored.

In Figure 4.2 we show a schematic relation between resistance and disease: by definition, resistance reduces the disease level, and in most cases disease undermines resistance. It does so through fever burning up nutrient reserves, through loss of appetite, through economic loss, by its psychological impact, by exposure to stressful hospital conditions and in ways specific for particular diseases. For instance, diarrhea reduces absorption of food nutrients. This creates a positive feedback relation that can be destabilizing.

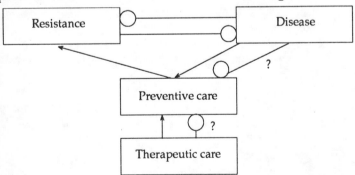

Figure 4.2
Resistance and disease in a larger feedback network. In the graph →
indicates positive and —o negative effect

The figure also includes the self-initiated preventive care that people engage in and that increases disease resistance. This self-initiated care can be increased by disease if the patient becomes more concerned about his or her health. It is typical that after suffering a heart attack people take up exercise, low fat diets and other health improving activities. But disease can also have the opposite effect, demoralizing a patient, causing losses of economic resources or energy for self-care. Therefore the link from disease to self-care will be different for people in different situations.

Finally, there is therapeutic care sought from the health system. The therapeutic care is not always sought when needed; there are social deterrants to going to doctors if the expectation is big expense, ineffective treatment or an unpleasant experience. The therapeutic care may be effective or harmful, and may result in either increased self-care or the undermining of self-care. With a feedback pattern that makes the whole system stable, disease episodes will be essentially independent events. But if it is unstable, one disease sets the person up for the next one, giving a pattern of runs of disease. Therefore the network shown in the figure will vary from person to person and is a major characteristic of that person's health situation.

5

Agricultural Ecology

Ill fares the land
To hastening ills a prey
Where wealth accumulates and men decay.

Oliver Goldsmith[1]

Agriculture marked a major turning point not only in human evolution but also in the ecology of the planet. The impacts of agriculture did not occur all at once but have emerged over the last 10 000 years or so:

[1] New ecological formations – cultivated fields, orchards, gardens and pastures – were created. Of the approximately 14 000 000 000 ha of land area on our planet, some 11 per cent was in cropland in 1981–3. Another 24 per cent was listed as permanent meadows and pastures, and 31 per cent as forests. The rest of the land area is lumped into the category 'other', including wetlands, deserts, tundra, etc. The figures are very rough, but they indicate that a major part of the earth's land area consists of habitats created by human activity.

These new ecological formations affect the climate of the earth. The heat balance of our planet depends on the absorption of the sun's energy and its various transformations. But part of that energy is reflected back into space by clouds or by the earth's surface. The fraction reflected back is the albedo, and stands today at about 0.14, that is, about 14 per cent of the sunlight that gets into the neighborhood of earth is reflected. But different surface materials have different albedos. The snow-covered Antarctic has an albedo of about 0.85, an oak forest about 0.15, grain crops or grassland about 0.23, and bare ground has an albedo which depends on its color. Thus the change from forest to crop land will lower the albedo of the earth during the height of the growing season, but raise the albedo when the land is bare. Irrigation also lowers the albedo and therefore raises the temperature of the earth.

More local effects also occur. The burning of sugar cane before harvest put so much ash into the Cuban atmosphere that it provoked increased rainfall just when this was least desirable because it interfered with the transport of the cut cane to the mills. The Cuban meteorologist Fernando Boytel (no date) argued that Cuba had a partly continental climate because the shallow, muddy waters along the north coast behaved like land with respect to the sunlight. Therefore erosion can contribute to the heating of the earth.

[2] Unlike many natural ecological communities, cultivated areas have sharp boundaries, forming islands of distinct habitat. Whether we regard microplots, even down to one or a few individual plants, as separate habitats or as part of a larger 'mixed crops' patch depends on the purpose of the analysis. From the economic point of view, the peasant may see a whole hectare as a mixed garden, but a bug that lives only on guavas may perceive isolated islands of single trees in a sea of weeds.

The nature of such island mosaics varies across agricultural systems. Plantation economies have often produced formations of thousands of hectares of a principal crop with isolated pockets of other land use, strips of forest along rivers and gulleys or the steepest slopes. Often the large plantations have fringes of minifundia around them, peasant homesteads where the farm laborers produced for their own maintenance.

[3] There has been a long-term trend toward reduced diversity of crops. Subsistence agriculture requires a certain diversity of crops both to provide for qualitatively distinct uses – different nutrients, medicinals, fuel and raw materials for construction and crafts. The development of commerce has allowed for local and geographic specialization. Trade makes crops interconvertible so that a single product can become many. This causes a drastic reduction in local diversity. One or a few principal crops and their associated weeds dominate the farmland, while the original native vegetation is banished to the inaccessible and waste land, and kitchen gardens preserve some of the original crop diversity. Plants which are not quite cultivated, yet are usefully gathered, may survive and be protected.

On a world scale some 3000 kinds of plants are used out of about a quarter of a million species described. Of these about 150 are grown commercially and some others are cultivated for home use without reaching the market. Finally, humanity depends for its food mostly on a few principal crops: the grasses wheat, rice, maize, sorgum and millet; cassava, yams and potatoes; the legumes chickpeas, pigeonpeas, dry beans and soybeans; sugar cane and beets.

[4] Along with reduced local diversity came the extension of ranges of a few principal crops. First they were introduced into regions similar to their native habitats in other parts of the world. But then they expanded into areas of less suitable habitat where production was less reliable unless special technologies, in the first place irrigation, protected them from the climate. Plant breeding led to the adaptation of plants to new habitats. For instance, for crops such as soybeans that are very sensitive to the day length, different photoperiod races with light responses suitable to different latitudes have been developed.

Today the geographic distribution of crop plants depends not only on their physiological needs but also on available technology and the costs of these methods compared to the prices of the crops. Growing seasons can be extended by irrigation, maize can be harvested before maturity and finish drying indoors with the help of heaters, smudge pots can protect orange trees against frost, vegetables can be grown hydroponically on islands that lack soil or in greenhouses in the tundra. The area sown to a crop varies from year to year according to market calculation, with both total production and yield per hectare responding more to prices than to weather.

[5] New species arose. The plants themselves have been selected under historically new conditions for traits desired by farmers. In some cases these traits made continued survival without human care impossible. For example, wild grasses shatter. While this is adaptive for the plants it makes harvesting more difficult although not impossible. The stick and basket are the appropriate tools for gathering shattering seeds and are used for crops like wild rice. The closed, non-shattering heads such as the ear of corn make harvesting much easier and bring in new tools such as the sickle.

The new cultivated habitat is also the environment for weeds. These are plants which have adapted to the conditions of cultivation, benefit from land clearing and fertilizers and irrigation. In a few cases, such as rye, the weeds themselves have been domesticated in turn and have become crops, while crops such as indigo have escaped from cultivation to become weeds.

Finally, new animal life has formed around the croplands. Many herbivorous insects are specialists feeding on only one or a few host species. It seems to be the case (Strong, 1979) that the number of herbivore species which feed on a plant in a given region increases with the abundance of that plant and its physical structural complexity. Trees provide more different habitats than bushes which provide more habitats than herbs and grasses. Crops are also fed upon by mites, roundworms, birds and mammals and are invaded by fungi, bacteria and viruses. It is estimated that various kinds of herbivores consume some 20 per cent of the world's agricultural production.

The herbivores themselves are the food resource for large numbers of predators and parasitoids. These are predaceous insects, mites and roundworms and parasites of the herbivores (microorganisms). Intermediate between the predators and the parasites are the parasitoids, mostly wasps and flies which lay their eggs in their hosts' bodies.

Other members of the community are the predators' predators, the parasitoids' own parasitoids, decomposers which feed on the plant and animal residues and their predators. A whole community is organized around cultivated plants and their associated weeds which may number hundreds of species.

[6] The pattern of human settlement has been dominated by agriculture and livestock. Cultivation can support many more people than can be maintained by gathering and hunting. As long as people had to be supported from local production, population concentrated in the most productive regions, often along rivers. But 'a region' is not defined by natural conditions alone. Is a single patch of meadow a region, or does the region include adjacent forests and mountains? This depends on the socially organized movements of goods. Anthony Leeds (1980) studied the historical ecology of the hill country around Austin, Texas. In pre-conquest times it was an agricultural region supporting native populations from local production. After conquest by European immigrants, it became a cattle region, no longer self-supporting but providing meat for the city and receiving other necessities by trade. Today it is a recreation area for Austin and no longer involved in significant food production at all.

At present the 5000 million people in the world are fed from perhaps 1400 million hectares of farm land. But the distribution is very uneven. Australian sheep ranches may have tens or hundreds of thousands of hectares while a Bengali farm might support a family from a single hectare and 90 per cent of the Salvadorean rural population is landless. Even in countries with high population densities the concentration of land holding allows some to have major investments in commercial agriculture while others can only supplement off the farm wages with a little gardening.

Over the centuries the productivity of world agriculture as a whole has been increasing slowly but unevenly. Japan and England have kept records for a long time. In Japan, rice yield in 800 CE was 1.2 tons per hectare. In 1600 it had risen to 1.5 t/ha, by 1820 it had reached 2 and now it stands around 6. Wheat yields in England rose from 0.4 t/ha in 1225 CE to 0.8 t/ha in 1600, 2 t/ha in 1900, and now stand at about 3.8. In recent times the improvement of agricultural yields has accelerated (for example, Braudel, 1981).

Machinery has allowed for large-scale extensions of cultivated areas through the pumping of water for irrigation and the tractor increased the area a single person could work. After the First World War, the nitrogen fixing industry developed to produce explosives became a chemical fertilizer industry. After the Second World War, chemical warfare was aimed at insects and microorganisms, and the expansion of pesticide industries led to further advances. Finally, plant breeding, more recently accelerated by 'biotechnological' methods, has increased the capacity of plants to use nitrogen and resulted in the 'green revolution' increases in productivity.

But the march of progress has been uneven. Indirect methods of estimation by anthropologists and archeologists have suggested yields of cassava of 20 t/ha in Mayan Central America in areas no longer cultivated. The Barind region of present day Bangladesh, once the heart of Golden Bengal and the breadbasket for the ancient Hindu capital at Gaur, is now a badly eroded semi-arid neglected area of that poor country. In some cases single crops have had to be abandoned due to pests and diseases, such as coffee retreating from Sri Lanka before the rust disease. The advance of agriculture is neither universal nor inevitable.

The Critique of Modern Agriculture

The successful long term increase in agricultural yields has given rise to a widespread optimism. It was believed that the development pathway that had proven so effective – increased and more diverse technical inputs to agriculture from off the farm – could continue indefinitely and that any problems created along the way could be solved by the same methods that created them.

This optimism was organized around the developmentalist ideas about progress: progress, or modernization, takes place along a single path from backward to modern. However, in recent decades a growing uneasiness with this pathway has emerged, for the following reasons:

[1] Modern, technical high-input agriculture is quite inefficient in terms of energy and resources. Its efficiency is limited to output per unit area, which is greatest in the Netherlands, Denmark and Japan, and to output per unit of labor, which is maximized in the US. The labor efficiency is usually exaggerated tenfold however: while one farmer may be involved in producing food for 40 consumers, food is really produced by one farmer plus five workers making the mechanical, chemical and energy inputs to the farm and another five handling, processing, storing, shipping, packing and selling the food. Therefore in the United States one food production worker on or off the farm produces food for about four consumers.

[2] Modern agriculture undermines its own productive base. The extensive use of irrigation uses up the reserves of the aquifers, making it necessary to dig ever deeper to mine water. Irrigation results in the salinization of the land. Heavy machinery or over-grazing of cattle compacts the soil. Annual cropping results in the loss due to erosion of some 5–7 tons of topsoil per hectare and year in the United States, in worst areas up to 50 tons per hectare, while natural processes can replace only 1–2 tons (Pimentel et al., 1987). In other parts of the world, where sloping land is farmed or attempts are made to cultivate the rain forest, erosion losses are greater, and when this takes place on shallow soils the impact is felt sooner than on the deep soiled prairies of North America.

Modern large-scale monocultures have lower organic matter content than the soil previously held. This increases the need for irrigation and nitrogen fertilizer and reduces the diversity of the community living in the soil. One result is increased pest problems. Another is the depletion of the minor nutrients which are not included in the mass fertilizer applications. This comes about because increased yield means greater quantities of material removed from the field and not restored. But in addition, the heavy doses of nitrogen, potassium and phosphorus interfere with the uptake of the minor elements such as boron, zinc, copper and manganese.

In affluent economies this declining productive capacity of the land can be hidden for a time by increased inputs of fertilizer, pesticides, irrigation water and mechanical energy. But the economic conditions under which this solution is viable become increasingly stringent and eventually the land has to be abandoned, first passing through stages of rainfed farming and pasture.

[3] Modern high-technology agriculture increases the vulnerability of production. Previously, diversity provided a buffer against the uncertainties of the environment. While some plants suffer from abnormally wet years, others prosper. Early frost might kill the corn but the oats will have been harvested. Pest outbreaks usually affect only one or a few crops, allowing the others to mature normally. A price decrease in one crop may be compensated for by a rise in another, or on-farm diversity can at least feed the family even if cash income is lost.

Diversity is lost when the single criterion of profitability excludes considerations of risk, food value, environmental impact, employment opportunities, taste and other factors. Not all crops are equally profitable. Since 'green revolution' plant breeding emphasized an increased capacity to respond to nitrogen fertilizer, grasses (grains) improved more than legumes, which have their own nitrogen fixing mechanisms. Therefore high-yielding wheat has tended to replace chickpeas in India. The absorption of Third World agriculture into the world market with its increased demand for meat has created situations in which it is more profitable to grow feed than food or divert farmland to pasture.

Large-scale monocultures are ideal environments for pests. Some of these pests have emerged as significant problems only with modern agriculture. Monoculture provides large expanses of available food where populations can spread continuously without barriers. Commerce often allows the pests to spread even faster.

Pesticides eliminate natural enemies, allowing minor herbivores to explode into major disasters. The brown plant hopper, so devastating for rice, seems to be a problem only after intensive pesticide use. Mites as pests of orchards, army worms (*Spodoptera* species), fruitworms (*Heliothis* and others), whiteflies and other common pests are referred to as secondary pests because their emergence as problems follows pesticide use.

Modern plant breeding, especially around the green revolution, has emphasized yield above all other considerations. For instance, a dwarf variety of wheat puts more of its product into grain and less into stems and roots. But this means that weeds can outgrow the wheat and more active weed control is required. Reduced roots means more need for irrigation. In general, the new varieties are bred for peformance along with a whole technical package. In its absence they perform poorly.

Fertilizer technology, especially large doses of inorganic nitrogen, makes plants more attractive to insects since nitrogen is often a limiting nutrient for them. And many plant diseases seem to be more severe with nitrogen fertilization. This seems to contradict the widely held belief that healthy, well-nourished plants are more disease resistant. However, abundant inorganic nitrogen is more favorable to the microorganisms in question than to the plants, which show increased vegetative growth but more succulent tissues and some imbalance of other nutrients.

In market economies, modern agriculture increases economic vulnerability. The use of irrigation, fertilizer and pesticides provides at least temporary protection against the vagaries of nature. But since these are produced off the farm and must be paid for, variation in prices can have a greater impact on the food supply than variations in rainfall. The root zone of a wheat plant in Argentina now has as part of its environment the politics of the Middle East by way of the price of oil and therefore fertilizer.

When variation in production passes through the market its impact is amplified. For example, only about 10 per cent of world rice production is traded internationally. Therefore a 5 per cent decrease in production results in a 50 per cent reduction in rice on the world market and corresponding to this, an enormous rise in prices. Finally, the inequality in a society usually means that a small fluctuation in production is allocated by the market in such a way as to affect the poor disproportionately. For instance, if there is a 5 per cent decrease in production of rice, this results in a price increase. The affluent will still eat as before, but if the decrease is absorbed by only the poorest 25 per cent of the population, then they eat not 5 per cent less but 20 per cent less rice.

Unpredictable economic fluctuations are sometimes exacerbated by deliberate refusals to sell to particular countries as a form of political pressure. Under these conditions monoculture and specialization are even more dangerous to a developing country.

[4] Modern agricultural technology harms the health of farm workers and their families and also the general public by way of pesticide contamination. In 1972 the World Health Organization estimated that there were some half a million cases of pesticide poisoning annually with a 1 per cent death rate. This is certainly an underestimate because the symptoms of pesticide poisoning are very variable and not always recognized.

[5] Modern high-techology agriculture pollutes the environment. Pesticides get into the air, the soil and the water. Fertilizer run-off gets into streams and lakes where it provides nutrients that permit bloom of algae. During this bloom, oxygen is produced which returns to the atmosphere. But when the algae die the organic matter sinks to deeper water and decays. The decay process uses up oxygen so that we get zones of oxygen deficiency which are lethal to fish and invertebrates. Fertilizers react with the soil conditions and sunlight to release nitrogen in the form of nitrogen dioxide (NO_2) which is a photooxidant effecting health and acid deposition and a green-house gas.

[6] The quality of food is debased. The single-minded pursuit of yield as a determinant of profit has often resulted in the sacrifice of protein content or other aspects of nutritional value to bulk. Heavy applications of nitrogen unbalance the mineral composition. The mineral content of vegetables can vary by as much as an order of magnitude depending on the conditions under which they were grown. The requirements of storage and transport take precedence over food quality. The competitive marketing of food has led to cosmetic criteria as spurious indicators of quality which encourage unnecessary pesticide use since many insects have effects limited to the appearance of the outer surface of fruits.

[7] Modern technology alters social relations in the countryside to the detriment of the poorer farmers and laborers. Differential access to the technology through access to credit or information contributes to the failure of many farms and the concentration of land holding and production in fewer hands. In the United States the initial investment in land and farm machinery prevent many aspiring farmers from entry into agriculture. In the Third World it is often more profitable to replace peasant labor, which uses some land for subsistence crops, by wage laborers dependent solely on the income from working the large farms. The displaced peasants may become landless laborers

or migrate to the cities. Jobs created by the new technologies are fewer than those eliminated except where year-round cultivation is made possible by irrigation and mechanization.

[8] The position of women is often undermined. Even in countries where women are responsible for most of the farming, new technologies are usually given to or fall into the hands of men. Modern post-harvest processing equipment displaces cottage level husking and milling which were usually women's occupations. And the greater unevenness of labor demand during the annual cycle works to the disadvantage of women with children, who can run farms with diverse crops making more level demands on their time.

[9] Agricultural science still operates on a very narrow intellectual base, emphasizing single inputs for each purpose and ignoring the broader implications of recommended technologies. Given the complexity of nature, many of the consequences of introducing innovation appear as 'unexpected' side effects. Research is dominated by the search for marketable input commodities rather than ecological knowledge to reduce the need for inputs.

This constrains the techniques to be applicable within the confines of a single farm. For example, if a pesticide is effective against the adult of an insect which does its damage as a larva, it will not protect the crop. If in addition the insect adult is highly mobile so that next year's invasion does not come from the survivors of this year's reproduction on this farm but from the survivors in the whole region, it will not benefit an individual farmer to use this product and the market researchers will recommend against its development. But a region-wide integrated pest management program might find the product useful.

Integrated pest management (IPM) (Levins, 1986) has a dual significance. On the one hand it reflects an awareness that promiscuous pesticide use is counterproductive and is a small step toward ecologically rational methods. Pesticide use is reduced by careful evaluation of what pest levels cause sufficient economic harm to justify intervention, and ingenious monitoring procedures have been invented to carry this out. The timing of applications is planned in such a way as to minimize impact on beneficial insects. The release of laboratory-raised parasitoids, the careful timing of planting dates, the breeding of resistant varieties, the use of pheromone traps and repellants have all contributed to the reduction of pesticide use.

But the other side of IPM is that it is a rear guard action by industry offered instead of biological control as a program which acknowledges ecology but still attempts to preserve a major role for the agricultural chemicals industry. Therefore the strategy of IPM has been to invent a much enlarged bag of tricks for farmers to buy. These include both commodities and services, as computerized decision-making consultants enter agriculture.

Since the selling of commodities as farm inputs is the most profitable way of turning agricultural research into profit, the dominant research strategy is one of increasing the diversity of off-farm inputs. An alternative to this strategy gives research priority to the design of almost self operating systems that require less intervention.

[10] Specialized research, carried out in the industrial countries or the major urban centers of the Third World, is part of a technical and economic package that confronts indigenous peoples as cultural invasion, disrupting their ecology, knowledge, technology, beliefs, land use system, autonomy and demography. Thus modern agriculture must be seen as a successional stage which creates the conditions for its own replacement. The question is whether it will lead to a wasteland or an ecologically and socially integrated pattern that protects nature, production and people.

Most of these criticisms are now familiar although usually not presented together. Nevertheless, the dominant pathway of development is still the high-technology package imbedded in a market economy.

Developmentalism

We argued in Chapter 2 that environmental destruction continues in the face of evidence of its destructiveness due to the various combinations of greed, poverty and ignorance that determine development policies in different parts of the world. In agriculture, greed takes the form of commoditization. Poverty acts to create an urgency to produce which is impatient with criticism of undesirable consequences and unable to take the risks of changing production systems or challenge the science and technology of countries that seem to be successful. Ignorance is structured into a complex system of beliefs, information and gaps in information, philosophy of science, and supporting institutional and policy arrangements which discourage any radical departures. Central to this structure is the developmentalist outlook which supports the following propositions:

Modernization is the transition from labor-intensive to capital-intensive technology, mobilization of energy to move or transform huge quantities of matter in order to free people from the overwhelming physical burdens of farming

This is indeed descriptive of some of the major changes that have taken place in agriculture in the last century. However it is still a nineteenth century thermodynamic model in which success is measured by the quantitative movement and transformations. An alternative model, however, is more concerned with the flow of information rather than bulk, and with very small inputs producing big effects. The energy involved in a nerve impulse or the total bulk of a hormone or even the power consumption of a super computer are negligible compared to the effects they have.

Thus we have some precedent for suggesting that the evolution of agriculture can be from labor intensive to capital intensive to thought and knowledge intensive, and that intellectual effort can be directed less toward inventing new inputs for agriculture and more toward designing agroecosystems that are as self-operating as possible and require minimum input of capital and labor.

Modernization simplifies for efficiency, so that the evolution of agriculture must be from diversity to uniformity and specialization at the level of the enterprise or region

This again is a roughly accurate description of what has happened. But this homogenization is more a consequence of the economic history and organization of the industry than of the nature of production. We have already indicated that monoculture is ecologically inefficient. The diversity of peasant production was partly a consequence of peasant technology, partly a deliberate choice to have a variety of foods or a hedge against disaster, and partly a consequence of a patchwork land tenure so that the countryside was a mosaic reflecting also the different needs and decisions of different farms.

We suggest that the evolution of agriculture can be from the partly random diversity of the tiny peasant landholdings through the uniformity of agribusiness plantations to an ecologically and socially rational planned diversity. An approach to such planning is outlined below.

Modernization requires a transition from small to large scale

The argument here is the one of economies of scale. Large fields allow for larger equipment; large farms allow for more investment in equipment and even to allot resources for gathering technical and economic information or hiring expert technicians and managers; large enterprises can have access to credit and will be less vulnerable to the whims of the market.

In opposition to the obvious harmful consequences of at least some giant enterprises, ecology-minded groups have put forth the counter proposal that 'small is beautiful'. This is partly an argument for diversity and partly for scaling down of machinery so that it will be compatible with small farms which are viewed as socially desirable.

However, large planned units are not always unsuccessful, and the uniform rejection of large planned units is more an ideological commitment than a careful analysis; we return to this question below. On the other hand, the widespread failure of family farms in the United States is well known. Here we have situations of economic failure with at least relative technical success in the short run. There does not seem to be any convincing evidence at present that one or another organization of agriculture is clearly, universally and overwhelmingly superior. Rather, the experience of each depends on its particular history and context.

When we discuss the scale of farming, it is necessary to differentiate between the unit of production and the unit of planning and remuneration. The often extremely localized qualities of different pieces of land due to topography, soils, flows of moisture and past history of use argue for small or variable sized units. Interactions between patches of land with different vegetation types modify the microclimate and can be used to improve the conditions of production. These effects occur roughly on a scale of ten times the height of the plants. Residues of one kind of patch can be used as inputs on another. Proximity makes this easier to do. The movement of beneficial insects, birds and other organisms from one patch to another is an essential part of ecological pest management. This requires that distances between patches be compatible with the mobilities of the creatures in question and would usually argue for modest-sized patches. The desirability of farmers' getting to know each of their dairy cows individually so as to care for them better and detect disease sooner argues for a maximum herd size below 100 animals, while epidemiological dangers also urge limits on poultry units.

But while individual patches of crop or other activity should be small enough to allow for the advantages, the whole array of patches may be quite large. The management of water is best carried out on the scale of a whole watershed and would require resources such as labor from all subunits. The management of disease or pests must take into account the range of a unit population of pests, their mobilities. The maximization of benefit for the ensemble as a whole, no matter how benefit is defined, is different from the maximization of benefit from each patch separately.

But if some patches will be more productive than others, and may be devoted to less productive activities than would be possible in order to improve the whole, people deriving their income from single patches of vegetation will be unequally rewarded for efforts that may be equally hard. It would not be feasible to ask some farmers not to grow the most profitable crop in order to protect their neighbors from pests. Rather, remuneration should in some way reflect the productivity of the whole set of patches.

Therefore the problem of scale requires combining the advantages of detailed local adaptation with larger scale coordination. How that coordination is to be achieved cannot be settled by ecological argument.

Modernization aims at an increasing control over nature, the freeing of farming from the unpredictable caprices of weather and pests

There is some truth in this assertion. The uncertainties of rainfall can be compensated for by irrigation, unexpected pest outbreaks by pesticides, unauthorized plant growth by weed killers, and so on. However it must be remembered that in some ways this merely shifts the focus of uncertainty from physical and biological factors to economic ones while contributing to the long-term vulnerability and productivity loss of the system. Further, the goal of increasing control has often led to the notion that any plant that wasn't sown is a competitor, any antenna that twitches threatens crop destruction. The vegetation between fruit trees is clipped to golf course height, the cows are kept in air conditioned boxes, nature is treated as an enemy.

The uncertainty of nature is a real problem for farmers. It can be confronted in several ways: we can enhance diversity, so that declines in one crop are compensated for by increases in others. We can breed for tolerance of extreme conditions such as deep-water rice, salt-tolerant grains and vegetables, drought-tolerant crops, etc. There can be systems of redistribution so that losses in one area are made up for by increases in others. And there can be improved prediction within systems that minimize the vulnerability to the unusual.

Good agricultural practice does not require complete control. Not all weeds or herbivores are really harmful. An insect that eats lower, shaded leaves of tomatoes can improve yield and ripening quality of the fruit. Some fungi improve the flavor of grapes. Many grains depend for production only on the topmost leaves (in maize, the leaves above the ear). Beans can tolerate heavy visitations of whiteflies after they are older than about three weeks, provided the whiteflies do not carry viruses.

An alternative to the impractical goal of increasing control is one of design of agroecosystems such that we can get away with not controlling most of what happens and rely on the resilience, robustness and feedbacks in the system to ensure that our needs are met. A diverse even if not censused fauna and flora is a protection against pest outbreaks. A rich soil with good organic matter and nearby forests would buffer against fluctuations of rainfall. Strong technical interventions could be held back as last resort emergency measures.

The smaller the object of study, the more scientific it is, and modern science is increasingly specialized
This is the reductionist bias which has dominated Euro-North American science since its inception, creating a hierarchy of the sciences and allowing 'modern' biology to be identified as molecular genetics. This also results in the typical errors of deriving programs for the large from tests of the small and places much of reseach out of reach of poor countries and non-specialists. When we recognize the legitimacy of science on all levels we also make possible mass participation in science and the mobilization of vast intellectual resources. It is particularly necessary to break down the barriers between social and biological sciences in agriculture and to give scientists an appreciation of the history both of their problem and of thinking about it.

Modernization requires the replacement of superstition by science
The term superstition implies that traditional or folk knowledge is necessarily wrong. Attitudes toward prescientific knowledge in medicine and agriculture have gone through many changes in recent times. The reality is that all knowledge comes from direct or indirect experience and reflection on that experience in the light of previous belief. Therefore each system of knowledge comes from a point of view and from a particular location in the world which carries with

it interests and indifferences and both insights and blindnesses. Modern science is a particular episode in the history of knowledge in which the creation of knowledge has become part of the social division of labor, organized around a special training and socialization of recruits, the organization of separate institutions and supported by a self-conscious concern for rules of inquiry.

The history of agricultural development schemes is full of examples of new technologies being rejected for apparently irrational reasons that proved to be well founded later on. Peasant knowledge tends to be local, detailed and intimate where scientific knowledge acquires its theoretical insights at a certain distance from the particular. Both kinds of knowledge are needed for an ecologically rational agriculture. Particularly, as we seek technologies that are gentler they are also more site specific: where the objective is to kill everything that creeps on the field it almost doesn't matter what they are or how they relate to each other, but if we want to nudge the ecosytem toward better production and productivity a detailed knowledge is critical. Things that work in one place will not work somewhere else, often for quite subtle reasons.

Therefore a precondition for an ecological agriculture is the creative combination of the detailed, intimate but very local knowledge that people have of their own circumstances with the abstract, theoretical and general knowledge that only scientific distance, comparison and intellectual detours can produce. This exchange of insights requires conditions where the farmers can meet with the agricultural scientists as equals on terms of mutual respect.

The Design of Sustainable Agricultural Systems

At the time of writing there is a growing concern about the sustainability of development. The notion of sustainability is itself an object of conflict. For those who are satisfied with existing economic and power relations it is the maintenance of productivity, keeping society as it is. For some it is the removal of the most obvious abuses and a democratization of access to opportunity for production and consumption while leaving both production systems and consumption patterns intact. For others sustainability is economically productive, ecologically rational and socially just.

Sustainability can be posed on the level of the single farm, the region, the nation or globally, and on time scales from years to centuries. As we expand the temporal and spatial scales we also usually have to expand the substantive scope since constraints which operate in the small become objects of decision making in the large. New problems and new degrees of freedom are added. Questions of land tenure, the availability of water in aquifers and rivers, the climatic and hydrological impact of forests, the choice of crops for a region, the structure of markets and prices, population and employment trends, dietary preferences and the organization and priorities of research are all givens from the point of view of the single farm but must be examined, questioned and decided about on a larger scale.

It is necessary for us to look at several scales. The smallest scale and shortest term horizon confronts the individual peasants, farmers and extension workers as practical issues of survival. There are severe constraints at this level, exerted by local custom, the availability of markets, transport and storage or processing facilities, the priorities of creditors, and access to information and seed. Tenants may not be sufficiently secure in their tenure to consider land improvement. They may be constrained by the priorities of landlords for whom farm income is only one part of their income. If they are also money lenders and food merchants and pesticide vendors, then the diversification of crops, expansion of the farming season and the reduced dependence on purchased inputs goes against their interests, and they oppose farm scale programs for sustainability and ecological and social rationality. Expansion of farming opportunities for women may improve the economy of the household but weaken the dominance by men and cause further conflict. It is not at all obvious that 'improvement' appeals to everyone and will be accepted once its merits are demonstrated.

Therefore the single-farm measures discussed below may not always be practical. However, they can be introduced where the social conditions permit and otherwise serve as models of the possible.

The individual farmer can in principle make decisions about land use within the farm, choose crops and techniques for water and soil management and pest control, especially for the less mobile pests.

The prevailing analysis of farmers' decisions is based on neoclassical economic models. They assume that the farm is a business with the goal of maximizing profits. A crop responds to an input such as water or fertilizer or labor, at first rapidly and then with diminishing return. The optimum level of input is that at which the cost of further input just balances the price received by increased production. A lot of sophisticated modelling has gone into describing the responses of crops to inputs of several different kinds simultaneously. Then development strategy consists of trying to manipulate the costs and prices in such a way as to get farmers to make desired decisions. In the research program of the 'green revolution', plant breeding was aimed at changing the response curve of crops so that farmers would decide to consume more inputs and produce more crops.

A more integral approach to farm decisions would differ from the neoclassical models in several major ways. First, instead of a single criterion such as profit maximization, multiple criteria are used including long-term social goals. Second, the constants of the neoclassical model which depend on soil, moisture, microclimate and pests and which determine the technical decisions in that model are here covariables with yield. That is, any use of inputs and any yield level affects the conditions for the following year, so that yield and productivity evolve together. Third, the neoclassical model assumes that almost any inputs can be bought, so that yield and price are weighed against input cost, but in the integral model there are constraints on inputs set by ecological and social factors.

The diversity of crops makes land use patterns and crop interactions a major concern. Crops interact at different levels. Through sharing of a common constraint, they compete for resources. Through having different responses to weather, different pest problems and separately determined prices they jointly provide buffers against uncertainty. Their chemical composition makes them partly supplementary and partly interchangeable in the provision of nutrients. Their different microenvironmental requirements will usually suggest where to place them spatially. The residues of one productive activity such as manure and straw for compost or mulch may serve as inputs to another.

There are also direct agronomic interactions which offer advantages to diversity: first, plants affect the microclimate around them. Wind is interrupted by the growing plants, altering moisture and temperature conditions for a distance of several times the height of the plants. Leaves can intercept the mud splash that sometimes spreads fungal spores from the soil to the susceptible plants. Mutual shading can be beneficial or harmful. Second, combinations of plants with dense superficial root mats and deeper taproots can be used to manage the flow of moisture and the building of the soil. Third, combinations of crops improve pest control. Some species serve as trap crops for the pests of others. For example, corn can divert fruitworms from green peppers, and beans can perform this service for tomatoes while also fixing nitrogen. Others repel the pests that affect their companions. Garlic repels slugs invading lettuce beds, marigolds repel soil nematodes. Mixtures can confuse herbivores looking for their preferred food plant, provide nesting sites or nourishment for beneficial predators and parsitoids or fungi and attract pollinators.

These interactions occur over different spatial scales from close intercropping to alternating strips or mosaics of fields. The desirable scale depends on enhancing positive interactions while minimizing harmful effects. For instance harmful shading is a close up effect, but the movement of predators can take place over greater distances. These considerations and the problems of mechanization can determine the spatial separation that farmers eventually use.

Because of the complexity of these interactions among different agricultural activities, ecological issues enter more directly into economic calculation than is the case with simple profit maximization.

Usually there are a few major crops produced for market in any region. The existing markets, credit, services, skills and knowledge are all focused on these crops with little room for major departures. However, a much greater number of potential crops are available for home consumption and small-scale local sales. Most peasant agriculture combines market and subsistence production. The subsistence crops provide a buffer against market uncertainty or disasterous weather, often absorb labor during the off season for the major crops, provide nutrition and medicine and raw material for crafts. Collective farms and state farms, even if specialized toward one or two commercial crops, generally also produce for the maintenance of their own members or workers. The subsistence fields on state farms are increasingly important in Cuba and provide the opportunities for agronomic innovation, crop interactions and learning how to manage diversity.

The combination of economic and agronomic interactions listed above would result in decisions in which crops are not necessarily grown only where they do best considered separately. For instance, only a small area is required to meet the garlic needs of a country. It can then be produced quite efficiently. But it may turn out to be preferable to grow all the country's garlic in protective bands around lettuce beds. The garlic production may be less efficient this way but the whole agricultural enterprise improved.

Some of the most interesting work on spatial patterns on the farm has been done by the Permaculture group in Australia. Their model is the independent yeoman farmer with sufficient land for diversity. In the permaculture scheme, concentric rings around the residence contain activities with diminishing demand for constant attention. Thus the kitchen garden is close to the house, field crops further out, then orchards, pasture and woodland. The farm is also divided into quadrants with land use related to prevailing sunlight and wind direction, and modified further by details of soil and topography. Since the growth of forest is a long-term project, permaculturists also consider the stages of tree growth, with temporary crops making use of the land between the young trees.

The rather specialized social assumptions of the permaculturist model make it less directly useful for the tiny peasant plots of much of the tropics or for large-scale production units that aim to feed cities. But their approach to serious consideration of spatial organization can be adapted to other systems.

Water is a flow-through on the scale of the individual farm. It enters by way of rain, run-off from uphill, subterranean water movement in the aquifer, and as irrigation water. It leaves as run-off, percolates down to the aquifer, evaporates from the surface or passes through the plants and leaves as transpiration.

As with any flow-through, the total input is externally determined (except for the purchase of irrigation water) and the output is equal to the input in the long run. Our object in water management is to regulate that flow so as to minimize the erosion caused by run-off and balance available moisture to the crop needs. In general plants grow best when the actually available water is equal to the potential evaporation from the soil and the transpiration through the plants, combined into the single term evapotranspiration. But the development of plants is never so integrated with rainfall as to maintain this balance throughout the growing season. Therefore various measures can be taken to approach that balance.

Water can be stored directly in ponds. Ponds can also provide for production of fish, ducks and geese. Residues from the land can fertilize the ponds and fish waste and algae can fertilize the land. Ponds modulate the microclimate to a distance about equal to their width in the downwind direction. The immature stages of dragon-flies and other predatory insects are aquatic so that ponds contribute to pest control. Finally, the water is readily available for normal domestic use, irrigation and fire fighting. However, the construction of ponds can be costly, there is evaporation from the surface, and land is removed from terrestrial production.

Water may also be stored in the soils of forests and in cropland with good organic matter content. This is perhaps the optimal way of storing water since there is no major outlay of resources for construction and the measures which are required are also desirable for other reasons, for instance, preservation of soil organic matter.

Soil moisture also serves to moderate the fluctuations of temperature and can sometimes prevent frost damage. The large-scale drainage of areas of Florida may be responsible for the more frequent losses of orange crops to frost despite an unchanged average temperature.

Sometimes the problem is too much water. This can be dealt with by improved drainage and also by the use of plants which transpire more water back into the atmosphere. Eucalyptus trees are especially effective in this regard and were used in Italy to drain the Po valley marshes.

Water requirements must be measured by the crops themselves. Sometimes it makes more sense to adjust the plants to the water regime than to try to create a water regime for the plants. Whenever crops are grown outside their zone of adaptation, water management becomes a major production cost and the year to year variability of the yield is usually increased. Water requirements can be reduced by selecting crop species whose water requirements match the actual water regime.

Pest and disease management within the single farm is most effective for some of the less mobile pests and diseases where the results of one year's efforts affects the next year's outbreak. Minimal input methods include mixed cropping, trap crops, repellant crops, resistant varieties, and the design of ecosystems which maintain populations of the natural enemies of the harmful organisms.

The first line of defense would be the predators such as predatory mites, spiders, ants, ground beetles, earwigs and some bugs and nematodes. They tend to be generalists and can maintain themselves even when the pest is absent. Sometimes they need help in the sense of protecting nesting sites or providing food supplements. They serve a preventive role since they are there before the pest outbreak, but usually respond slowly to the outbreak if it occurs.

The next line of defense consists of specialized parasitoids, usually wasps and flies. Because of their specialization on only a few host species they will be rare or absent before an outbreak and lag behind the pest. But their dependence on the pest population also means that they respond rapidly to the outbreak and can become very abundant.

The adult parasitoids usually require a source of nectar for their maintenance, so that nectar sources should be grown to attract them. Sometimes it is even desirable to maintain pest populations at low levels so that when the outbreak occurs the parasitoid will not lag too far behind. For instance the scale insects which attack citrus in Cuba are very seasonal, coming with the rains and the flush of new leaves. But they are less seasonal on guavas. The guavas can keep a population sufficient to maintain the wasps that prey on them.

Insect diseases can be both preventive at an endemic level and can increase rapidly when an outbreak occurs. The fungi *Metarhizium*, *Beauvaria* and *Hirsutella* have been used for this purpose.

There are technical constraints affecting the use of these methods on the scale of a single farm. If a very mobile pest can be killed only after the damage is done, it will not protect this year's crop. And if the outbreak next year comes from a wider area than a single farm, post-damage control will not help that farm very much. Further, populations of parasitoids, birds and bats (excellent predators) usually depend on larger areas than a single farm.

Some kind of coordination on a larger scale is necessary. But this is often quite difficult to achieve. The Hessian fly is a major pest of wheat in North America. One remedy is the growing of resistant varieties which yield satisfactorily during an outbreak but which are inferior to the susceptible wheats when the flies are absent. During the rising phase and peak of an outbreak it is to the advantage of all farmers to switch to resistant varieties. Their joint efforts cause a decline in the Hessian fly population over a whole region. But once the outbreak is receding it is to the advantage of each farmer to return to susceptible varieties before the neighbors do so as to derive the benefits both of the higher yielding variety and the protection their neighbors' resistant variety provides for all of them.

Regional Agroecology

When we shift focus from the single farm to the region, new degrees of freedom become available but also new requirements for an effective system.

The availability of water, pretty much a given for an individual farm, can be managed regionally. Now the exploitation of the aquifers, the land use around rivers and the preservation of forests become objects of decision making.

The prices and costs which are givens for on-farm decisions are affected by what all the farmers do. Here the inequality among farms plays a role. If the prices received, the costs of marketing or of inputs, and the constraints on inputs vary from farm to farm, not only is there inequality of living conditions but also an increased total accumulation of profit despite reduced total production. Therefore the farmers and planners interested in total production would favor those measures which reduce the variation such as rural roads, market integration and eased access to credit. And the goals of production and equity are compatible. But merchants who can benefit from the variation or investors interested in the total rate of accumulation would find these measures deleterious and oppose them.

On the other hand variation in natural conditions and in the responsiveness of the crops to inputs has the effect of increasing both total profit accumulation and production while increasing inequality. Therefore technical innovations which benefit mostly the better off farms will have a greater impact on production than measures which improve the yields of the poorer farms. This means that planners with interest in increasing total production will have common interests with the better off farms even if they have no direct personal ties to the wealthier landowners. They will tend to sympathize with strategies of 'building on the best' and to accept growing inequality as a 'cost of progress'. This makes research strategy a political issue imbedded in class conflicts of other kinds.

Regional land use policy will affect the food supply, equity, employment, resource use and population movement. Therefore planning on the regional level might proceed as follows:

[1] Classify land areas by potential uses as determined by topography, soil, access to water and climate. For instance the steepest slopes may be unsuitable for any direct production and conserved under natural vegetation for environmental protection, gentle slopes may be available for natural or managed forests or tree crops, and so on.

[2] List potential crops including forest, orchard and field crops and grazing. 'Potential' here refers to immediate potential and therefore to foods which are part of the diet or export market.

[3] For each crop, give its use value as food, industrial raw material, contribution to water management, soil improvement, effect on local climate, conservation and effects on other crops, and additional

values such as recreational. For each use we can combine the contributions of different crops.

[4] List the economic value of each land use as providing foreign
exchange, farm income and jobs and having requirements of water,
labor, organic matter and so on. For instance the pasturing of beef
cattle has a very low demand for labor, provides an export product,
ruins soil and makes manure available for vegetable crops.

So far these are technical evaluations. Of course they can be refined
further to take into account the impact per year and long-term trends.
The next stage is more a political matter. The existing information has
to be combined in order to contribute toward policy. For instance, it
may be decided that all the food requirements of the region be met
locally, that in order to discourage migration to the cities there must
be an average of at least one full-time job equivalent per hectare, that
average water needs cannot exceed one cubic meter per year, that a
given amount of firewood be harvestable within 15 minutes walk of
each household, that half the land area be wooded, that manure
production suffice for 1000 ha of vegetables and that pesticide use be
kept below some tolerable threshold. The formulation of such goals
is both a political and a technical process requiring both scientific
expertise and broad democratic participation both to set reasonable
goals and to make their implementation likely.

But this is still too abstract a formulation of the problem. The
various actors in the agricultural decision process have different
goals, and the planners themselves are part of their society, formed
from particular social groups, empowered by particular classes. We
cannot assume that planners and decision makers will share any of
the goals listed or consider that it is their task to work toward them.

National Level Agriculture

Although national agricultural policy must include the same issues
as we encountered regionally, these are subordinated to several
other macro-scale issues: the land tenure question, the relation
between production for consumption and export, land use,
urban–rural balance and so on.

The first question is, who owns the land, who works the land, and
how are they remunerated for their labor.

Some caution is required here. The notion of ownership is itself bound to particular societies and has many different meanings. Ownership really arose under capitalism. It includes the rights of use and abuse, sale or rent, and complete diversion from agriculture. Sometimes these rights are restricted by zoning laws, or some rights such as 'development rights' might be sold separately from the agricultural rights.

At present there are several forms of land holding in agriculture: the owned or leased family farm of Europe and North America is a modern capitalist enterprise producing for the market and making use of purchased inputs. It has a high ratio of capital to labor and adds only a small although essential part of the value in food production. Economic decisions are based mostly on profit maximization.

The trend, especially in the United States, has been toward the decline in the number of family farms and an increase in their size. Family farms are faced with the double uncertainties of nature and the market, and have a precarious existence which discourages risk and subordinates long-term planning to short-term solvency. Since the objective of farming is to support the family, it is advantageous to keep working through as long a season as possible and on all the land. Therefore even crops which yield a lower profit may still be cultivated when other crops cannot be grown, or on land that won't support the principal crop. This encourages a certain amount of diversity. The major advantages of the family farm are the direct personal motivation of the farmers which encourages intense and disciplined labor, and the detailed intimate knowledge of the land and of individual animals, which allows for locally directed technical choices.

But even farms of several hundred hectares are usually too small to determine their own pest populations and water relations, which must be treated as givens.

The large corporate farm in the US is usually only one of a number of investments by its owners. It is often held only for a short time, used for tax purposes and then sold. Agricultural production does not allow for a more rapid turnover of capital than the reproductive cycle of plants or animals permits, and is beset with the dual uncertainties of nature and market. Therefore it is not the investment of choice. Large corporations have tended to control the manufacture and sale of the inputs and the processing and marketing of the harvests while leaving to the farmer the risks and constraints of production in the field. However, in some areas such as California corporate agriculture has been profitable for fruit and vegetable growing.

The economic rationality of the corporation is somewhat different from that of the family farm. The objective is the maximization of total profit from all investments taken together, not from each enterprise separately. Therefore if a farm yields a maximum profit which is below the average rate of return of the other enterprises of the corporation it is regarded as unprofitable. Since labor can be hired and fired, there is no need to produce when profits would be low. Further, since the corporation is not committed to any particular farm or even to farming as a whole, it can decide to use up the productivity of the land as quickly as possible and invest the earnings elsewhere. If the rate of reproduction of productivity (soil formation and leaching of salt) is slower than the discount rate of the economy then this kind of exploitation becomes 'rational'.

In Third World countries much of the agricultural land is in peasant households, large estates and corporate plantations. Peasants are farmers living at the periphery of modern capitalist societies and producing both for subsistence and for exchange with the surrounding markets. They may have title to their land or be tenants paying rent in money or kind, and may also engage in wage labor and craft production. The majority of the rural poor are landless and work for wages, sometimes in the form of housing and small plots as well as money. Peasant farming becomes increasingly incorporated into the wider economy so that, quoting Marx (*The Eighteenth Brumaire*), 'the small holding of the peasant is now only the pretext that allows the capitalist to draw profits, interest and rent from the soil while leaving it to the tiller of the soil himself to see how he can extract his wages.'

The degree of land concentration varies widely, and struggles over the land are a major factor in the political and social processes of these countries. Revolutionary movements in China, Vietnam, Kenya, the Philippines, Guatemala, and El Salvador have been motivated in part by a struggle for land reform. In El Salvador some 90 per cent of the rural population are landless. Indigenous communities in the Andean and Amazonian regions of Peru, Bolivia and Ecuador have seen their own survival as dependent on retaining or recovering control of their land.

Collective agriculture occurs in a number of different forms: the Soviet and East European collective farms, the Israeli kibbutz, the Saskatchewan group farm, Cuban cooperatives, the Chinese commune. They differ in inputs consumed, internal organization, relation to the surrounding economy, and the extent to which participation is voluntary or coerced. This seems to be a major factor in determining the success or failure of the enterprise. Where collectivization was imposed coercively, production is often reduced by low motivation and resentment toward the administration experienced as coming from the outside. Even in voluntary collectives uneven motivation is often a problem. Where the collectivity is imbedded within a capitalist economy, as in the various experimental communes in the US founded for religious or political reasons, the Mexican ejido or the Israeli kibbutz, the pressures of the market act as coercions on the long-term development and lure the younger members of the collectivity away from farming. Some collectives such as many kibbutzim have resorted to hiring labor from off the farm, the farm then functioning as a collective employer.

The Chinese commune system was one of the largest, most integrated collective systems. The commune included many villages and often thousands of people, and assumed state functions below the provincial level in rural China. It organized diversified agricultural production, industrial enterprises processing the harvest and manufacure of inputs and tools, and engaged in watershed management, irrigation projects and reforestation. The results were mixed, and the system was abolished after the death of Mao Zedong. Subsequent criticism of the communes have to be seen not as the self-critical admissions of error but as accusations by the winners of a political struggle against the losers, so that a full evaluation of the experience is not yet available.

Perhaps the best assessment comes from William Hinton. He claims that about one third of the communes were highly successful, a third were disasterous and the rest survived. The crucial difference between success and failure seems to be the extent to which democratic organization had real content or was perverted into an authoritarian hierarchy allocating resources and privileges in an atmosphere of corruption. At any rate, in the post-commune system of privatized farming, collective assets passing into private hands has produced some prosperity, while large-scale ecological projects have fallen into decay, class differentiation is reappearing, and a get rich quick mentality has shifted decision making away from sustainable models.

State farms are a common form of landholding in revolutionary societies. The state farm has the advantages of economies of scale, an on-farm scientific staff and better access to equipment and supplies. Its major failings have been a developmentalist, industrial model leading to high chemical and mechanical input, low-diversity, short-term economic urgency, and a management system which undercuts motivation and prevents adaptation of production to very local circumstances.

In Cuba, some 80 per cent of the farm land is in state farms. A comparison of Cuban agricultural performance with that of neighboring countries is inconclusive. Yields are higher than in the other countries in some crops, lower in others. Rural health, educational and cultural resources are generally better than those of the other countries. This has helped Cuba slow down the rural–urban migration and prevented Havana from becoming a smaller scale Mexico City. Ecological rationality is spreading, with a policy of replacing pesticides with biological and natural control, and reforestation exceeds cutting in contrast with the regional trend.

Whatever the pattern of land tenure, the governments attempt to determine what happens on the land. This is done by positive planning, by price manipulation, subsidies and services, with different degrees of motivation and success.

The first priority has to be meeting peoples' consumption needs. This can be done both by national production and by exports exchanged for products that can be produced better elsewhere. Governments have wrestled with the balance between export and consumption agriculture. Exports can be exchanged not only for food imports but also for industrial inputs that are so important in development. Especially for tropical countries, it is possible to produce crops that the industrial temperate zones cannot produce, and therefore have almost guaranteed markets. However there is an element of uncertainty here: industrial countries look for substitutes for their imports, such as corn syrup to replace cane sugar, or synthetic fibers to replace cotton. A second problem with agricultural exports is the increasingly unfavorable terms of exchange for Third World agricultural products compared to industrial goods. A third issue is the vulnerability of the economy to international price fluctuations or discriminatory trade policies.

In terms of ecology, export production requires large volume, and this encourages specialized enterprises with monocultures and all the attendant dangers. Competition on the international market often imposes standards of appearance of products which lead to excessive use of pesticides. Yet export is necessary both to help finance the economy as a whole and in order to exchange for foods that cannot be produced locally. For instance, it does not make sense to grow wheat in the tropics. Yet bread has become an important part of the diets of the peoples of almost all countries, especially in the growing urban sector. Therefore wheat flour has to be imported, and this requires the export of tropical products.

It would seem that a mixed strategy is required which combines production for export and for home consumption.

Meeting the consumption needs of the people means satisfying first the existing diet and dietary aspirations. For instance, in most poor countries where meat was rarely seen, the consumption of meat is a basic consumer aspiration. This has led to the priority expansion of poultry and cattle production in Cuba. However, there are both ecological and health reasons to consider dietary changes. Meat production is one of the least efficient ways to turn solar energy into food. One kilo of beef requires 100 times more water for its production than 1 kilo of wheat, and consumes 16 kilos of feed grain. And Cubans already consume 79 grams of protein daily per capita, perhaps double the recommended requirements from a nutritional point of view. Already cardiovascular diseases are a leading cause of death in that country, and increasing meat consumption must be a contributing cause.

Grazing is also destructive to the land, mainly through compaction. In the US, western rangelands have lost about one third of their carrying capacity for cattle as a result of prolonged grazing. Large-scale meat production unlinked to field crops is also a major nitrogen polluter of water supplies.

Therefore a long-term land use program should consider promoting changes in diet while satisfying present demand, but changing the eating habits of a population is not easy. Eating is a social activity as much as a nutritional one.

Within each region, land use provides employment as well as harvestable goods. Since different land uses have different demands for labor, the mix of activities must be in equilibrium with available and anticipated labor. Rangeland and conservation areas have the lowest demand for labor, basic grain crops are intermediate, and vegetable crops the highest. Additional requirements enter from ecology. For example, it may be that for every 1000 ha of field crops we need 5 ha of forest for pest control purposes, or 10 ha of forest to provide the firewood to cook the food, or 100 ha to modulate the water supply.

Agriculture does not affect only agriculture. Any large-scale land use pattern also affects health and climate. The effect of farming on health enters through the use of chemicals, the role of soil in determining the nutritional qualities of food and as a detoxifier of the atmosphere and the effects of water management on mosquitoes and other vectors of disease. The climatic effects come about through the altered albedo of vegetation of different types, the impact of irrigation on albedo, wind erosion putting dust into the air and reducing the transparency of the atmosphere, the effect of moisture on the variability of temperature.

As we become more sophisticated in understanding the necessary relations among parts of a system, we find more requirements on that system and more different degrees of freedom to achieve them. Thus there is no final perfect scheme for agriculture but a strategy for designing the system which is open-ended.

6

Social History of Nature

It is worth bearing in mind, when the relations are discussed of biology to the social sciences, that an essential social science is likely to prove history.   Bernard Williams[1]

That *nature* has a *social history* is of course beyond doubt. Whether *societies* have *natural histories* can be disputed. Natural conditions certainly set boundaries for social development – there are no agricultural societies in the Arctic – but this is far from showing that nature would in a stronger sense determine social development. Anthropologists such as Mary Douglas, Julian Steward and Eric Wolf, and historians such as Fernand Braudel, Perry Anderson and Immanuel Wallerstein have assessed the role of ecological and geographical conditions in history.

In this chapter we introduce conceptual tools for investigating the role of society in changing nature, and the role of nature in molding social development. The concepts we use are *ecohistorical period* and *ecohistorical formation*, respectively.

Somebody may question the relevance of historical inquiries on the grounds of the immediate urgency of the ecological crisis. Why does history matter? In addition to our own personal disposition we can give three reasons.

First, the question 'How does humanity change nature?' requires an empirical answer. We already noticed that human-induced change in nature is intermingled with changes of non-human origin. It is difficult to distinguish between these two types of change. But this means that the boundaries set to humanity by nature are not immediately visible. We want to know what nature allows and what she forbids, but can never know for sure. Although the present ecological crisis is qualitatively different from those in the past, understanding of the crises of the past helps us today.

Second, we have also noticed that the 'carrying capacity' of nature relative to human populations is not a constant but a historical variable. 'Carrying capacity' changes in two ways. The resources that are used change as a result of use or for extraneous reasons, and human needs also change.

Third, 'changing nature' is not carried out by human individuals but by social formations. This follows from the fact, recognized already by the Greeks, that division of labor is a basic feature of human societies. Human beings are no Crusoes scratching along independently of others but depend entirely on social networks. Natural resources are acquired and transformed into social wealth in social praxis.

It is useful to distinguish between the inadvertent changes that result from human activity, and intentional change. The former resemble the impacts of other species on the environment in being essentially random with respect to their benefit or harm. They are, of course different in detail, in magnitude, in diversity, and in the profundity with which they penetrate the biosphere. The change is intentional when rivers are diverted, land dug or filled, forests planted or cleared, species slaughtered or propagated according to some plan which is formed on the basis of past experience for specific purposes. This is a new kind of impact, an interaction between the natural system and a whole social context of various congruent and conflicting interests and accumulated knowledge. The outcome may or may not correspond to the intention. Typically, the immediate intended results are at least partly achieved (that is, the trees do fall to the axe, water does fill the artificial lake) but other, more far-reaching and long-term effects, do not correspond to anyone's intention and are faced as surprises.

A further complication is the fact emphasized by cultural historians such as A.O. Lovejoy and Raymond Williams that the very concept of 'nature' is culture-laden. What has been regarded as 'nature' has varied enormously through history and across societies. How do *we* know what is 'real' nature?

How Does Nature Change?

The motion of objects is extremely complex, subject to large numbers of influences   Isadore Nabi[2]

What is permanent and ubiquitous in nature is change. However, there is no ecological change 'in general' but a broad array of specific albeit complex processes. At every level of analysis there is an inside and an outside, internal dynamics and external inputs that enter across the boundaries of the object of study. If the object is very small, there is relatively more boundary; what happens is more determined by external events. Some of these external impacts are essential for the survival of the system such as flows of energy and matter. If they are more or less constant we look on them as parameters of the system. If they are inconstant but frequent, they are seen as 'disturbances' or 'perturbations', and if rare but drastic, they are 'catastrophes'.

But we have already argued that the distinction between the internal and the external, between 'organism' (or system) and 'environment' is not absolute. In various ways the external may even become necessary, for instance, fire or flood for seed germination. The external in a sense becomes internalized.

Some types of disturbance such as falling down of old trees in a forest, creating space for regeneration, are due to processes internal to the ecological complex. This is not always the case, however. Characteristic of ecological change is that the causes, external influences, are usually triggered by chance factors relative to the units that are responding. Life itself is a process that produces and reproduces regular patterns from a background of unstructured flow of energy. The non-linear thermodynamics of dissipative structures gives a fruitful general framework for understanding the origin and evolution of life; the ideas are technically difficult but conceptually relatively simple, but their presentation is beyond the scope of this book (see Prigogine and Stenghers, 1984; Dyke, 1988; Weber et al., 1988).

By an *ecological complex* we mean any ecological entity that is separated from the surroundings by differences in the rate and intensity of processes inside versus processes outside. An individual is obviously an entity – individuals are kept together and distinct from the surroundings by the high rate and specificity of biochemical processes in cells and tissues. In death, as enzyme systems break down, the basic biochemical processes that characterized the organism submerge into the sea of background processes, and the organism loses its dynamic identity even before anatomical integrity has been drastically breached. A forest pond is an entity – the chemical and ecological processes and interactions in the water differ greatly from those in the surrounding forest.

But all entities are relative, that is, their boundaries are permeable and they receive energy from outside sources. That is one reason why recognizing ecological complexes is a problem in its own right. The human phenomenological perspective is biased – to us it appears natural to acknowledge multicellular organisms of similar size with ourselves as 'entities' whereas larger complexes such as ecosystems or smaller complexes such as individual bacteria avoid recognition.

Ecological complexes can be viewed as hierarchies comprising levels of organization; this view is introduced by Allen and Starr (1982), and O'Neill et al. (1986). It is entirely a matter of convention where 'ecology' is located in the hierarchy of life and depends on whether an ecological perspective is fruitful for investigating a given entity. What is important for our present discussion is that each level of organization is held distinct by processes that have specific space and time scales. Actually, as we have seen, the processes making up the complexes constitute the characteristic space and time scales (Chapter 2). Molecules within a cell are reproduced faster than the cell. Cells are reproduced faster than the whole organism. Organisms are reproduced faster than the population in which individual organisms belong. Numerous local populations are established and go extinct during the life span of a species. Species come and go in ecological communities which maintain their structural features for longer periods of time.

For evaluating the significance of a particular type of external disturbance for a particular type of ecological complex it is important to compare the characteristic space–time scales of the disturbance and the complex. Consider, for instance, the following disturbances:

- particles emitted by radioactive decay;
- localized concentrations of organic substance dissolved from dead soil bacteria;
- vole burrows;
- tree-fall gaps;
- water erosions along river shores;
- forest fires;
- extreme weather conditions such as exceptionally hot and dry summers;
- secular changes in climate over decades or centuries;

- glaciation cycles;
- changing configurations of the continents due to continental drift.

Some disturbances are highly localized and practically instanta-neous (radioactive radiation), whereas some cover vast expanses and long periods of time (glaciations, continental drift). Each of these disturbance types has a decisive influence on some ecological complexes, but not on the same ones. This is a matter of space–time scales.

However, it is not only the duration and the spatial extension of single disturbance events that are of consequence but also how often they occur, their average frequency. Elementary particles emitted by radioactive decay cause changes in the structure of biological macro-molecules, both in hereditary and in structural compounds in the cells. However, a single change caused by a single particle is extremely unlikely to have any effect on an organism, while intensive, high-frequency radiation certainly does. Every forest fire causes a dramatic change in the locality which is burned down, but ecological effects of forest fires depend on how frequently they occur, and how large an area on average is burned by one fire.

The relationship between external disturbances and ecological complexes that are 'disturbed' can be evaluated by the following guideline: such situations manifest relevant ecological change in which the characteristic space–time scale of the disturbance and the ecological complex approximately correspond to each other. For instance, a single radiation particle is totally irrelevant for a population, but it may destroy vital biochemical substances in the cells of an individual member of the population. A vole individual digging her burrows in a meadow does not affect plant populations, but individual plants are uprooted. On the other hand, fluctuations in con-tinental ice affect tree populations, but are irrelevant for metabolic processes in individual trees. Continental drift shapes species richness and composition of whole continents, but has no effect on popula-tions which turn over much faster.

Ecological units have a characteristic ability to maintain structure not only despite but also because of external perturbations. The integrity of the systems depends not only on their isolation from their surroundings but on their special way of integrating with the sur-roundings. This is called self-regulation in the case of individual organisms (Chapter 4), and resistance or resilience in the case of larger ecological complexes (Chapter 2). Individual organisms have a whole range of mechanisms available for self-regulation, depending on the character of the disturbance, as we discussed in Chapter 4. Ecological complexes on higher levels of organization also respond differently to different types of disturbances. These alternatives are summarized in Figure 6.1.

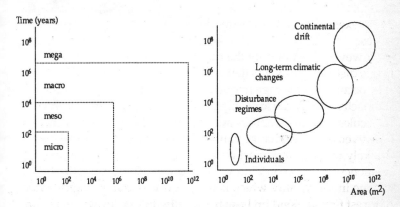

Figure 6.1
Scaling the space–time dimensions of ecological change. Values on the x-axes range from 1 m^2 to 10 000 km^2, and on the y-axes from 1 to 1 billion years. Different types of disturbances occur in different parts of the space.
Source: Adapted from Wiens (1981), Delcourt et al. (1983) and Birks (1986)

Disturbance types distinguished in Figure 6.1 can be loosely separated into *micro-*, *meso-*, *macro-* and *mega-scale*. 'Mega-scale' refers to processes covering whole continents and demanding tens of millions of years. The convergent evolution of the Australian marsupial fauna and placental mammals of the other continents is a phenomenon on this scale. 'Macro-scale' can be equated with processes covering parts of continents and demanding hundreds of thousands of years such as glacial cycles. This is, by and large, the spatial and temporal perspective determining the species pool from which extant ecological communities are assembled. 'Meso-scale' refers to years or decades that correspond to demographic and microevolutionary changes within populations. 'Micro-scale' is constituted by processes characteristic of individual organisms and relates to physiological time.

Disturbance Regimes

An important class of environmental perturbations can be called 'disturbance regimes'. This refers to local-scale events which occur with a characteristic frequency in a certain landscape type, for instance, wildfires in northern boreal forests or Australian eucalyptus bushlands, or hurricanes in tropical forests. What is apparently 'stable' in such a landscape is the regional average. The disturbances are often, but not always, triggered by factors external to the landscape – the occurrence of hurricanes is certainly unaffected by events within a particular area of rainforest, whereas the probability of a forest fire is a function of the time elapsed since the previous one.

Other examples of landscapes created and maintained by frequent disturbance include the marine intertidal continuously perturbed by irregular wave action; wetlands subject to variable levels of flooding; rivers changing their course due to erosion of the banks (called 'meandering' – this process is astonishingly rapid in some landscapes, for instance 300 m per year in the Peruvian lowlands beneath the Andes (Salo et al., 1986)); deserts and arid grasslands getting variable amounts of rainfall which continuously modifies local vegetation patches, additionally disturbed by grazing herbivores.

It is natural to locate regular disturbance regimes in the 'meso-scale' of Figure 6.1 because they have an immediate and readily observable effect on ecological complexes. They initiate successional cycles in local communities in the disturbed patches, but the patches representing any given successional stage in the patchwork are not identical with each other. Small-scale variation in the landscape is enhanced by differences in site quality, and by the stochastic nature of perturbations and colonizations. Species diversity of frequently disturbed landscapes is often high; in general, the smaller the area of individual perturbations and the larger the element of stochasticity in the composition of the community that is established, the larger the total species richness in the whole landscape (Connell, 1978).

This gives a general norm for planning human intervention in the landscape: human modifications should be comparable to those disturbance regimes under which ecosystems exploited by humans took shape in order that ecological diversity and productivity be preserved.

Natural Catastrophes

The notion of disturbance refers to recurring events that have a characteristic frequency. In addition, there are also natural events that can properly be called catastrophes, for instance, the 'mass extinctions' revealed by the paleontological record. These are fairly short periods during which a disproportionate number of species suffered extinction. Methodological problems make distinguishing mass extinctions from the normal background extinction level complicated, but five such events are beyond reasonable dispute and another 20 periods with increased extinction rates have been suggested (Nitecki, 1984; Raup and Jablonski, 1986).

The most recent one of the five major extinction waves occurred some 70 million years ago, at the transition between Cretaceous and Tertiary epochs in the earth's history. Some 50 per cent of all animal genera in both marine and terrestrial environments went extinct during some hundreds of thousands of years, which is a very short time compared with the 600 million years that multicellular organisms have lived on the earth. The mass extinction exterminated dinosaurs, and this probably facilitated the diversification of mammals. There is some geophysical evidence that the mass extinction may have been provoked by the collision of a large meteorite with the earth.

With the help of Figure 6.1 we can give a more general characterization of natural catastrophes. They are (unique) events which have spatial and temporal dimensions dramatically exceeding the resistance and resilience of the ecological complexes affected. Catastrophes are disturbances, but of a peculiar sort – they have effects way beyond the disturbance regimes ecological complexes have been shaped by. This implies that the definition of a 'catastrophe' depends on the ecological complex considered. Mass extinctions were catastrophes on evolutionary and biogeographic level, but lower level units are subject to catastrophes as well. Ordinary wildfires are catastrophes for individual trees, and an exceptionally fierce fire burning down a whole continent would be a catastrophe for the whole forest biota.

Human-induced catastrophes may be similar to previous ones in severity, but unique in the particulars and pace. After all, the cretaceo–tertiary extinctions took hundreds of thousands of years, while present changes are on the scale of decades to centuries. Exceptional catastrophes in the past imply that there is little that humans can do that would not already have happened in geological history. But this is a bleak consolation. The recovery of the biosphere took tens of millions of years after each major catastrophe. That is not the time scale in which human populations lead their lives.

Ecohistorical periods

Civilization is the grandfather, the patriarch of world history.
                                                    Fernand Braudel[3]

It is against the background of natural change that human impacts must be projected, and from this comparison criteria must be sought for identifying human-induced changes in ecological complexes and for assessing whether the changes matter. Humans change their environment by all their activities. In assessing the significance of such changes it helps to identify the characteristic spatial and temporal scale of the human-induced disturbance and of the ecological complex supposed to be affected. Purely local disturbances, however drastic, are irrelevant on large spatial scales. On the other hand, locally minor modifications that extend uniformly over vast regions may have unexpected consequences.

Thus, changes in nature significant in a historical perspective are brought about by human activities exerted systematically over vast regions and long periods of time. This brings social formations into the picture. No individual human has ever had continent-wide, let alone century-long influence on the environment. In analysing the historical dynamics of human modification of nature one is facing a two-sided challenge: one should recognize such modifications that have been significant, and identify the social structures that caused them. It is often imagined that human-induced changes in nature can be attributed to a single factor such as population growth or technological development, and the whole process pictured as linear deterioration, but this is patently false. Historical variation both through time and across societies is huge and must be taken seriously.

With the concept of *ecohistorical period* we refer to such periods in history in which human activities have led to (relatively) uniform changes in nature over vast areas. The concept is borrowed from the Soviet ecologist S.V. Kirikov (1983) who analysed historical changes in southeast European steppes. His analysis was, however, closely tied to political and administrative changes. This seems too narrow a perspective. Alterations in ways of exploiting nature relate to structures that change more slowly than political conjunctures.

We discuss some important historical transitions in this section. Our scope is necessarily very broad, but the notion of ecohistorical period is also sensitive to historical detail and allows refined historical analyses of society–nature relationships in particular regions. For instance, the Finnish economic historian Sven-Erik Åström (1978) analysed the role of nature in the economic history of Finland and distinguished four major periods in which the dynamics of the society–nature interaction clearly varied.

The French historian Fernand Braudel has emphasized the need to distinguish between different layers of time in human history. Braudel's slowest time scale is *geographical time*, which refers to how natural conditions and social history mingle. Geography sets the stage for humans who modify the stage in turn, and the slow motion of history goes on. Geographical time is the time scale of civilizations, which have developed partly independently of each other in different parts of the world. The shorter time scales distinguished by Braudel are 'social time' and 'individual time', the former referring to conjuncture, the latter to events shaping the lives of individual humans.

Another point emphasized by Braudel is that no society develops as a uniform whole. On the contrary, the pace of different spheres of social life – economy, class relations, administrative structures, culture, technology, material ways of life – causes differentiation, the more so, the finer the scale in which comparisons are made across societies. This means that the social dynamics of nature modification varies as well, depending on which spheres dominate a particular society. Generalizations about transitions in the society–nature relationship are necessarily abstractions, but they are useful abstractions as in other contexts.

Behind ecohistory there is, naturally, biological evolution. What makes humans different from their closest relatives is not single critical characteristics – one cannot name a single characteristic that is not shared with some other species – but a new combination of those characteristics. This is associated with a new type of sociality not found among other animal species. Social cohesion of early human groups, based on their subsistence and on the intelligence and behavioral flexibility of the group members necessary for coping with long-lasting, complicated social relations, evolved as a complex. The whole process was facilitated by a new type of collective memory, human language.

By being integrated within, human societies grew open toward the world, that is, a secondary generalization began concerning relations to the environment. A break occurred from natural history to history in human evolution, but from an ecological point of view this break presents a formidable paradox: it is a break off from ecology based on ecology. Characteristics acquired by natural selection made it possible for humans to establish a new, social mode of existence in which human individuals are not immediately subjected to the environment, but the relationships are mediated through social groups, kept together by behavioral skills on which culture is based. With these permanent groups a new type of history started, and assessing the degree of liberation from ecological conditions reached by human societies in different historical periods is a basic task in analysing eco-historical periods.

Human influence in the ecological systems of the earth is irreversible and has roots extending to ancient times
Our biological species *Homo sapiens* is something like 100 000 years old – that is, a child of the latest glaciation. Our species originated in sub-Saharan Africa. The growth rate of the early human population was apparently very low, well below 0.001 per cent before the origin of agriculture some 10 000 years ago; the global population at that time was approximately 8–9 million persons. The growth rate is far below the biological potential of our species, and it is obvious that social mechanisms of regulating population growth have been universally in use in human communities (Hassan, 1979).

The geographic range extension of *Homo sapiens* is better documented. Anatomically modern humans had colonized most parts of the Eurasian continent by some 20 000 years ago and displaced their predecessors, the Neanderthalers, which are biologically considered a subspecies of *Homo sapiens*. They crossed the Bering Strait along a land-bridge that connected Old and New Worlds during the latest glaciation, swept through both American continents in 2000–3000 years, and arrived at the southern tip of South America by about 10 000 years ago. The Malayan archipelago and Australia were colonized earlier, and humans arrived at major Pacific island groups, including Hawaii, by 1500 years ago. Some relatively large but isolated islands such as New Zealand and Madagascar were reached quite recently, about a millenium ago.

The dating of human settlements both in the Americas and in Australasia has been revised often in the direction of greater antiquity. It now seems that the spread of our species throughout the world's continents was very rapid compared to the time required for our evolution. Even at the extremely slow spread of 1–2 kilometers per year, we would have reached all accessible areas almost instantaneously on the geological time scale.

Early humans are usually described as hunter–gatherers. The distinction between hunting and gathering is not sharp, since 'gathering' includes the capturing of small animals and insects as well as plant resources. Perhaps the distinction corresponds to a presumed sexual division of labor that endows 'hunting' with the aura of masculine high adventure and hand to hand combat with dangerous beasts. Although the relative weights of 'gathered' and 'hunted' food can vary greatly across regions and seasons, in the anthropological usage hunting is placed first.

There is some evidence that the early hunting cultures had a strong impact on their main prey, big herbivorous mammals. This evidence comes from the sudden extinction of a major part of large animals, particularly mammals, on all continents for about 20 000 to 10 000 years ago. Remarkably, the extinctions of big animals coincided locally with the arrival of human populations. On the other hand, very few species of small animals or plants suffered extinction. This pattern supports the hypothesis that the early hunters contributed substantially to the big game extinctions (Martin and Klein, 1984). Human impact is beyond doubt affecting the most recent extinction waves, namely, the disappearance of moas (large birds unable to fly) from the fauna of New Zealand (Brewster, 1987), extinctions of birds in the Hawaiian Islands (Olson and James, 1982), and the disappearance of giant lemurs (primitive primates) and elephant birds from the fauna of Madagascar. The use of fire by primitive hunters was an equally drastic influence of early humans on ecosystems; at least some of the savannas are of human origin (see Thomas et al., 1956).

The big game extinctions brought an irreversible change in the world fauna, and indirect effects have certainly been large as well – the most immediate among them were extinctions of predators preying upon the big herbivores, and of plants that used the big grazers as dispersal vectors. Thus, the prehistoric extinction wave started the era of social history of nature.

Preagricultural cultures are strongly influenced by local ecological conditions but they modify the environment in turn, and the variable ways of life of these peoples show a spectrum of local ecohistories

The influence of ecological conditions on preagricultural cultures is indisputable. This is easily said, but what are the precise ways and mechanisms of this influence? Basic alternatives would be nature as a constraint, or nature as a constitutive factor. As a constraint nature sets limits within which the way of life of a local people has to take shape. A stronger assumption is to regard nature as a constitutive factor and interpret all cultural features as functional adaptations to the external environment. This is the claim of strong environmentalism.

Strong environmentalism has had its proponents among anthropologists of our century. However, the basic problem with environmentalism is the very definition of *the environment*. The 'environment' of a society is not a constant, but a historically changing complex of variables. Similar environmental conditions have 'constituted' vastly different social formations in different phases in history. The relation of local cultures to the environment is no one-way adjustment, but a two-way interpenetration. The new type of 'memory' facilitated by social cohesion, communication and language is the basis for widening the margins of social adaptation to the environment.

Strong environmentalism faces yet another problem. The adaptation of a human society to the environment is realized through material reproduction. Reproduction is, however, by its very nature connected with values. What is picked up from nature is first evaluated, designated, represented. The elements of nature get reified, and their meaning for society cannot be deduced from their natural characteristics (Ellen, 1982). This factor became fortified when exchange started among societies which increasingly had material ties not only to the immediate surroundings but, via other cultures, to a far wider region.

It is often claimed by contemporary defenders of the environment that indigenous peoples protect their resources with elaborate sets of rules restricting the hunt to particular times, places or animal types. This is undoubtedly partly true. But these practices depend on knowledge of nature which was not always available to them.

First, peoples migrate and are not always living in the same place for millenia. Most peoples have legends of coming from somewhere else. In some cases historical, archeological or climatological evidence supports these claims, for instance, people have inhabited the high

Arctic for only some 4000 years and the tropical rain forest for perhaps 3000. When peoples move and climates change new knowledge has to be acquired.

All peoples are curious and innovate on the basis of experience, and some of it takes a long time. Hunters who hunt local populations of beaver or rabbit can see a direct connection between what they do and what happens later – how present hunting affects future animal populations. But the hunters of the large migratory herds have a different experience: their own hunting efforts are only a small part of what determines the numbers of bison or mamoths that come by next time. Some years are better than others, for no reason apparent to observers at any one location. Thus the possibility of over-exploitation of a resource is perfectly compatible with our notion of peoples living close to nature, observing, and acting accordingly.

Because of these problems ecology is not an appropriate starting point for anthropological theory although some features of the mode of subsistence of local cultures such as settlement patterns, size of local groups and group cohesion, depending on how the environment is exploited in different seasons, are greatly influenced by ecological conditions. Ecology can help in evaluating constraints, and thus also the ways in which technological innovation has helped to overcome those constraints.

Another problem is that local cultures cannot be dismembered into single cultural traits, still less into human individuals with their character traits. Culture is a *context* within which individuals lead their lives – the more binding the more complex the means of subsistence have become. The means of subsistence of local cultures are flexible and amenable to change. Primitive cultures have histories, and each one of them constitutes an ecohistory of its own; on small islands in the Pacific variation among local ecohistories is overwhelming (Kirch, 1984). However, such human influences on the environment that would cover uniformly large areas and long periods of time are lacking in this stage.

Agriculture and urbanization, and the ensuing growth of human populations, mark the onset of ecohistorical periods on a new, large scale
The transition of prehistoric cultures to agriculture is a series of events of tremendous importance for the social history of nature. Since at least the late Pleistocene times (35 000–12 000 BC) people have used plants for food, fuel, medicines, fiber, shelter and tools. The transition

from collecting to growing plants may have passed through a number of intermediate stages where plants may have been helped along with watering and weeding before they were actually planted.

But the knowledge of plants was not sufficient for agriculture to arise. For that step it was necessary that people stayed in the same area long enough or returned to it regularly enough to tend the plants. This depended on the abundance of game and of gatherables. It is likely that rather than some dramatic moment when some ancient woman cried 'Eureka, it grows!' and agriculture began, the beginnings of agriculture were uneven and reversible as conditions varied. The commitment to farming was not the result of discovery but of calculation: is it worth hanging around while that thing grows? Sometime in the Neolithic period the growing of plants became common enough to leave archeological residues.

The domestication of plants took place in a number of geographic areas. The earliest records are from the middle east in the broad sense, roughly from Egypt to central Asia. Direct plant remains, impressions of plants in pottery, and the implements and utensils used with agriculture suggest that by 8000 BC people in this region already cultivated grain and had domesticated animals. Unambiguous evidence of agriculture appears in China and India around 2500 BC and in the Americas before 3500 BC A closer examination of the crops suggests multiple centers of domestication of plants although it is still uncertain how many times agriculture arose independently.

Most peoples know a lot more botanical facts than they apply in practice. Gatherers have a rich plant lore even if they do not farm, and data from North America suggest that in the course of their migrations the ancestors of present day Apache shifted back and forth between an emphasis on hunting and cultivation according to the changing conditions along their route. The introduction of the horse to the plains encouraged a number of peoples to shift from a mixed horticulture–gathering–hunting economy to one dominated by the buffalo hunt. There is no directional law that requires peoples to evolve from gathering and hunting to agriculture.

But where agriculture was adopted, the transition was a complex process with a plethora of factors involved. Ellen (1982) suggested that the mechanism of the transition can be viewed as a positive feedback loop with population pressure – often presented as the basic independent variable in the process of agricultural growth – and technological innovation, including 'innovations' within the social sphere such as division of labor and centralized administration, as mutually enforcing factors.

The role of population pressure in social evolution is an important issue that we discuss in the last section of this chapter.

The ancient civilizations developed on the basis of agriculture, permanent settlements and division of labor. From the beginning there were important differences in social structure among the civilizations, for instance between ancient Mesopotamia and Egypt, the latter being much more hierarchical and centralized than the former (Clark and Piggott, 1965). The differences in social and administrative structure were even more pronounced between Old World and New World civilizations. In intercontinental comparisons one comes across striking ecohistorical differences as well, beginning with a different array of domesticated animals and plants. A curious fact is the dramatic imbalance in the number of domesticated animals originating from the two continents. Apart from the guinea-pig, dog (an apparently independent invention on both continents) and fowl (turkey), the guanaco (or llama) is the only important domesticated animal originating from the New World, and its use has, moreover, remained restricted to the area of origin. This may simply be due to ecological contingency – quite naturally, only such animals can be domesticated and such plants cultivated that are around.

Geographic conditions apparently also had a great influence on the development of early civilizations by enhancing or impeding exchange which originated with permanent settlements as an element in the dynamics of cultural systems – a central emphasis in Braudel's *Civilization and Capitalism*. While for a completely self-supporting community growth is restricted by the resource in shortest supply, exchange permits growth to be limited by the surplus of the most abundant. Conquest plays a similar role. Ancient Assyria could acquire more grain than the diminishing productivity of the river valley soils allowed by producing armies and extracting tribute.

Here may be another important difference between the Old and the New World: geography in the source areas of Old World civilizations was far more facilitative of permanent exchange than in the New World (Wolf, 1982).

Development of agriculture led to systematic, extensive growth of human influence on the environment, as we discussed in Chapter 5. This was fortified by the far more efficient social 'memory' than anything known before which originated in the aftermath of urbanization: written language. Writing actually constituted 'language' as a permanent cultural structure (Illich and Sanders, 1989).

Agriculture thus marks the origin of ecohistorical periods on a new scale. Local conditions gradually lose their significance in explaining how human populations get their subsistence, and the transmission of social and technological traditions across cultures gains importance. Basic agricultural technologies were transferred to Europe from Asia, mainly over the Black Sea coast and the lowlands along the Danube river system. Shifting agriculture prevailed early on. Local settlements were quite small; according to estimates of Clark and Piggott (1965), a population of 150 persons required about 1 km^2 of cereal cultivation per year which means, taking into account declining crop returns in later years, some 80 km^2 in the long run.

Nevertheless, early agriculture had a great effect on vegetation as documented in pollen deposits. Clear changes took place in local floras of central and northwestern Europe some 6000–5000 years ago. The Danish botanist Iversen (1941) originally proposed that these changes be attributed to the 'early occupation phase' (or *landnam*, an old Scandinavian word that Iversen used) of agricultural settlements. Detailed analyses of such changes are now available; they were recently summarized in Birks et al. (1989).

The early 'landnam' apparently consisted of a cycle of forest clearance, cultivation and grazing, and abandonment and subsequent forest regeneration. The whole process covered a couple of centuries at any single locality but occurred within a total time span of less than a millenium in most sites favorable for early agriculture in central and northwestern Europe. Such local cycles are attributed to formation and gradual disintegration of non-migrant population units which were able to subsist for a while but fell victim to gradual exhaustion of the soil. The early 'landnam' thus represents a complex ecohistorical period in northwestern Europe.

Ecohistorical periods are related to changes in the mode of production
Agriculture, urbanization, technologial innovation, trade, transport, division of labor accompanied by the swelling of administrative structures and differentiation of class relations within societies, and literacy have an interrelated origin. They mark the origin – or origins – of history. The Neolithic period also triggered – and was triggered by – a rapid growth of human populations, the total world population climbing from about 8–9 million to 50–100 million persons. Growth rates may have reached 0.5–1 per cent in periods of maximum

increase (summarized by Hassan, 1979). The result of the Neolithic transition was a diverse array of complex societies, or 'organized pluralities' as called by Wolf (1982).

Mode of production is a term introduced by Marx for analysing structural characteristics of societies. The term can be used without commitments to fixed theoretical positions, as a general description of basic features of social structure. Such a use of the term is based on the simple assumption that human societies get their means of subsistence from the environment, and the way this is obtained and divided among members of the society will, in turn, influence and shape all aspects of the society.

Mode of production describes basic economic dynamics that shape the relationships between society and nature. It is, however, a notion of far higher historical generality than ecohistorical period – the former sets the stage for the latter. In the following exposition we adopt the scheme of Wolf (1982), who recognized just three basic modes of production, namely, *kin-ordered mode of production*, *tributary mode of production*, and *capitalist mode of production*.

Wolf's kin-ordered mode of production covers the whole array of societies where the division of labor was by gender and age, and formal administrative structures were poorly developed. Kinship in kin-structured societies can be understood as a way of committing social labor to the transformation of nature through appeals of filiation and marriage, and to consanguinity and affinity. '*What* is done unlocks social labor; *how* it is done involves symbolic definitions of kinsmen and affines' (Wolf, 1982: 91). Kinship is a social more than a biological category. In kin-ordered societies strangers become members by establishing a formal kinship relation, by adoption, or by inventing a common ancestor. There can also be far-reaching networks of exchange among unrelated kinship groups. Kin-ordered societies are characterized by a fairly direct interaction with local natural conditions, as we have already discussed. This restriction of scale is clearly an inherent property of the kin-ordered system itself – the ties of kinship set a limit to the complexity the society can reach.

The characteristic feature of the tributary mode of production is, according to Wolf, extraction of surplus wealth from primary producers in the form of tribute by political or military coercion. Social labor is mobilized primarily through the exercise of power and domination. The most elementary form of coerced exploitation is direct plunder, which avoids all problems of administration. Sporadic plunder is not limited to the extraction of a surplus since the plunderers have no stake in the continued survival of the plundered. But when it becomes regular, a long-term relation is established, and periodic plunder can become formalized into tribute.

Tribute leaves the subjected society more or less intact. The exploiter is interested only in the prompt and full arrival of the tribute, and intervention is limited to the removal and replacement of local rulers who fail to deliver. At a more sophisticated stage, tribute can become organized into systems of taxation, often creating new social strata of tax collectors. In each successive stage of exploitation, the exploiters penetrate more deeply into the society of the exploited.

Tributary societies had two faces in their relations with nature. On the one hand, local systems delimited more or less strictly by natural conditions were broken, and the collection of tributes extended to all areas within the reach of the central power. Direct influence from the central power gained in importance in shaping the relationships of any particular community to its environment. On the other hand, being coercive rather than economic the external pressure did not lead to uniformity of means of subsistence in local communities. Regional and local differentiation was preserved. In the Mediterranean world, for instance, broad, geographically defined regions such as mountains, plateaux and plains retained their specific economies fairly unchanged through centuries of varying tributary pressure from the outside. Similar regional differentiation is characteristic of the economic history of India. Consequently, the ecohistorical periodization of a particular region within a tributary system is partly independent of the development of the central power.

As regards the (semi)independence of particular regions from economic centers, the development of capitalism marks a new break in the development of humanity–nature relationships. The essence of capitalism was identified by Marx in the ability of monetary wealth to buy labor power. A prerequisite for this was that producers were 'freed' from means of production and thus compelled to seek employment from the owners of wealth. Through the mechanism of surplus value this leads to accumulation of riches to the owners of means of production. It also leads to the formation of the capitalist market which is controlled by exchange value – different products are compared with each other using the same economic standard whatever the material composition of those products. Elements of capitalism appeared early in history (Braudel, 1984), but as a developed mode of production capitalism is the product and creator of modern Europe.

The spread and increasing sovereignty of the market had two decisive consequences for the ecohistory of humankind. First, institutionalized greed became the primary motivation of economic activities. Second, substances of nature lost their specificities and became measurable by the same basic unit, exchange value. It does not matter whether your particular product is wheat, coffee, timber, coal or parrot feathers once a demand can be created for it on the market. Exploitation of nature during capitalism is universalized because all elements of nature are brought within the sphere of economic activities and subjected to the same external measure, exchange value.

However, the increasing uniformity is only a tendency and important regional differentiation reappears secondarily by the fluctuations of the world market. Even under capitalism, ecohistorical periods differentiate regionally. The rapid cycles of change in nature created by the capitalist market are beautifully analysed by William Cronon in his book on Chicago and the Great West (Cronon, 1991).

Large-scale trade has created structures that have defined ecohistorical periods over vast regions

Trade is a process mediating material influences from one area to another and from one culture to another and, consequently, has a unifying influence on regional ecohistories. Cultures become less dependent on local conditions and means of modifying the environment spread. Large-scale trade in bulk products is a fairly recent phenomenon, but the volume of what is transported is not the whole story: necessities of every-day life such as tools, weapons, and salt and other foodstuffs were economically important very early in the history of societies.

Trade has often in history consolidated into structures that remained unchanged for centuries and thus promoted uniform exploitation of nature over vast regions. This has happened the world over; a central emphasis in Braudel (1982) is that the huge advantage of Europe over the other continents as regards scale of trade – and concomitant economic domination – appeared only with the dawn of modern society.

We use fur trade as an example of trade creating ecohistory. In northern Europe intense fur trade began in Roman times, was upheld through the Middle Ages by the demand in the Byzantine Empire, got great impetus when Britain opened trade connections to the East in 1553, and gradually lost its importance with the decimation of populations of fur-bearing animals first in the West and in the eighteenth and nineteenth centuries even in Siberia. In northern North America fur trade was equally important since the establishment of permanent connections by European traders. Fur trade had a major influence in shaping the traditional societies of northern regions such as Finland (Wolf, 1982; Cronon, 1983; Merchant, 1989).

Kirikov (1960) summarized the gradual decline in distribution and abundance of major game animals in the Russian empire since the Middle Ages. The most dramatic is the case of the Sable (*Martes zibellina*), a forest-dweller, related to the weasel and otter, with a highly valued fur. In the sixteenth and early seventeenth century sables were still found in western Russia including the Baltic states, but they disappeared from areas west of the Ural mountains by the end of the seventeenth century. In Siberia the decimation of the population proceeded rapidly; for instance in western Siberia around the commercial center of Tomsk, average capture per hunter and year decreased from 9 to 1.8 between years 1632 and 1710. In the nineteenth century the range of the sable had shrunk to central Siberia, and it was close to extinction when a special preserve was established at Lake Baikal in the early 1920s.

Large game animals such as bear and elk disappeared from southern parts of their ranges in the sixteenth and seventeenth centuries. Such species would be considered taiga animals according to their current distrubution but this is actually not true: they have disappeared from more favorable southern environments because of hunting. The beaver is an analogous example. The European beaver was hunted into extinction in northern Europe, and in North America beavers were decimated from coastal Massachusetts by about 1640, and from inland New England by the end of the eighteenth century.

The Middle Ages in Europe were a dynamic period of population growth, land reclamation, technological development, and local and regional economic differentiation

Historians have in recent decades become aware of the dynamic character of the European Middle Ages, in contrast with the traditional view of the Middle Ages as dark stagnation (Postan, 1972; Anderson, 1974). The Middle Ages coincide with the era of European feudalism, a new social formation, which consolidated as a synthesis out of the collision of deteriorating western Rome and the surrounding kin-structured societies. Some important features of the dynamics of the European feudal society were as follows:

[1] New rural relations of production gave incentive to the spread of agricultural technologies such as the iron-plow, the stiff-harness, the water-mill and new methods of crop rotation. Some of the technical inventions such as the water-mill originated in the antiquity, but the Greco–Roman slave societies lacked economic stimulus necessary for their application (Finley, 1983). New technologies facilitated extensive reclamation of new agricultural land in heavy clay soils in lowland habitats. This brought about shifts in the settlement patterns of human populations all over Western Europe.

[2] Population grew steadily and new areas were claimed for cultivation until the onset of a subsistence crisis in the fourteenth century. The crisis was aggravated by the Black Death, but there is good evidence that population growth and land reclamation came to a halt several decades before the spread of the Black Death to Western Europe. This is usually attributed to gradually diminishing returns due to exhaustion of the soil.

[3] Growth of population brought about increasing trade, specialization and division of labor quite early on in medieval Europe. This stimulated the revival of European cities which, in the words of Braudel (1981), marked the beginning of the continent's rise to eminence. The autonomy of medieval cities – 'non-feudal islands in feudal seas' (Postan, 1972) – was the key to later social and cultural development in Europe. Stabilization of the legal system made long-term economic activities feasible.

[4] 'Europe' was regionally highly differentiated at the end of the Roman era, Roman heritage being much stronger in the Mediterranean than further north, although the Roman impact on, for instance, medieval England is usually underestimated (Postan, 1972). Roman rural structures such as the slave latifundium shaped, on the other hand, patterns of agriculture everywhere in Europe, especially in the East which lacked mature civilizations to resist their influence (Anderson, 1974). Increasing trade created new differentiation: in antiquity the Mediterranean was the primary stage of commercial exchange, but during the Middle Ages river and land connections through Western Europe increased in importance. This created

important markets and fairs in northern France and southern Germany (Braudel, 1982). Later on there came to be constant tension between Mediterranean and North Sea–Baltic trading cities. The integration of Flemish textile industries and English wool in the thirteenth century is an important early example of regional division of labor between industry and raw material production (Postan, 1972).

Critical features of the European Middle Ages in terms of ecohistory were the intensification of agriculture, the occupation and reclamation of new habitats and the consolidation of new mechanisms for regional differentiation. But this brief overview also allows drawing methodological conclusions about ecohistorical periods in general.

First, several social processes may modify the existing relations of a given culture to nature, for instance, technological development, social innovation, population growth, shift of economic activities to new areas, or trade creating division of labor and regional differentiation. None of these factors can be *a priori* considered primary; their relative importance varies from time to time and region to region. A corollary from this conclusion is of course that any longer period in the history of any other part of the world would, on closer inspection, turn out to be equally complex as the European Middle Ages.

Second, the structures that shape the society–nature relationship at a given point in time originated often much earlier. This lesson is clearly brought home by historical analyses of the structure of the English countryside. But this of course implies that significant transitions in nature modification occur slowly. Cultures are prisoners of their past.

The European expansion, beginning with the great explorations in the fifteenth century, was a decisive step toward a uniform, global ecohistory
Two periods in history most deserve the attribute revolutionary, namely, the Neolithic revolution and the birth of industrial capitalism. A preliminary to industrialization took place in Europe in the sixteenth century, and it brought about changes that have had far-reaching consequences for the whole world. This was the consolidation of commercial empires such as Portugal, Spain, France, the United Provinces of the Netherlands, and Britain, and their global expansion.
What happened?

Main elements of commercial capitalism were already present in the Italian city-states of the thirteenth century, but large-scale expansion only began in the sixteenth century. Immanuel Wallerstein (1974) dated the break to the period 1450–1640, and located it to an old dual core area of the Mediterranean in the south and the Flanders–Hanseatic trade network in the north, supplemented by new commercial connections to Eastern Europe on the one hand and to the Atlantic islands and swelling New World settlements on the other.

Wallerstein's (1974) thesis is that the essence of the break consisted in the creation of a new world system. The thesis underlines that the European transition was not something that first happened in Europe in isolation and was later to have consequences for the rest of the world, but rather a gradual emergence of a new configuration of economic relationships in the Western world as a whole, a process in which both core areas in Western Europe and peripheral areas were involved from the very beginning. A critical role in this change was played by a tremendous increase in the volume of trade and the significance of the market, in connection with upheavals in socio–political relationships in Western European states.

In the sixteenth century the market for primary products such as cereals, timber and, somewhat later, wool expanded; gold and silver flowing to Europe from the New World contributed to strengthening commercial ties. Trade in bulk products brought into fruition a new type of exploitation of natural resources, namely, monoculture, extensive cultivation of agricultural products over vast areas solely for the market. The first extensive experiments in monoculture since Roman latifundia were undertaken by the Portuguese on the Atlantic islands in the fifteenth century, and the invention was rapidly exported to the West Indies.

Wallerstein (1974) distinguished four regionally separated ways of organizing labor in agricultural production in the European world-economy: *slavery* was adopted in the plantation economies in the New World in areas where indigenous labor force was in short supply but where slaves could be readily exported from Africa. *Serfdom* spread again in parts of southern America and in Eastern Europe which came to be the granary of Western Europe. Why serfs and not slaves in these areas? Because import of slaves was not economically feasible and because the relatively sparse indigenous population could not be enslaved for logistic reasons. *Share-cropping* developed in areas that Wallerstein characterizes as 'semiperiphery', for instance, southern

Europe. Lastly, in the core areas agriculture was based on *yeoman farmers*, and in some regions pasturage dominated, for production of meat as well as raw materials such as wool. In these core areas the productivity of agriculture was to grow much more rapidly than in the other zones.

This zonation, a product of social and economic differentiation, led to future regional divergence in Europe. This was not a straightforward reflection of natural conditions, as is shown by the development of agriculture in Eastern Europe. Eastern European agriculture has traditionally made use of large areas and extensive, labor-demanding methods. This, however, was due to the internal differentiation of the emerging European world system. Development in Russia ran parallel, although the Muscovite empire was an independent economic region until the early eighteenth century. In the Middle Ages, productivity in cereal cultivation was comparable, about 1:3, all over Europe. The productivity began to increase in the West in the sixteenth century, but remained constant in the East for another two to three centuries.

Why?

Because Western states were able to reap the profit of the growth of commerce and industry within the whole European system, and their domination strengthened in the periphery in Eastern Europe social structures that reproduced this disparity and hindered agricultural innovation. Trade outposts in eastern Baltic such as Danzig (Poland) hoarded profits from agricultural hinterlands in the East, and trade centers in Western Europe hoarded profits from Danzig *et alia*. In Russia, a system of serfdom took shape in the fifteenth and sixteenth centuries to produce cereals for the internal market of the expanding Muscovite empire and innovation was likewise hindered. Since the reign of Peter the Great in the seventeenth and eighteenth centuries, contacts to the West strengthened and the old, semi-feudal system in the countryside was retained until the late nineteenth century.

Thus, the consolidation of the capitalist world system in the sixteenth century induced rapid changes in nature but these changes were not similar in all regions belonging to the system. Pasturage caused overgrazing and ecological impoverishment in the Spanish highlands, ruthless exploitation of share-croppers desolated hillsides of southern France, extensive wheat cultivation changed landscapes in a wide belt from the eastern Baltic through Poland and Bohemia to the Hungarian plains, and slave-driven plantation economies led to the destruction of habitats on the Caribbean islands – all as parts of the same, interconnected economic network.

The other major consequence of European expansion was characterized as 'ecological imperialism' by Crosby (1986). This refers to the spread of European domination to other parts of the world. Crosby's major thesis is that ecological factors played a prominent role in facilitating the European expansion, which resulted in the establishment of what Crosby calls 'Neo-Europes'. They are parts of the world geographically distant from each other but sharing populations derived from the European stock, and agricultures based on shared methods and shared species of plants and animals, the bulk of them originating from the Eurasian continent (maize is the important exception).

Major Neo-Europes are Australia, New Zealand, southern South America, and North America. These areas have in common a temperate climate and natural environment favorable for creatures adapted to Mediterranean conditions on the Eurasian continent. Thus, a critical historical preliminary for the establishment of Neo-Europes was a long cultural development that had shaped methods of agriculture and husbandry adaptable to Mediterranean-type climatic and geographic regions anywhere on the earth.

The Neo-Europes hosted of course indigenous people and local floras and faunas before Europeans arrived, but local human populations were decimated by diseases, and local floras and faunas gave way to plants and animals that Europeans brought along. Uncountable herds of cattle, horses, sheep, goats, swine and smaller creatures such as cats, dogs, rats and mongooses filled local habitats, decimated native animal populations and modified vegetation beyond recognition. European weeds invaded local plant communities and pushed aside native species.

The European sixteenth century opened a new page in the social history of world nature. There is, however, still a question that needs to be briefly touched upon. Why Europe, why not, for instance, China, which was far ahead of Europe in technology and agricultural productivity? Chinese ocean-sailers were ahead of their Portuguese contemporaries in exploring African shores in the fifteenth century, but they stopped whereas the Portuguese, and other Europeans after them, kept going. Why 'Neo-Europes' instead of 'Neo-Chinas'?

This is an ongoing discussion among social historians, but from the point of our argument a major conclusion is that there are no natural *a priori* reasons that could explain the difference. The answer must be sought from historical, social and economic factors. This conclusion is different from what we claimed above about Neolithic revolutions, which were to a larger extent influenced by ecology and geography. During the millenia that separate the Neolithic from the sixteenth century, the role of natural and geographic factors diminished in relative importance in influencing social processes – and, as the other side of the coin, social modification of nature became more and more liberated from the immediate constraints of local ecological conditions.

The final breakthrough of industrial capitalism in the early nineteenth century created the modern world burdened by environmental problems of a new type

Ecologically minded interpreters tend to view the industrial revolution too narrowly as a technological process. However, the basis of the revolution is not technological innovation but a series of revolutionary tranformations in the whole economy and society. Eric Hobsbawm characterized the industrial revolution as follows:

> Some time in the 1780s, and for the first time in human history, the shackles were taken off the productive power of human societies, which henceforth became capable of the constant, rapid and up to the present limitless multiplication of men, goods and services.
>
> (Hobsbawm, 1962)

In other words, the national economy of industrial capitalism commenced a self-sustained growth. Growth of production began to stimulate new growth of production and so on, apparently (and for the time being) without limits. How was this possible?

According to Hobsbawm, the revolutionizing feature of modern capitalist industry is its ability to create its own markets and so to escape the limits of existing demand, in contrast to earlier small-scale industries that were strictly limited by the immediately available market. The revolution originated, as is well known, in the cotton industry, but in the long run an adequate capital goods capacity was critical. The spread of railroads provided the incentive that revolutionized the capital goods industries in the mid-nineteenth century. The construction of railways was, according to Hobsbawm, a sponge large enough to hold the huge amounts of capital produced by the expanding textile industries in the early decades of the nineteenth century. Thereafter, the basic expansion of capitalism was secured for several decades, and ever new fields of production were swallowed into its profit-making mill.

In the social sphere capitalism produced a fundamental change in the social organization of labor, but capitalism brought about fundamental changes in land as well. The breakthrough of industrialism was actually predated by revolutionary transformations in agriculture. In the core areas of Britain and the Netherlands agriculture was getting modernized, technologically efficient and market-oriented, and it paved the way for industrialism. Eastern Europe and the colonies, in contrast, produced bulk products such as grain for export with extensive and labor-demanding methods.

The first large-scale effect of capitalism on the social history of nature was the transformation of the countryside, brought about by the spread of capitalist-type, market-oriented agriculture. The process was slow in the beginning, in the early nineteenth century, primarily because traditional social ties prevented rapid changes in rural areas in large parts of the world including Britain (Williams, 1973) and North America (Merchant, 1989). However, the transformation gathered momentum in the second half of the century (discussed by Hobsbawm, 1975). It meant rapid expansion in new, virgin areas such as North America, Argentina and Australia, but also in older peripheral regions in Europe such as southeastern Russian plains. It meant vast clearance of new cultivated land all over Europe and destruction of forests. It also meant intensification and technological innovation especially in areas with a shortage of labor power (US), or profitable peasant economies (central Europe). Finally, the transformation brought about the abolition of slavery in the New World and the abolition of serfdom in Eastern Europe, but also intensified violent assimilation of native peoples.

The second major consequence was increasing production of raw materials for export on a world-wide basis. The old patterns of colonial trade were fortified and spread to new areas. Cotton is the prime example of a product that conquered vast tracts of cultivable land particularly in the Caribbean and the southern United States in the footsteps of the industrial revolution, but other raw materials were to follow later. As a rule this entailed extremely rapid transformations of the nature of vast regions. Another example is the spread of rubber plantations in coastal Brazil in the nineteenth century, and later on – after rubber plants were successfully smuggled out of Brazil – in the Malayan Peninsula.

But also the new plants and factories themselves transformed nature. In the beginning industrial units were small and their pollution problems local albeit serious, not least because of the crowded living conditions of workers in the surrounding area. Large-scale ecological consequences and irretrievable changes in large ecosystems began to accumulate with the growth of chemical industries.

Urbanization, a counterpart to the change in the countryside, has produced new environments and habitats. Industrial metropolises resemble geological formations, only changing far more rapidly. The flora and fauna of big cities include species that have literally conquered the world, such as the house sparrow, Norwegian rat or fire-ant.

Uniformity is brought to the social history of nature under capitalism by economic trends that cover the whole capitalist world system and by the spread of similar industrial methods to every corner of the globe. The history of industrial capitalism consists of cyclic fluctuations, so-called 'long waves', first studied by Nikolai D. Kondratief, an economist and statistician active in Moscow in the 1920s. By and large, they have followed the shifts of investments from one branch of the economy to another. Colonial economies also showed long-term cyclical behavior, driven by the exploitation and exhaustion of resources, as discussed by Eduardo Galeano in the case of Latin America (1973).

The analytic status of the concept of 'long waves' may be disputable, but it is valuable for describing the phases of capitalist development and the modification of nature by capitalist industrialization. Global economic trends have produced unity all over the world, due to increasing integration of the world market, but this is accompanied by divergencies due to regional differences in the composition of industries. Different branches of production and, accordingly, different regions have reaped the profits during each phase of growth.

It would, however, definitively be a mistake to view industrial capitalism as always and everywhere leading to a more intense and ruthless exploitation of nature. Three important qualifications are needed. First, during recession phases economic 'hinterlands' are simply left behind, and nature can recover (as far as possible). Second, traditional subsistence methods resulted often – under heavy population pressure – in more disastrous changes in the natural environment than has been the case after capitalist modernization. The history of Finnish forests is a good example (Åström, 1978), but the pattern is probably true everywhere, including many Third

World countries today. Third, although the basic goal of capitalist production, maximization of profit, is in contradiction with the sustainable use of natural resources, it also gives strong incentives for rational management whenever this is profitable in the short run. Pollution control, for instance, may be very efficient once it is made compulsory and thus creates a steady market for new technology.

The ecological crisis is a new stage in global ecohistory

Global ecohistory has entered a new stage sometime after the Second World War. Ecological crisis is an apt name for this stage, characterized as it is by the dramatically increased human capacity to cause irreparable destruction in nature.

Paradoxically, however, it is difficult to give a precise definition to the ecological crisis. The crisis has two dimensions: the material basis is that human activities have reached the potential of modifying such geophysical processes that determine the basic boundary conditions of the very existence of human life on the earth. This prospect has caused an explosion in the cultural consciousness about environmental hazards. But the paradox is that neither are the boundary conditions of human existence on the earth visible to us, nor are we able to distinguish between 'allowable' and 'forbidden' human activities. This is due to the very complexity of the interplay between society and nature. A demonstration of this dilemma is that concrete 'ecocatastrophe' scenarios have, as a rule, been social utopias – beginning with Paul Ehrlich's classic article 'Eco-Catastrophe!' in *Ramparts* in September, 1969.

'Ecological crisis' is better viewed as a metaphoric expression for a multitude of specific environmental problems accumulating all over the world, some of them extremely serious. There is no need to give a list of the problems here; such lists abound. The ecological crux of the matter was recently crystallized by Eugene P. Odum (1989) in the words 'our endangered life-support systems'. Deterioration of ecosystems all over the world threatens the life-supporting potential of nature. This threat is real – although we do not know how actual – even on the global scale. The conditions making life possible on the earth were produced by life itself, and there are no transcendental guarantees that those conditions cannot change.

The ecological crisis means that the consciousness of risks of the future permeates the modern society. This is the concept of 'risk society' of Ulrich Beck (1986). Beck claims that risk scenarios shape modern society irrespective of whether they are literally true or not, and that this defines the fundamental social significance of environmental issues in modern society. Environmental risks are not primarily problems to be solved by scientific and technological means, but risks to be coped with in the whole cultural and social sphere. As a consequence, environmental science may primarily aim at manipulating the risk-consciousness of people instead of addressing the risks.

The issue of nuclear safety is a good example. It can be endlessly discussed from scientific and technological perspectives but the fundamental fact remains that there is a risk as long as there are nuclear plants or concentrations of nuclear waste around. The issue simply cannot be settled by scientific and technological means alone.

Beck refers with his term 'risk society' to a broad range of social phenomena that stem from the dissolving of the social structures of industrial capitalism and the resulting individualization. Environmental issues are only one, albeit a major manifestation of the trend. According to Beck, the label 'risk society' is applicable to all industrial societies, and Third World countries are also increasingly being brought into the same picture. This is certainly true in the sense that many risks are global. However, this does not mean that differences in political situations and practical possibilities of coping with environmental issues would be evened out; we return to these problems in the last chapter.

But there is a deeper cultural dimension to 'ecological crisis' and 'risk society': our well-established views of nature and of the relations between culture and nature become increasingly doubtful. Our conception of 'nature' draws partly from the antiquity, particularly Plato, and partly from the rationalism of the Enlightenment. 'Nature' is to our culture a unified, harmonious whole, external to ourselves, which can be modified and exploited once the laws governing its behavior are known. Progress is increasing knowledge and increasing domination of nature. Williams (1980) sketched some major shifts in ideas of nature in Western culture since the Enlightenment, from the 'capricious ruler' of Shakespeare to the 'progressive breeder' of Darwin and Spencer.

This idea of nature lies in shambles. Unified nature has been dismembered, the privileged position accorded to humans in nature has disappeared, the foundation of the idea of linear progress has collapsed. This of course also implies that Romantic ideals of the inherent harmony in nature, adopted as the other side of rationalistic exploitation, are no longer viable. The era of ecological risks calls forth a fundamental revision in our cultural view of nature.

Ecohistorical Formations

The world of humankind constitutes a manifold, a totality of intercon-nected processes, and inquiries that disassemble this totality into bits and then fail to reassemble falsify reality.   Eric Wolf[4]

The notion of ecohistorical period refers to changes in nature as a con-sequence of human activities. The complementary notion of ecohis-torical formation allows us to recognize distinct ways in which societies relate to nature. We should characterize these formations by features which will help distinguish different kinds of dynamics both in the mode of production and in the related ecology. Our discussion of ecohistorical periods above was primarily descriptive. In this passage our emphasis is more on process.

A given mode of production can span many ecosystems. Simple gathering and hunting societies can occur under the harsh conditions of the tundra or desert or rain forest but also in the rich northwest coast of North America, where abundant fish permitted relative abundance. Capitalism can also invade these same habitats, and with much greater population densities. Societies with extensive exchange can flourish in regions where the habitat is too impover-ished to support much food production but where mineral wealth is available and can be exchanged for food produced elsewhere. Thus there is no one to one relation between the mode of production and the habitat.

A comparative analysis of ecohistorical formations presents us with two broad problems: first, recognizing similarities in the relations to nature of a particular mode of production across different envi-ronments, and second, detecting relevant differences between different modes of production in their relation to nature in similar environ-ments.

We ask the following questions of an eco-historical formation:

What is the habitat, vegetation, array of soils and climate?
This is at first glance a question of natural geography, the space within which we will insert a society. But that is not the case. First, the habitat is already the product of previous human activity. All

regions of the earth except the Antarctic and the highest mountain tops have already had a history of human occupation or at least sporadic impact. But more importantly, the size of the social unit determines whether a particular mountainous area is itself an eco-historical formation or only one kind of patch in a mosaic of habitats which, taken as a whole, is the environment of a society. As an example we discussed the study of Anthony Leeds (1980) on the historical development of the hill country of Texas in Chapter 5.

What is produced? With what raw materials and by what tools?
All societies produce food and at least some clothing and shelter. Food production may consist of gathering what is already present, or of the deliberate growing of plants and animals. Whatever the initial stages in the production of food, the final stages require the trans-formation of inedible into edible material. This may be simply peeling or cutting, or it may involve cooking, grinding, fermenting, etc. These later stages prior to eating are usually included under con-sumption rather than production. However, from an ecological point of view, production and consumption are different aspects of the same process. The consumption of primary production is at the same time secondary production. Until the recent invention of nearly inde-structible plastics, all produced materials were also consumed somewhere in a process of new production and the wastes were the raw materials for subsequent production.

Whatever the way in which food is produced, the final stages of consumptive production of food usually take place on a small scale, within households, and have generally been carried out by women. Since this productive activity is engaged in directly for consumption it takes place outside of what is thought of as the economy and is often ignored. Yet much of human labor is still expended in these tasks.

In gathering–hunting and simple agricultural production systems, the primary raw materials are mostly of biological origin and recycle relatively quickly and locally. But the extraction and transformation of minerals has acquired a growing importance over the millenia. It changes production in several ways: the distribution of minerals on the earth's surface is much more irregular than that of arable land, so that mineral products are transported from one place to another at an early stage of human history. Even in Neolithic times objects made from Mediterranean shells were moved to central Europe and flint quarries served larger areas than single populations. The extraction process has a long lasting effect on the places where it takes place. In addition to the holes in the ground left by mining, the bringing of heavy metals to the surface often poisons plant or animal life.

The extractive processes are much more drastic than the processing of biological materials, requiring (at present) high temperatures and often strong reagents. And the final products, both usable and waste, recycle only very slowly. Industrial societies have increased both energy consumption per capita and per unit area. In some regions, the oxygen consumed in the burning of fossil fuel exceeds the capacity of photosynthesis to replenish the oxygen so that these areas are net importers of oxygen.

In recent times in some countries the proportion of human labor devoted directly to material production has decreased. There has been an increased proportion of human labor devoted not to material production but to services of various kinds. The question 'what is produced' includes not only what materials are transformed and what do they leave behind, but also what do most people do? And an increasing part of the population is removed from both agricultural and industrial production. Some are engaged in distribution of goods or public service activities which have become necessary – health care, education – while others are involved in sales, public relations, insurance or finance, or in police and military.

Who does the work, and in what way (individually or socially)? Who owns or controls the means of production, who disposes of the product? What becomes of the surplus? Of what does wealth consist? What is the relation between production and reproduction?

These are the classical questions of relations of production and reproduction, of class structure and the gender-based division of labor. They are especially relevant for ecology because of their role in determining which of the possible products are produced, how much and with what means. Where surpluses are used mostly for consumption there are limits, no matter how lavish, to consumption and therefore to the expansion of production. But where the surplus becomes a means of new production, expanded production and resource use can be more rapid than population growth or the natural reproduction of resources.

The dual role of women in production and reproduction is a significant determinant of the situation of women in different societies. In slave societies the allocation of women's labor between these two functions was direct, obvious, and linked especially to the availability of cheap slaves. As long as slaves could be acquired cheaply a very high mortality was acceptable and deaths were replaced by purchase. But as slaves became scarcer, prices rose and the reproduction of the labor force became important enough for slave breeding to become an economic option. In other societies the forces governing the allocation of women's work is less transparent.

The shifting allocation of women's activity between production and reproduction not only responds to the supply and demand for labor, but also affects the fluctuating demography, giving rise to bursts of births (baby booms) and periods of lower recruitment.

The feedback between economic fluctuations and women's activity takes place through intermediate variables of beliefs, opportunities, institutions and laws in complex patterns unique to each society. Through the relative roles of women in production and reproduction and their impact on demography and back to the economy, the situation of women is an inseparable part of the dynamics of all societies.

Margaret Mead (1950) compiled a classification of different ways in which labor is organized within societies: there is group production in which everyone does the same thing individually but in the same place; cooperation without stable division of labor as in hunting or weeding; and more stable division of labor with the development of the crafts. Since these different ways of doing things affect the distribution of the final product and often have different values attached to different roles, they have a profound influence on beliefs and human relations.

In class societies different people may own land and tools, and neither of them work the land. Producers may own some of their tools (for example agricultural laborers may have to provide their own machetes, plowers may be contracted to prepare land, providing their own oxen) and may receive a share of the product of their labor or a fixed compensation. Tenants may make the day to day management decisions or may be under supervision by the landlord's representatives.

Questions of ownership are not as clear cut as they might seem, as we discussed in Chapter 5. The form of wealth determines whether or not present wealth is the means for future wealth and therefore whether transitory differences in economic success (however defined) are the basis for future wealth. Wealth may take the form of rights to use a resource for hunting or fishing, but in most societies such wealth is not self-reproducing. Having a good fishing area does not allow someone to acquire additional good fishing areas or to speculate in the leasing of fishing grounds.

Land may be the main source of wealth. Where there is a struggle for land, it is often the case that new lands are opened up for cultivation by the landless seeking to escape from dependency on the owners of large tracts. These small cultivators move up the mountains, sow on steeper and steeper slopes, clear the forests. And if they are successful they are later displaced by the estates of the landowning class. Therefore the destruction of the forests and erosion of the mountainsides is sometimes the work of the displaced poor. This is especially the case in countries such as Mexico where the political power of a landed oligarchy coexists with a public ideological commitment to give land to the tillers. Since it cannot be taken from the landowners it is taken from the forest.

Under capitalism wealth takes the form of capital, the physical embodiment of previous human labor. Capitalism is a more fluid system than previous modes of production: its stability requires change, increasing consumption, and more radical transformations of raw materials to create new products. The economic rationality of capitalist production is profitability. Therefore under this mode of production there is often an economic stake in environmentally destructive practices which leads the owners of production to resist acknowledgement of the environmental or health impacts of their activities. Further, the livelihood of the workers depends on employment, their ability to sell their labor power regardless of how it is employed or for what products. Therefore we have the common phenomenon of industrial activities which may be 'good for the economy' but bad for people.

Although it seems that all societies have a gender-based division of labor, the particular division of labor is highly variable across cultures and over time. Farming, tending sheep, marketing and many crafts such as weaving or brewing have variously been male or female occupations. Furthermore, the assignment of status is linked to this division of labor.

The question of who does the work and who owns the product must be answered along the two dimensions of class and gender, and in some societies also by race or nationality.

Why are things produced?

At first glance this is obvious: things are produced to be used, because they satisfy some human need. But it makes a big difference whether things are produced for direct consumption by the producer's own household, for sharing in a larger community, or for exchange. The distinction between production for use and production for exchange, between production of use-values and of commodities, is a crucial one both for society and for ecology.

When goods are produced directly for local consumption, there are natural limits to the quantities which are required. Therefore production is aimed at guaranteeing an adequate food supply, clothing, shelter, etc. If natural conditions become harsher, more effort is required and when conditions are milder there is more leisure. Innovations which make production easier would then result in less effort spent and production of the same amount rather than in increased production because it promises a higher profit.

The uncertainty of nature and therefore of food production can be confronted to some extent by storage of surplus food. This is limited however by food technology, by the attractiveness of stored grain for insects and rodents and its vulnerability to microorganisms. Some of the uncertainty is highly crop-specific such as outbreaks of plant diseases. Or some crops are more sensitive to drought or flood than others. Therefore a mixed cropping pattern is common. Uncertainty may be highly local, in which case networks of mutual obligation may serve as a redistributive system that acts as insurance. Further, even in the simplest economy different kinds of goods are needed. Therefore people have to engage in a variety of activities and acquire a broad range of knowledge about nature and technique. In some ways, societies with the most elementary tools have to be even more knowledgeable about subtle nuances of nature.

Marx was the first to explore systematically the dual nature of commodities as objects of use and exchange. Commodity production has existed long before capitalism, and has persisted into all post-capitalist societies to date. For our purposes it has the following importance:

[1] Exchange is the most effective way of transforming one object into another. There is no technology that will turn wheat into shoes, but this can be accomplished quite easily in the market. The interchangeability of goods endows them with an abstract value, an equivalence in exchange that has no relation to their physical composition or shape. This makes possible all kinds of specialization, and when supported by transportation allows populations to grow not only where all their needs can be met, but also where any single need

can be met sufficiently so that a surplus may be exchanged for the others. This results in a total change in the meaning of habitat requirements of human societies.

Exchange over wider areas provides more protection against the local fluctuations of nature. A system of trade allows the movement of surpluses from areas of abundance to areas of need and is therefore a large-scale protection against even regional production disasters. However, as commodities they only flow to where sales are profitable. The terms of exchange turn out to be more volatile than the weather, and the market itself can become the major source of uncertainty.

[2] There is a separation between the production of an object and its use. Its usefulness is replaced by 'demand', that is effective demand, the possibility of sale. Of course, the ability to produce something requires raw materials, skills, markets and connections so that industrialists cannot in fact shift product capriciously to follow short-term trends. But as the financial markets become more flexible, investments can move more freely from one branch of the economy to another so that it becomes increasingly a matter of economic calculation whether to invest in production, labor relations, research, sales or bribery, or to hold the money idle until some clearly lucrative alternative emerges.

The same sort of calculation influences the choice of technology. Whether a resource is nurtured and replenished, extracted with care or used up all at once depends on economic calculation. For resources which reproduce only slowly, it can be more profitable to exhaust the supply as quickly as possible and invest the profits in some other activity than to harvest only as much as can be replaced. Also scientific and technical knowledge itself becomes increasingly a commodity and this has a powerful impact on the pattern of knowledge and ignorance, as we discussed in Chapter 3.

[3] With commodity production, it becomes necessary to create abstract forms of representing wealth, such as money, credit, shares, etc. The significance of these instruments for us is that in this form wealth is insatiable. Surplus food can be eaten up to a point and even stored within the body as fat. This provides some protection against hard times, but the quantity is limited. It can be stored in the ground in jars, dried, smoked, or pickled. This extends the possibilities of accumulation but is limited by the decay of the stored product and its attractiveness for rats, insects and fungi. It could also be shared and

converted into social obligations of mutual aid, but this is limited by the area of direct personal contact and the frailty of human memory. But in its abstract form wealth can be stored indefinitely and in unlimited quantities.

[4] Since the object of commodity production is to sell products, a major effort must go into sales. The encouragement of consumption as a way of life becomes a necessity, and with it the active creation of new needs. Thus the model in which goods are offered to satisfy independently arisen needs no longer holds. The needs are actively created to demand the new products.

Although commodity production reaches its most pervasive development under capitalism, even here simple production for consumption persists as a subordinate activity of many farmers, as some supplementary hunting and fishing, and most important of all within the household. The distinct nature of production for use can be seen by posing the question, would a housekeeper decide to spend a whole week cleaning while postponing food preparation for the next week and bathing each child eight times a day in the following week out of considerations of efficiency? The different household tasks are not interconvertible because they are not commodities and are evaluated by their utility.

The core of our theoretical analysis is an emphasis on process rather than description. Therefore, for each ecohistorical formation we shall go on to ask two major dynamic questions.

What keeps the ecohistorical formation as it is?
This is the general ecological question, why are things the way they are instead of a little bit different. It is the question about the regulatory processes, the homeostasis of the system. All societies have such processes, ranging from the within-household reproduction of the division of labor to region-wide changes in animal populations from hunting.

Among the pre-revolutionary Chukchee reindeer herders of Siberia, herds could expand only up to a point. As they increased in size, they had to be moved more often because they exhausted the local forage. They were also more subject to disease. Therefore owners of large herds would divide them, giving parts to different sons or dependents. But these different herds had to be separated spatially, and the original owner could not retain effective control for long. On the other hand, very small herds were more readily lost to predators or the lure of wild reindeer. Thus herd size was kept within boundaries by negative feedback, and successful herding did not lead to an indefinite accumulation of wealth.

But negative feedback is not sufficient to provide stability. If the regulatory process has delays in it, this can itself induce oscillations. For instance the commercial production of livestock or orchard crops for market requires decisions to be made now about market conditions when the animals or fruit are ready for harvesting. But many investors have made similar decisions, so that at harvest time production may be so great as to drive down prices and discourage further planting or breeding. The cyclic abundance and scarcity usually has a period that depends on the length of the delay, the generation time for livestock or the time to reach production for the resource considered.

The time lag itself could result in cyclic glut and scarcity. But it is reinforced by external events (for example new technologies, new markets) and by positive feedbacks. In the animal production system, a decline in the price of meat while the animals are growing may lead farmers to calculate that it is not worth raising them to maturity. Then younger animals are dumped on the market, driving prices even lower. And when they would have matured, there is a shortage which stimulates new production. Since its inception capitalism has shown cyclical behavior in several time-scales, as we discussed in the previous section.

For the economy as a whole, the concentration of wealth exhibits positive feedback. Large enterprises have reserves to buffer against short-term fluctuations, easier access to credit and resources, and other economies of scale. Further, they have the flexibility to shift investments. The major tobacco companies in the US are already highly diversified in anticipation of a continued decline in smoking while they conduct a ferocious rear guard action to protect present investments in cigarettes.

What forces lead to change in the system?
Although ecohistorical formations show enough self-regulation to persist for long periods and retain a recognizable identity, they are not really constant. Each system has its own dynamics of change.

The processes which cause long-term change are not the same processes responsible for short-term fluctuation and its regulation. They are often ignored in describing the short term, because they change slowly enough to be treated as constant. Or, like the erosion of topsoil, they may progress unnoticed until some critical point is reached. Or they may act only during periods of extreme stress, when they show that the system has lost its resilience. Some changes are multiplicative, such as population growth. Small differences in growth rates accumulate and may rapidly acquire great significance. Events in the social sphere such as the concentration of land holding, or the penetration of the market to new spheres of society, can alter the relations with nature.

The natural resources are not givens of nature. A mineral becomes a resource when there is social use for it and technical means to extract it. The availability of a mineral or plant can encourage finding the use for it and the means to produce it; on the other hand, the extraction may deplete it or competing sources may make it unavailable economically if not physically. Then it loses resource status and becomes again merely a mineral or a wild plant. Therefore, the depletion of resources or the eradication of ecosystems on which a particular society has subsisted is a complex process.

In general, a community which produces mostly for its own use will make use of a greater diversity of raw materials and species of plants and animals than one which produces for the market. Commodity production makes different useful things equivalent as values and measurable against each other on a single scale. This creates the oscillation between diverse productive basis and monoculture that we discussed in Chapter 5.

Many authors have argued that population is a major factor in longterm social change. The formal analysis of population is quite simple: population growth or decline depends on births minus deaths plus or minus migration, and reaches a stable level if these balance and remain constant. But these parameters depend on the particular natural and social forces at work in each formation and change over time. Stability is therefore the exception.

Population is relevant in four major ways: total population size, population density, population growth rate and age distribution.

Total population size sets limits on the division of labor and the maintenance and reproduction of various cultural traits. When populations get very small, part of the common fund of knowledge is lost. When the Pawnee tribe was reduced by conquest, displacement, disease, the destruction of the bison herds and harassment from thousands to a few hundred individuals, ritual and healing knowledge was lost as their bearers died without being able to pass them on.

Total population also determines the extreme values of individual quantitative traits that are found in populations. This is seen most clearly in the Olympic records: big countries get more prizes. There is some distribution of athletic ability which is produced by the interaction of many biological and social factors, with most people performing close to some average score and fewer and fewer examples in the tails reaching out to both extremes. But this logic is misleading in one major respect: if a large part of the population has no access to sports, it doesn't matter how many they are. It is the *effective* population size that is relevant. Cuba, with only some ten million people, is a world power in sports because of the widespread participation.

However, for a given social organization, total population size produces some scale effects. For instance, suppose that a city has a circular shape. With a fixed density, the total population is proportional to the area, which is the square of the radius. But access to and from the city crosses the boundary, which is only proportional to the radius. Therefore as the city grows in size the demand on the boundary for exchange between the city and its surroundings increases.

Population density can be important for questions of contagion, resource use, waste production, etc. But this depends not only on average density but also on its unevenness. For instance, if we calculate the land available to farm families in Panama from total figures, we find some 20 ha per capita, a generous allotment in most conditions. But land ownership is very uneven and if, instead, we calculate how many people are living at each density, we find that most people are crowded, experiencing about 0.27 ha per capita.

There are many different kinds of density. Density for land use, density for contagion, crowding on public transportation or in traffic jams, residential crowding and noise exposure, people per job, per meter of beach, per liter of water per day, etc. Even something that seems a simple natural calculation turns out to be complex.

Yet it is true that, for a given social organization, as population density increases so does the demand on resources. Less suitable land, less accessible minerals, more distant sources of water all have to be mobilized to continue supplying the existing levels. Thus increasing population density necessarily creates new relations with the environment and consequent social changes.

Population growth rates are important both for their direct economic impact and indirectly through the age distribution: growing populations are young populations. The growth rate has to be measured against the growth of the means of subsistence. In recent years, the gross national products of most countries have been growing at rates of from 1-5 per cent per year, and agriculture somewhat slower. Population growth has been comparable so that many countries have been falling behind in production per capita. However, once again we note that national averages are misleading. The unequal distribution of the products of agriculture and industry, rather than total population, seems to be the direct cause of poverty in most places.

If production does not keep up with population, this means that the newly created labor force is less productive than the previous cohorts. People preoccupied with population often cite figures such as 'every second there are x new mouths to feed' without noting that there are also 2x new hands to produce and x new brains to invent new ways to produce. Yet their arithmetic is justified if employment is not created for the new people.

Finally, the rate of population growth influences the age distribution. In a growing population, people are young and the proportion of the total population which does the work to support the whole is reduced. This creates pressures favoring child labor. In a population which is stable and with low mortality, a large proportion are old, post retirement. This can give the same result – a small part of the population doing the work for everybody. In this case the pressure will be toward raising the retirement age and the restructuring of jobs to take into account an older work force. We see that for a given social organization and technology, population changes have some rather obvious consequences. But social dynamics lie behind: social organization and technology are influenced by demographic changes.

7

Political Ecology?

I am on nature's side. Man the scientist, white *man the scientist, white* ruling *class man the scientist, the enterpreneur, the corporation president sets out to control nature – to make it behave!*

But I'm a Third World, born working-class woman. I look at it from nature's point of view, from the insects' point of view, the insect out in the cornfield sucking the sweet juice of the crunchy cane or the nourishing mealiness of the newly pumped kernel. Rosario Morales[1]

Ecology has come to stay on the political agenda. However, it is clearly not true that ecological problems automatically constitute a 'political ecology'. The social and political implications of the ecological crisis are not transparent. The role ecology should have in social development needs scrutiny.

Environmental movements have tended to fall prey to naturalism and objectivism, that is, scientific facts are not seen as historical and often temporary conceptions stabilized by prevailing theories, and theories are taken too literally. We began by discussing constraints of ecological knowledge in Chapters 2 and 3. We continued in Chapters 4 and 5 by giving a detailed account of how ecological knowledge can be integrated into actual social practice in agriculture and health. In Chapter 6 we presented a broad historical framework for viewing human culture against the natural background. In this Chapter we elaborate explicitly the political implications of the ecological crisis.

Defining Ecological Problems

> *The abolitionists succeeded in revolutionising the image of man. In the same way, the ecology movement will succeed in changing the idea of nature.*   Mary Douglas[2]

Because the notion of 'ecological crisis' is nebulous, concrete approaches are needed in order that something realizable in practice could be suggested. A way to start specification is clear posing of problems. We ask first the general question, what is an ecological problem?

A preliminary definition might read as follows: an ecological problem is a condition of the environment which prevents pleasant or preferable activities and is threatening either human health and wellbeing or the productive potential of nature. In the short term, human health and wellbeing are critical, in the long term, the productive potential of nature is critical. However, a tension between these two criteria is unavoidable because the conditions under which we live were produced during millenia of uneven and unequitable social development: only too often the poor and oppressed are forced to exploit nature in ways that threaten her productive potential. Whatever we may wish, the burden of history lies heavily upon us.

A problem is a social category; it is something people are conscious and worried about as demanding solution. But this implies a paradox again: a catalogue of ecological problems is necessarily simultaneously a chart of consciousness about those problems. We cannot separate material and ideological determinants from each other. Are the issues people view as problems the most serious problems? Are the most serious problems included among the issues popularly talked about? (What could possibly be a 'serious problem' nobody knows about?)

Therefore our preliminary definition of an ecological problem is far too general. It needs to be tied to specific social and historical circumstances. This of course brings social controversies into the open. Specific ways of defining problems already presuppose answers as to where and how solutions to those problems ought to be found.

Problem for Whom?

Environmental threats, whether they concern primarily human wellbeing or the productive potential of nature, are distributed highly unevenly in society. This is almost a platitude. We already discussed related issues in Chapters 4 and 5.

The benefits derived from the use of resources are also distributed unevenly, usually opposite to costs. Therefore a balancing of costs and benefits all too easily ignores that benefits accrue to some, usually those who can hire the cost/benefit analysts, while the costs fall on others, usually those who are already disadvantaged and disempowered.

The fact of uneven distribution of threats and benefits has several implications. First of all, those who benefit from the production of hazards or can avoid hazards naturally try to downplay them. For instance, the myth is wide-spread in some parts of the world that climatic warming would make life easier. While this is disputable even as a technical prediction – increase in mean temperature simply does not equal the climate becoming more favorable – it is a wishful illusion on the societal level. A very small global warming trend, displacing the westerlies winds toward the poles, changing rainfall patterns and growing seasons, might improve conditions in some areas at the expense of others, but the social consequences of a considerable warming would certainly be negative the world over. The geographical unevenness both of natural conditions and power of course imply that any climatic change will have consequences that are redistributed internationally, giving different governments unequal interests in averting the changes or their effects.

A more fundamental implication of the unevenness of threat is that ecological problems are internally tied up with social relations. All assessments of ecological problems, and every design of a sustainable future for humankind must take stands with regard to injustice and inequality. The future of humanity simply cannot build on pleasant life for a few and suffering for the majority.

This principle should influence definitions of and approaches toward specific problems. Take the biodiversity crisis and Amazonian rainforest. The problem is unsolvable without a firm commitment to guaranteeing decent conditions of life to the local people. Similarly, the success of conservation in South Africa is tied up with the fate of apartheid. The South-African government has aimed at buying goodwill in the world with nature protection programs which sometimes directly violate the rights of local people, but there is a time-bomb hidden in such programs – it will prove fatal if nature protection becomes viewed in Africa as another form of foreign oppression.

The social dimensions of a large class of ecological problems thus merge with traditional issues of social class, poverty and inequality. This is particularly true of Third World problems. Humanity will suffer from the heritage of colonialism for a long time to come. Every honest human being can agree upon this connection. After Auschwicz, Western people have no justification whatever for staying detached, or for imagining that cruel oppression is a characteristic of 'less-developed' cultures and mentalities but does not concern us.

It is exactly at this point that the most frightening prospect concerning the social consequences of the ecological crisis arise. This is the prospect of an overt and violent preservation of the privileges of Euro-North-Americans in control over the resources of the earth, the prospect that people on other continents will be made to suffer the consequences of what is done in Europe and North America. It is fair to remember that this prospect is becoming reality with, for instance, the refusal of the US government to take the greenhouse effect seriously. The Gulf war is a part of this scenario too.

In the highly industrialized countries the social setting of ecological problems is new, however. This is due to several factors. One reason is a growing awareness that there is ultimately no escape from the genuinely global threats. Another reason is the versatile and nebulous character of the ecological crisis. The crisis calls forth fundamental changes in Western society and culture, but the changes required cannot be identified. This contradiction may readily result in an impotent *Weltschmerz*; this relates to the notion of 'risk society' of Ulrich Beck (see Chapter 6).

Existing social structures are at present clearly unable to cope with the problems at hand; consider the records of the Reagan–Bush or Thatcher–Major administrations. But of course this will, to some extent, change. Ecology and the environment will be superimposed upon the society as a new set of constraints, and a new 'technology of the environment' will be established in a similar fashion as a 'technology of hygiene and health' was established in the eighteenth century. This will mean measures that are, apparently, simply necessary and rational in securing order in society. But social order is never innocent as regards social power. 'Technology of the environment' will create new structural elements of power, analogously to the structures of power inherent in the control of physical or mental health; this perspective we can recognize thanks to the work of Michel Foucault (summarized in his *Power/Knowledge*, 1980).

When power is tied to apparently innocent structures maintaining rational order and common good in society, it is constitutive of views and behavior of people; it is not only power as the capacity of somebody to rule over somebody else. That 'nature' is deeply merged with such constitutive structures of social power is nothing new. Mary Douglas (1975) argued that 'nature' is an important element in the power structures of primitive societies, for instance, in purity myths. 'Natural dangers' have been socially defined and they have set checks on what actions are possible. In male dominated societies an efficient way of securing the sexual fidelity of the wife while leaving the behavior of the husband unconsidered is to postulate a 'natural danger' to which female physiology is exposed; for instance, that the wife's infidelity will hurt the children.

The ways in which 'nature' is incorporated into structures of power in the era of the ecological crisis will of course be new. The crisis can be used as an argument for a deep-going control of people's actions. Indeed, a tendency toward environmental policing on the global scale is already detectable. We do not know how the structures of order and power will look like in detail. But we can already identify two contrasting, fundamental alternatives: either 'order' to maintain social privileges and inequalities, or 'order' through increasing public discussion, participation, democracy and empowerment of the people.

The Spectrum of Problem Definitions

'Facts' do not speak out, it is the significance of facts – for whom and for which purpose? – that matters. Consequently, in all assessments of ecological problems the context of interpretation is critical. Controversies about ecological problems are controversies about a proper interpretative context.

Problems and risks are recognized and their severity assessed through social mechanisms. It is easy for us to accept the analysis of Mary Douglas that 'natural dangers' in primitive societies are inherently tied up with power structures within those societies. It is equally easy to extend the conclusion to, say, medieval views of illness and sorcery, but we tend to deny the validity of the conclusion concerning our modern culture. This is naturally completely unjustified (Douglas and Wildavsky, 1982).

An important, new element in the perception of ecological risks in society is the growing role of environmental movements. Movements are, by and large, subjects that are able to define ecological risks in public awareness. This explains the serious weight given to control of movements in governing quarters all over the world. This also explains the rapid divergence of 'environmentalism' from the fairly homogeneous concern in the late 1960s and early 1970s to the present, bewildering array of movements that define problems in very different ways; these are considered below.

Environmental reformism

Since the early part of the century, enlightened capitalist developers and apolitical conservationists have been concerned about the rational exploitation of resources for long-term development. As ecological problems multiply, this current has become more visible and informs most established organizations and campaign groups. The challenge is seen as regulating greed for its own ultimate good. Since a market economy is itself taken for granted, the greatest ingenuity is devoted to finding ways to make the market behavior of self-seeking individuals or companies work out for the common good. There are several major variants with different views as to the antagonism or harmony of interests and the appropriate means for improving practice:

[1] Ecology is everybody's job; we all pollute whether on micro- or macro-scale. Blame rests with 'us'. Therefore we should all be committed to moderation in consumption, recycling wastes, picking up litter. A rational world arises as increasing numbers of people behave rationally. The thing to do is to educate and set a good example. This variant allows corporations to join in the Earth Day festivities and praise their own commitment to 'the environment'.

[2] Action is also needed through government. Legislative and legal initiatives can regulate harmful practices and contain greed. Communities must organize to prevent corporate interests from being short-sighted and from overwhelming the concerns of the politically marginalized. Therefore the potential political power of the people has to be made actual by laws about making information public, requiring consultation with affected communities, and expansion of effective grass-roots democracy. Then we can raise the costs to the destroyers to the point where their own self-interest will impose ecologically sound practices.

[3] Technocratic. People are ignorant, not well informed enough or intelligent enough to grasp the complexity of the world. They misconceive or over-simplify problems. What is needed is more objective analysis using cost/benefit models in which ecological concerns are balanced against 'the economy' or competitive position. This view is popular among scientists who see themselves as the advisors of 'decision makers' toward whom they maintain a slightly condescending but non-antagonistic stance. Credibility is the highest asset, not to be squandered by putting forth far-out ideas.

Although these variants are listed separately they coexist in the same people in a loosely articulated reformist ideology congenial to a sector of those in power, their actual or potential advisors, and liberals caught between their commitment to 'the system' and repugnance at its behavior. (For an analysis of US environmentalism, see for example, Schnaiberg, 1980.)

Radical community movements

These often arise out of the perception that people in a particular locality are being poisoned or their livelihood or neighborhood is being destroyed. Their stance is therefore confrontational at the start, seeing their adversary as either the public or private destroyers or the government's complicity or indifference. Starting from very local particular concerns, they often expand their scope to explore the 'environmental problem' more globally.

The political cultures of community movements are variable and typically reflect popular traditions of each country. The movements have been relatively strong in the US, where the civil rights movement was an important recent background (Boyte, 1984). In Europe local alternative movements have been particularly important in Germany, as a reaction to the corporativism of the political system, and in countries with long liberal traditions such as the Netherlands and Denmark. The alternative movements in West Germany were important in the early stages of the German green party (Spretnak and Capra, 1985), but in other countries the ties between community groups and parliamentary actions of green parties have been loose or absent.

Third World environmentalism

This starts from the perception that the destruction of natural resources or the dumping of toxic waste or the pushing of pesticides or the export of hazardous industries is done by foreign, colonial exploiters and their inheritors on behalf of foreign investors. It is sometimes an autonomous movement defending part of the nation's wealth as in Mexican biologists' opposition to the drug companies' plunder of medicinal plants or Puerto Rican opposition to polluting industries, or may be linked to anti-imperialist political movements. It sometimes merges with nationalisms that challenge the justifications for exploitation and development from the perspective of defending indigenous culture against alien value systems. While some variants favor rapid development controlled locally for local benefit, others counterpose the virtues of village life. Environmental problems of the Third World countries – degradation of land, hunger, plunder of forests, pollution – are typically viewed in broader contexts of world economy and development strategies; recent accounts can be found in Caufield (1986) and George (1976, 1988).

In India this debate is particularly sophisticated. Do we criticize 'Western' science or 'modern' science, its misuse or its underlying philosophy, Western culture or modernity, development or vulgar development (for example, Goonatilake, 1982, 1984)? The memory of Mahatma Gandhi is ever present, and he is invoked by opposing sides for different arguments. Also the Bhopal catastrophe was important in India by demonstrating the hazards brought to Third World countries by the activities of multinationals (Everest, 1985).

Ecofeminism

The basic insights are that modern capitalist man has broken the organic unity with nature that guided previous thinking and feeling about nature, that an ideology justifying exploitation, domination, conquest and so on makes science and technology a destructive, masculinist and exploitive force, that women are regarded as in some way more natural beings, closer to nature and treated the way nature is treated. Therefore sexism and the destruction of nature are linked ideologically. A way out would be a society guided by feminist ways, organic rather than fragmented, nurturing rather than exploitative, uniting thinking with feeling. Carolyn Merchant (1980, 1989) emphasizes the interdependence of production and reproduction in shaping the interchange between society and nature; see also Griffin (1978).

Deep Ecology

A life-centered rather than human-centered solidarity with all living things or with 'the planet' sees all civilizations as going beyond our rightful modest place in nature, so that we are a weed species like the Norwegian rat or Russian thistle. Our goal should be to retreat to a less intrusive way of life informed by harmony with nature, sometimes with strong spiritual overtones. Ancient hunters and gatherers are seen as the last legitimate society. The movement was founded by the Norwegian philosopher Arne Naess and has found many adherents particularly in North America (see for example, *The Ecologist* Vol. 18, No 4/5, 1988). Some variants are social Darwinist and applaud famine or the AIDS epidemic as nature's ways of restoring balance. Others are less misanthropic. Deep ecologists have often engaged in militant direct action to protect forests.

Social Ecology

A primarily North American movement connected with the name of Murray Bookchin (1982). It sees 'domination' as the central injustice, with capitalist exploitation as one particular expression of domination. Social ecologists attempt to derive lessons for society from nature. For example, they emphasize the mutual dependence of species in ecosystems as urging cooperative social arrangements. They see this mutual dependence as prohibiting hierarchical structures. Promulgators of social ecology are not biological determinists since the core of their program comes from social analysis, but they do give greater weight to ecological imperatives than do Marxists. Social ecologists have also been influenced strongly by (eco)feminism.

Marxist Approaches

Marxism has been an important stimulus behind several of the directions mentioned above – community and Third World movements, feminism, social ecology – but there is not one unified Marxist approach to nature.

Historical materialism emphasizes the inseparability and yet distinctness of our species, the interconnectedness of what we do in the world and what happens. It also looks at science as a social product. This encouraged a critical scepticism toward capitalist science and technology which might have led to the self-conscious search for alternative pathways.

But Marxist movements were also strongly influenced by 'progressivism' and scientific optimism inherited from the Enlightenment.

In capitalist countries, socialist labor movements concentrated on jobs and contracts so that the expansion of production was always seen as desirable. In socialist countries the critique of science came into conflict with the predominant politics. The holistic focus of Marxism led to very farsighted legislation in the Soviet Union in the 1920s aimed at protecting nature and planning for integral development of regions. These laws were also emulated in the Eastern European socialist countries after the Second World War. However, the environmental reality has proven grim everywhere in Eastern Europe. Ecologically imaginative measures coexisted with the most flagrant disregard for the environmental laws. The laws were praised but not enforced, and fines for violations of the law were built into the costs of production of many enterprises.

The full power of the dialectical and historical approach of Marxism remained a marginal influence, strong in theoretical studies and in rhetoric but very limited in guiding national policy. The theoretical critique of capitalist science, under conditions of top down leadership, easily turned into a caricature of itself imposed rather than debated, a fertile field for opportunists to build careers around 'correct' ideology. This had disasterous results in Soviet genetics from the late 1930s to the mid 1950s.

But despite the perversions of Marxism in Eastern Europe, and to some extent in direct opposition to it, there has been a growing body of Marxist thought which sees the relations with nature as inseparable from social development and includes environmental struggles in its vision of a struggle for socialism and its vision of the future.

What is common to almost all variants of environmentalism is a new way of understanding the political. It is not formal positions in the decision-making apparatus that matters, but influence on public opinion and behavior, popular participation. Indications of the change in body politics include, on the surface, the growth of green parties, the growing green of old parties and the attempts by even the most polluting industries to co-opt Earth Day. At the heart of the process is the increasing role of movements and popular initiative on the one hand, and mistrust of old political structures on the other. Here ecology joins hands with other issues such as race and gender. Is green a path to red?

The green parties, with their activities circling around the agenda of the parliament, are faced by a dilemma that stems from the heterogeneity of ecological problems and, in particular, their social dimensions: how to create a political subject out of ecological movements? Is it possible? And of course we need to add: Is it desirable? Or is it rather the case that ecological problems underline with a new force basic demands such as democratic participation, and environmental movements bring their own contribution to the strengthening of democratic movements and procedures?

Quite obviously consciousness alone is not sufficient but it must be grounded on real comprehension of and experience about the society. We can perceive an analogy with feminism: some feminists argued that history will enforce feminism. However, it was later realized that issues have to be raised prior to their ripening into crises, and crises do not automatically lead to positive outcomes but they can be solved in different ways. Conscious social involvement and continuous struggle are needed.

Local Versus General Solutions?

Problems need concrete solutions, in this sense they are always unique. We are not interested in probability distributions of environmental hazards, but in avoiding particular hazards. Ultimately we want to maintain conditions favorable for human life and wellbeing on the only earth we know.

This situation specificity creates tensions with our accepted ways of thinking. The ideal of modern science is universality, but this is problematic in the face of variable and unique, local situations. Adequate addressing of ecological problems requires participation on the local level, not control by specialists from the outside. For instance, the site-specificity of ecological conditions opens up possibilities for a diversified agriculture taking advantage of local opportunities, but this requires reorganization of agricultural practice on every level, as we discussed in Chapter 5. The requirements are analogous within other social practices.

The recognition of site specificity is not an argument against theoretical generalization; this would be a misuse both of the hetrogeneity of nature and of theory. The heterogeneity of nature is itself a major theoretical point, the starting point for understanding adaptation, diversity, distributions of organisms and strategies of production. Recommendations then do not take the form of 'always do this when growing corn': but rather, 'this is what to examine in deciding how to grow corn.'

The notion of scale is crucial in approaching the problem of specificity versus generalism. Intensive change at one site may be acceptable if the potential of life represented in that site is preserved on nearby sites. Criteria for evaluating intensive, localized activities such as industries and urban development come from their influence on external areas, the ecological consequences need to be scaled. It is no problem that a piece of land is covered by buildings in a city. Basically, a new habitat is created, not that different from unproductive natural habitats such as bare cliffs. But intensive exploitation indirectly influences surrounding areas, and therefore special measures for buffering such effects should be considered.

Scaling is also critical in traditional conservation activities such as preservation of biological diversity and individual species. In the short run the major task in conservation is to establish adequate preserves. This implies the task of defining criteria for the adequacy or inadequacy of preserves and preserve systems. In the long run, however, the future of ecological diversity is determined by what happens in areas that are under economic management. Preserves are not insulated from their human-modified environments – 'no park is an island', to paraphrase Daniel Janzen. The long-term task is to modify management practices everywhere such that preservation of ecological diversity is maximally taken care of. Until this is achieved, preserves may act as a bridge to the future.

Issues of appropriate scaling are among the fundamental theoretical challenges in the understanding of society–nature interactions; we have repeatedly come across the problems of ecological scaling in Chapters 2, 4 and 5.

Nature: Appropriation Versus Appreciation?

All my means are sane; my motives and objects mad.
Captain Ahab (Herman Melville)[3]

Some people would find it arrogant that we have explicitly taken the human standpoint in defining ecological problems. Would not 'health of nature' be a more adequate point of reference? Is it correct to give a privileged status to humans compared with other living beings?

Humans are in fact privileged precisely by asking the question about privileges. There is no escape from the human standpoint because it is the only standpoint available to us. But it is exactly the human standpoint that gives rise to ethical issues. Humans need to ponder upon the rights of lions, but do the lions ponder upon the rights of humans?

Ethics means conscious and simultaneous consideration of the goals and the means of human action. The human capacity for considering means and ends together was called 'practical reason' by Aristotle. 'Practical reason' evaluates in specific situations what kind of action would in that situation advance the attainment of aims that are valued and pursued. An element of 'practical reason' is thus included in all human decisions.

Ethical traditions are strongly historical, as emphasized by Alasdair MacIntyre (1985). The historicity stems from the dramatic historical variation in conditions under which people have lived. In the history of ethical thinking there is a cycle of means becoming goals; principles demanded as absolute goals are extracted from practical ones. For instance, democracy was originally conceived as a means for avoiding continuous clashes within the highly stratified Greek city communities, but was later transformed into a goal. Ethico–religious goals were originally means of keeping social groups coherent. The opposite of absolute ethics is not arbitrariness, but socio–historical imagination and sensitivity.

Some variants of ethical thinking, reaching back to the nineteenth century utilitarianism, tend to deny the historicity of ethical ideas and instead construct universal standards. Utilitarianism claimed that one commensurable criterion can be found for evaluating ethical consequences of human actions, called 'happiness' by Jeremy Bentham, and 'pleasure' by John Stuart Mill. It was supposed that every human action can be appraised by the sum-total of happiness that it entails to all persons involved. The search for ecological ethics is often based on utilitarianism by assuming that nature can be viewed as another participant in a situation of conflict, and different interests concerning nature can be compared using the same unit of measurement. In environmental economics this standard is simply money.

However, as MacIntyre points out, utilitarianism fails because different pleasures and different happinesses are to a large degree incommensurable. The notion of the greatest happiness of the greatest number is a notion without any clear content at all. Concerning the value of nature utilitarianism fails precisely for the same reason: nature means different things to different people. There is no way of adequately measuring the 'pleasure' derived by South African industrialists from extracting diamonds in the Kalahari against the 'pleasure' of the !Kung people living there.

We are advocating ethical principles concerning nature, but see no possibility for formulating absolute laws. Ethical principles grow from the realization that 'nature' is an internal prerequisite of human life and culture, and humans need to respect the general potential of life in nature. That is, nature is a value-in-itself as an inseparable part of human existence. This contrasts with a purely instrumental view of nature as providing 'external' means for reaching particularly defined goals.

This suggestion does not imply ahistoric norms of behavior toward 'nature' that would be applicable always and everywhere. This is because humans do not have general relationships with 'nature'. Humans have only specific relationships with nature, molded by specific social relationships and realized through specific practices. Thus, environmental ethics and norms of conduct towards nature are inseparably associated with historically constituted social practices. This connects our ethical considerations to the notion of ecohistory.

In more practical terms, respect for nature as a general potential of life means that human-induced irretrievable changes of nature that threaten this potentiality are proscribed. Changing nature is not *per se* ethically forbidden for humans – indeed, how could it possibly be, as humans are equally dependent on exploiting the environment as all other organisms? We need to avoid misuse of ideals such as 'passivity is harmony and balance and equals good, use is exploitation and disruption and equals bad.'

Ethics merges with practical considerations, which is what the Aristotelian 'practical reason' is all about. Practical experiences and considerations also modify ethical views. Ethical views shared among community members help to preserve social cohesion – this is the view proposed by Emile Durkheim. But ethical views also draw upon knowledge. For instance, ecology can help in evaluating what kind of modification of a particular habitat leads to loss of the potential of life. The type of answers that can be given to this type of questions is important, namely, ecological knowledge emphasizes preparation for the unexpected and adoption of safety margins that are not derivable from short-term utilitarian calculations. A broader view of 'nature' than promulgated by utilitarian calculations is needed.

Somebody may wonder whether we mix 'values' with 'facts' and thus violate the principle known as the Humean guillotine, that facts and values must be distinguished from each other. We indeed do, because the 'Humean guillotine' is obsolete. The conception that facts are value-free is a misunderstanding which ultimately derives from a false notion of a 'fact' (see MacIntyre, 1985). 'Facts' are not atomic entities that we become aware of one by one through our sensual perceptions, as imagined by eighteenth century empiricists. 'Facts' are statements created about states of affairs that are of concern to human existence and wellbeing. Such statements cannot possibly be ethically neutral. From the fact that lack of adequate nutrition for poor people in New York causes illness and suffering it follows an ethical demand to allow those people to improve their nutritional situation. From the fact that forest cutting in tropical countries is an immediate threat to the potential of life and ecological diversity on the earth it follows an ethical demand to stop unscrupulous destruction of tropical forests. And so on, and so on.

Perspectives for Action

Those who will ultimately effect change are the known and unknown heroes and heroines, from North and South, working to show that democratic development is possible. Susan George[4]

Ecological problems must be analysed in their concrete totality, that is, with the aim of identifying serious problems and finding solutions to them. Perspectives for action derive from several sources and need to be formulated on several levels.

Formulate positive metaphors
Because society is not transparent, claims about social and societal prospects have the nature of metaphors. The importance of metaphors has been emphasized by many feminists both concerning our relationship with nature (Merchant, 1980) and our scientific thinking (Harding, 1986). Metaphors are different from formulating 'blueprints' – which is impossible because specific requirements do not come out of ecology. Positive metaphors indicate the direction we ought to take, they do not specify the steps. For instance, the notion of 'sustainable development' is best understood as a metaphor standing for a different trajectory for global development from the one we experience today.

But once a metaphor becomes popular, it becomes a battleground for interpretation. We discussed conflicting definitions of sustainability in Chapter 5.

Social metaphors are backed by ideological commitments. The spread of capitalism and the most wanton destruction of nature have been supported by an ideology of domination and conquest. And socialists have inherited some of the same beliefs and have often continued with similar practices. It is therefore necessary to take these ideas into account and challenge them.

The question we have to confront at this point is, are harmful ideas a necessary derivative of particular social systems or are they more or less autonomous causes of social practice? Can we hope to stop the destruction of nature by changing how people think about nature, or must this be accompanied by changing the social relations that make that thinking seem 'natural'? But if social relations must be changed first, what role does changing ideas have in changing society? Clearly these are political questions of really basic importance.

It is possible that the answer to these questions will be different for different societies. The competitive, aggressive, dominating view of nature is consistent with the norms and values of capitalist society and is reinforced by capitalist experience. The boundaries of legal liability readily define the boundaries of concern, so that impacts for which a company is not formally held responsible are of little interest. They are dumped onto society as a whole. Environmental protection measures can be evaded, resisted or defied with the justification that they create employment, as if there were not more useful things to do, build, clean or create.

There is much talk today about 'the market' or 'the free market'; these are widely used apologetic expressions for capitalism. But the notion of 'free market' is another metaphor, used to give a positive connotation to capitalism as a system. What is ignored all too often is that capitalist markets are not 'free'. Fernand Braudel in his *Civilization and Capitalism*, defended the contrasting view that monopolization of markets is a diagnostic characteristic of capitalism. In his view 'market economy' is a broader term than capitalism; markets have existed everywhere as a necessity for exchanging products between and within societies.

The regulation of the market has been a major activity of the state for a long time now. But in addition, the markets are controlled by the major participants in the market. In the United States, hundreds of thousands of farmers buy their equipment from a handful of machinery manufacturers and chemical and seed suppliers (the seed companies being in large measure subsidiaries of the chemical companies). They sell grain and soybeans and vegetables and meat to a relatively few buyers such as Cargill, Campbell's, MacDonald's and Kentucky Fried Chicken. The market is a place where people come with unequal power, and exchange goods and labor at rates determined by these inequalities.

These inequalities are even more striking in international trade where the gap between the costs of manufactured goods and raw materials has widened to the increasing disadvantage of the former colonial countries. Departures from this increasingly unequal exchange are regarded as 'subsidies'. The widening of the price gap is a basic reason for the debt crisis of the 1980s which has demonstrated the inadequacy of the prevailing, developmental approach toward Third World problems (George, 1988).

The enthusiasts of 'the market' also ignore monopoly, the concentration of production in the hands of very few producers who might agree among themselves explicitly or by monitoring each others' decisions to leave certain options out of bounds for competition and to combine efforts to prevent regulation.

The behavior of an entrepreneur seeking to maximize profits may lead to many different investment decisions: increase production; reduce production and the labor force; reduce costs of production by engineering measures or wage cuts or tighter supervision; increase sales efforts; invent a new product; improve the quality of a product; degrade the quality of raw materials; or manipulate financial instruments and taxes. Some outcomes of these decisions may benefit consumers while others are clearly harmful. The point is that they have no necessary relation to what they do to people, let alone to nature.

The present state of nature on a global scale is the result of the operation of the market over the last 500 years especially. It seems that a market economy can sometimes promote expansion of production and innovation, but has never increased equality or spontaneously used natural resources to promote human ends. It has proven highly efficient on a small scale, at the level of a single enterprise and within the confines of its own book-keeping, but grossly inefficient at the global scale.

'Planning' is another social metaphor. The naiveté of recent socialist planning has been the assumption that once something is decided it will happen; that information used to develop the plan is accurate; that the methods of planning take into account everything that should be considered both globally and locally; that the planners act only to meet social needs as efficiently and fairly as possible; that the administrators of enterprises within the plan act to provide the most accurate information possible; and that the plan has the flexibility to meet new situations and to encourage innovation.

The centrally planned economies have been most successful in the allocation of national priorities toward perceived national needs. They have succeeded in developing social consumption and relative equity in the face of scarcity. But they have been notoriously inefficient at the level of enterprises. The various indices of performance that were intended to make local goals coincide with public ones almost always leave a gap between the two which allows enterprises or their directors to maximize the income-generating indices without really meeting the goals for which they were designed. This discrepancy accumulated into serious structural distortions in the whole national economy, for instance, in the Soviet Union.

The first political reaction in Eastern Europe following the fall of old regimes there in 1989 seems to be a fierce defense of what people think is 'free market capitalism' (supported by a conscious policy of Western powers, tied to their economic aid, see Gowan, 1990). Socialist perspectives became equated with the policies of the oppressive regimes that were in power, and when the regimes are gone, farewell to the perspective. However, capitalist reality has already proven grim compared with the unrealistic expectations, and it is largely a matter of political visions and perspectives as to which direction peoples' thinking will take in the future.

We are witnessing a struggle of contradictory metaphors. Launching of positive metaphors is participating in this struggle. But of course they ought to be substantiated on other levels of societal activities.

Integrate general principles with specific social practices
Integrating ecology into social development is a joint challenge for ecology, social planning, and engineering and industrial design. The first need is to formulate questions that relate to practices in different spheres of activity. No specified conclusions can be derived from general principles.

A particular task is diversification of the role of planning and markets relative to each other: capitalist exploitation and one-plan command-economy are not the only alternatives. The unit of production and unit of planning are not the same. Unit of remuneration is larger than the unit of production. That is, productive units should have free space for decisions, on this level competition and markets enhance innovation and strategic planning within single companies, which is also positive for the environment. But constraints should be set not only from the market but also from societal principles such as: first, production so that it takes care of people's demands; second, bans on dangerous production; and third, collective needs must be subsidized because they do not create the 'effective demand' required according to a market economy ideal.

Local production may be necessary even though it would not be equally profitable as complete division of labour among specialized regions. This is to avoid intermediate costs (transportation, storage losses both in quantity and in quality) and also to preserve productive potentialities; as a hedge against uncertainty; to even the use value of products; and to ensure uniform demand of labour at all localities.

Disasters are likely in routine operations. An event of very low probability becomes virtually inevitable given enough opportunities. This emphasizes care: if you cannot get rid of it, do not make it; and asking: is this really necessary?

Be aware of individual actors in social processes

We need to look at contexts in which people's actions and ideas develop together and possibly feed back to the society. Productive units form a critical link in which autonomy and consciousness develop together. This is clear to the Third World critics of modern development: equity, empowerment, democracy and participation are seen as imperatives that increase people's ability to act. Sigmund Freud triggered a revolution in our view of human action by discovering the submerged layers of the unconscious which influence the behavior of each individual. But human individuals mold themselves through the very activities they get involved in. Practical action is the starting point for the emancipatory educational program of, for instance, Paulo Freire.

There are also social elements involved. Success in economic activities allowed and supported by the prevailing system is very much tied to people's sense of worth, especially for men. And the opportunity to reinforce one's sense of self is easily transformed into an ideal goal. Freedom is seen as equivalent to the opportunity to advance, conquer, dominate and compete. Therefore additional feedbacks among ideas and practices link the beliefs to the real social necessities of their advocates. This does not mean that people are incapable of acting from a perspective that is much broader than their narrow economic interest, and in fact they often do. But two types of feedbacks operate against these dissident viewpoints prevailing. If a public corporation fails to achieve maximum profit levels its leadership will be called into question by its stockholders or by financiers capable of organizing a takeover. Or if the owners agree to a non-aggressive, humane policy the company itself may go under.

There are many historical examples of individuals or groups who refused to go along with the unbridled pursuit of economic self-interest. The colony of Pennsylvania was led by Quakers for a long time, and maintained relatively peaceful relations with the Native Americans. But the expanding colonial capitalism was on a collision course with its neighbors. The interests of the two systems of living became increasingly incompatible, and the Quakers, unable to sacrifice either their economic interests or their peaceful ideology, withdrew from government.

The history of the Catholic Church in colonial Latin America is another example. While its religious faith called for acceptance of the native population as brothers in Christ, its links to Spanish and Portuguese mercantilism made it an ally of the conquerors. Individual priests such as Bartolomé las Casas exposed the brutality of the conquest and agitated for constraints on the abuse of the conquered. The Spanish government even decreed various rules aimed at ameliorating the sufferings and destruction of the subject peoples. But these were generally ignored, and beliefs more compatible with the needs of the conquerors prevailed.

All colonial powers had ways of legitimizing their conquests although the particular legitimizations varied according to the traditions of each culture. Expansion could be justified as a Christianizing mission to save souls, as the white man's burden to spread civilization, as Manifest Destiny, as the right of a superior race needing *Lebensraum*, or to defend democracy, free enterprise and human progress. Alternative beliefs challenging these dominant views would be seen as illegitimate, subversive, impractical, or irrelevant, and dismissed from serious consideration with or without reprisals against their advocates. They survive around the edges, as minor themes troubling the consciences of those who partly uphold them, and in 'fringe' groups that are effectively shut out from power.

It follows then that the beliefs that justify conquest, domination and plunder are not sufficient causes for those behaviors but are closer to being consequences of them. But the structures of cultural consciousness are not really understood. What is obvious is that they are grounded in practical life situations; they create differences between different cultures; they mold the relationship of societies to the environment; and they influence international relationships.

We suspect that basic ingredients in the justification of the international system today, not precisely known for its equity, are slogans and metaphors such as 'democracy' and 'free enterprise', supported by a Western biased view of 'human progress'. This is very different from the genuine solidarity that is needed.

Trust in popular participation
Popular participation is an imperative when the political systems of the future are envisaged. There is ample evidence that things go astray if it is lacking. Participation requires that preconditions for participation be met. Popular participation is a former 'means' becoming an 'end' in the era of the ecological crisis.

The political form must allow the mobilization of intelligence and creativity. Many features of social life around us give proof of the high capacity of 'common sense' to solve problems; but this creativity is directed to harmless activities such as sports because it is denied access to more relevant ones such as decisions concerning work. Popular participation requires an intellectual climate in which people have confidence in what they are doing.

Red and Green

Another event that was memorable to me was 'Fly', at Naiqua Gallery in Tokyo. People were asked to come prepared to fly in their own way. I did not attend.   Yoko Ono[5]

We need practical experience and not only formal ideas of favorable development. But simultaneously we clearly need long-term perspectives.

We elaborated in the preceding passages upon the relationships between cultural consciousness and social structures. A consequence of the analysis would be that the cause of environmental destruction under capitalism lies in the structure of that society rather than in bad ideas, and that changes in the structure would be necessary to stop destruction. This does not make questions of changing ideas unimportant, but the sequence would be changing ideas to change social structures to change environmental practice to change thinking about the environment.

But in that case, how do we account for the environmental destruction observed in socialist countries? Throughout the history of Soviet Union and East European socialism, the most rapid expansion of production has been a dominant concern of public policy. This ideological framework was reinforced administratively by a heavy, inflexible and inefficient organization of planning and by the ruthless suppression of the needs of human individuals or local cultural groups. Concern for the environment was administratively diffuse without a single strong power base, while destructive activities emanated from powerful ministries. On the level of cultural consciousness concern for the environment was fatally weakened by the suppression of popular initiative.

Although ideas themselves are not a sufficient explanation for major social trends, when political decisions shape the structure of a society they acquire a material base. Early Soviet perceptions about development, technology and science gave rise to decisions about the organization of production which produced a particular kind of stratification in society and created groups with interests distinct from those of the society as a whole. These groups then found the ideas which led to their creation to be congenial, and interest now reinforced theory. Those aspects of theory which conflicted with what they were doing for other reasons were abandoned completely. The decline of open debate after the first few years made criticism of the prevailing policies difficult, frustrating and even dangerous.

Meanwhile, the continuation of capitalist forms of organization of work continued to reinforce the alienation of labor from production. In the gap between the decline of capitalist motivation for work – the fear of unemployment – and the development of new collective social motivation, alienation persisted as indifference to production and the quality of the product. There have also been dramatic exceptions to this, periods of great enthusiasm and dedication, where voluntary labor has played an important part in production. But the problems of labor under socialism, how to combine autonomy and organization, security and discipline have not been solved on a large scale.

It was argued in Chapter 2 that environmental destruction and ecological irrationality are consequences of greed, poverty, and ignorance. Greed, institutionalized under capitalism as the demand for profit, is the dominant cause in developed capitalist countries. It reinforces a structured ignorance by determining the priorities of research and the disdain in high places of warnings.

In socialist countries, poverty and ignorance are dominant causes, with greed operating in a subordinate role through the narrow ambitions of administrators pursuing their personal goals. The ignorance is shared with capitalism through a shared science, but structured in a developmentalist framework. Therefore ecological irrationality is less built into socialist relations than inherited. If that is the case, it should be easier to win environmentalist battles in a socialist context.

Richard has participated in the struggles to promote ecological agriculture in Cuba; in the following we discuss briefly his experiences. During the early period (the 1960s and 1970s) pesticides were not only used widely but also seen as an indicator of progress. Awareness of their health impact was expressed through careful screening of the workforce. Workers who showed depressed acetylcholinesterase activity, a sign of organophosphate poisoning, were transferred to other work at the same pay. There was no real ecological presence although some of the botanists and zoologists had ecological ideas and some people were already issuing warnings. The botanists were especially vocal in opposing (unsuccessfully) the monoculture and clear-cutting technology of the forestry service. But the prevailing view was that ecological concerns, appropriate technology, polyculture and natural control were either backward-looking yearnings for the simple peasant life, flourishing among people who had never lived its harsh realities, or else luxuries for some future more prosperous economy. Progress was seen as adopting the 'most advanced' technologies.

By the 1980s several factors began to operate against this view. The harmful side of high-tech agriculture is not an economic externality under socialism but an internal cost. Therefore the balance sheet is different from that in capitalism. A community of self-conscious ecologists had arisen among the botanists and zoologists, and in the plant protection institutes and universities, who were actively educating the public and government about ecology. In 1980 the first Congress of Ecology was held which included not only botanists, zoologists and economic entomologists, but also representatives of polluting industries looking for ways to protect the environment and the tourist industry starting to think about nature as a resource for tourism. In 1987, the Institute of Systematics and Ecology was organized within the Academy of Sciences, and its physical plant constructed during 1988 by the staff of the institute.

Arguments about the wholeness, dynamic interconnection and complexity of the agroecosystem fell on more receptive ears than elsewhere because of the Marxist worldview. The philosophy was relevant in two ways: first, it insisted that science is a social product so that its theories, priorities, criteria of quality and methodologies must be seen not as dictated by nature but as the result of a strong interaction among natural phenomena, economic interest and the sociology and philosophy of scientists. This allowed for a sceptical look at what world science proclaimed as modern, countering the popular progressivist technocratic view which sees science and technology as developing along a single inevitable path.

The popularity of biological control was enhanced by a few dramatic successes involving the use of ants (*Tetramorium bicarinatum* and *Pheidole megacephala*), wasps and fungi, and trap cropping in the protection of crops. By the mid 1980s the Ministry of Agriculture had adopted biological pest control as one of its national scientific priorities, and the five year plan proposed the expansion of the area under natural and biological control.

Other developments in the economic and political spheres encouraged ecological approaches. The world economic crisis, with its decline in the prices received by Cuba compared to most imports, created a foreign exchange squeeze which led to efforts to reduce imports. The costs of pesticides compared to biological control agents began to weigh more heavily among economists.

At the same time, in the context of a general turn to the left, Cuban political leaders began to criticize narrow specialization in education and urged administrators to look at the whole impact of their decisions, not only the balance sheet. This injunction conflicts with the urgency to obtain or save foreign exchange, giving rise to a very fluid situation. But it generally seems to be the case within socialist countries that leftward turns of politics place greater weight on the long term and encourage ecological measures while shifts to the right, favoring the criterion of economic returns, promote short-sighted exploitation.

Socialism is a less stable system than most of us thought a few years ago. Concrete realizations of socialism are in trouble. But this does not of course mean that capitalism is a viable system. Neither does it mean that no viable alternatives to capitalism can be envisaged.

We believe in the necessity of socialism, but do not derive this view from ecology. We believe that a society capable of long-term planning on human terms is a historical necessity. However, the basic arguments for socialism stem from social considerations lying outside the scope of this book (for an elaboration, see Levins, 1990).

Nor can we prescribe the particular kind of socialism, how to resolve the contradictory demands on a rational and equitable society. Our reluctance to prescribe is not simply timidity in the face of tragic experience. In part, any specific program would depend on a social and political argument which we have not developed in this book rather than on ecological principles alone. But most importantly, we do not think that there is an *a priori* formula for a future society. The kinds of organization that would be successful in one place and time would be disasterous in others. In order not to thwart social and ecological goals, local autonomy must also presuppose solidarity across localities. The right to decide requires the capacity, information and self-confidence to decide well. The possibility of making decisions based on their long-term consequences requires at a minimum that the short-term is more or less secure, and so on.

What Engels wrote about the future of the family applies as well to the future of the society:

> What may we anticipate about the adjustment of sexual relations after the impending downfall of capitalist production is mainly of a negative nature and mostly confined to elements that will disappear. But what will be added? That will be decided after a new generation has come to maturity: a race of men who never in their lives have had any occasion for buying with money or other economic means of power the surrender of woman; a race of women who have never had any occasion for surrendering to any man for any other reason but love, or for refusing to surrender to their lover from fear of economic consequences. Once such people are in the world, they will not give a moment's thought to what we today believe should be their course.
>
> (Engels, 1986)

Engels' archaic Victorianism only reinforces his argument against prescribing for the future.

But although we cannot propose a particular way that society must be organized, we can outline some of the criteria for that society.

[1] Our relationship with nature must be developed thoughtfully and consciously as a principal human objective. It cannot be left as the

accidental by-product of the pursuit of other goals, whether these be private aggrandizement or a public imperative to produce. Nor can it be an afterthought, a secondary appendage to that pursuit. This applies equally to the parts of nature that we conserve untouched and the parts that we use and live in.

[2] The goal of a rising standard of living cannot be identified with increasing consumption of energy and raw materials. Rather, after the meeting of some basic needs which people will have to decide on, further progress will have to emphasize the improvement of the quality of life.

This could entail increasing the effort and thought devoted to caring for people, for our health, education, cultural life, opportunities for creative and healthful work and recreation. We expect that the richness of the natural world will be recognized as an important element in that quality of life, not only as resource but also as the medium within which our lives take place and which conditions our perceptions, our feelings and our physical selves. We will then be making very different decisions about the environment. These decisions will require careful evaluation based on understanding of both nature and ourselves. What we decide will also be determined by, and help to form, our culture, our attitudes and esthetics and values that guide the evaluation and that in the long run must be compatible with the decisions.

[3] The solving of the problems of our species' global relations with nature requires first of all a global community of interest based on equality among peoples and within peoples so that nature does not remain a battleground for the clashing of more particular interests and an instrument of domination. Secondly, it requires the mobilization of the collective intelligence of our species. No modern society has yet succeeded in tapping this collective intelligence although some have succeeded in rallying the collective energy, courage, enthusiasm and dedication.

The community of interest can only come about with the end of exploitation within and between nations and the elimination of racist, sexist and national chauvinist modes of oppression. As long as the benefits from using the environment go only to some and the costs are born by others it is not possible to arrive at rational decisions about how to use nature. As long as some regions are coerced by poverty into accepting the dumping of toxic wastes or allowing polluting industries, even the most democratic decision making only ratifies their subordinate state and negotiations end up in agreements that reflect not human need but relative power. As long as some live on the margin of survival, long-term concerns must seem to them a distant abstraction.

Only when there is a real equality can people have an individual and collective control of the conditions of their own existence which would allow for ecologically sensible decisions, and only then can they have ties of solidarity which permit this control to be exercised in compatible and reinforcing ways.

[4] Mobilization of the collective intelligence of humankind implies broad empowerment, a deeper notion than simple democracy. Empowerment includes the practical capacity, education, knowledge, self-confidence and finally formal opportunities to determine what happens. This in turn requires sufficient security to have the freedom for long-range considerations: decisions based on long-range considerations presume the short-range is taken care of.

In order for the creativity of our whole species to be included in the common enterprise of establishing a humane and ecologically sound way of life, there must be an end to those practices and beliefs which block the full participation of the members of the oppressed majority of humankind, undervalue their contributions, deprive them of access to the knowledge that would allow them to develop their potential, and sap their confidence.

Thus we must have a real common human interest and work together to promote that common interest. If we want ecological sanity we have to struggle for social justice.

The solutions of the complex problems of society and nature depend on a combination of the intimate knowledge people have from their own experience and the scientific knowledge that requires some distance from the particular. This suggests that we must reject the technocratic strategy of relying only on expertise and replace it with some combination of specialized knowledge and democratic participation. It also demands a rejection of the facile anti-intellectualism of some populist responses to academic elitism and to the placid technocratic complicity with injustice.

[5] The heterogeneity of nature demands sensitivity to the particular; the global interconnectedness requires understanding of the whole. This sets the agenda for working out appropriate ways of combining

local and central decision making. Neither a single universal uniform scheme nor completely independent local decision making are commensurate with the problems, rich interconnections, the uniqueness of the particular and yet the commonality of society–nature.

The uncertainties inherent in natural–social processes require diversity of thought and practice. After deciding what our best knowledge and wisdom suggests is the best course, we always have to consider, 'But what if we're wrong?'

This suggests a diversity of decision-making constituencies to allow for experimentation on different scales and to compensate for or challenge each others' biases. This diversity would provide alternatives for all of us in organizing our lives; many more options for organizing production, communities and social affairs than we can imagine now are likely to be tried somewhere, leading to a rich mosaic of patterns. We could therefore encourage diversity as a practical human strategy.

[6] Intellectual strategies for understanding the world should take into account the diversity, variability and uncertainty of nature and society. This should encourage us to avoid those abstractions which, presenting themselves as universal and self-evident, merely disguise the particularities of their origin. It should also argue against an obsession with precise prediction of where the world is going. There is not only one pathway of development, or even only one pathway of desirable development. Instead, our science should identify the contradictory processes that move society–nature on its course or displace it from its course, and project possible alternatives from which we can make informed choices. A future which is not determined is a call to the exercise of freedom.

References

Chapter 1

1. Friedrich Engels, *Dialectics of Nature*, International Publishers, New York (1940), pp. 291–2.

Chapter 2

1. Leo Rybak, *personal communication*.
2. Lawrence Ferlinghetti, *Open Eye, Open Heart*, New Directions, New York (1973).
3. Yuri Chernov, *The Living Tundra*, Cambridge University Press, Cambridge (1985), p. 193.
4. Herbert Simon, *The Sciences of the Artificial*, 2nd edn, MIT Press, Cambridge, Ma. (1982), p. 195.
5. Larry Niven, *Ringworld*.
6. A.A. Milne, *The House at Pooh Corner*, Methuen Children's Books (1928).
7. Raymond Williams, *Socialism and Ecology*, Socialist Environment and Resource Association, London.

Chapter 3

1. Marjorie Grene, in: Nancy J. Nersessian (ed.) *The Process of Science*, Martinus Nijhoff Publishers, Dordrecht, Holland (1987), p. 71.
2. Leo Rybak, *personal communication*.
3. Ian Hacking (1983), p. 210.
4. An anonymous Finnish biology professor.
5. Nelson Goodman, *Ways of Worldmaking*, Hackett Publ. Comp., Indianapolis (1978), p. 23.
6. Mary Hesse, in: John B. Thompson and David Held (eds), *Habermas. Critical Debates*, Macmillan, London (1982), p. 113.
7. Evelyn Fox Keller (1985), p. 5.

Chapter 4

1. *Leakage*.
2. J.B.S. Haldane, *oN BEing the rIGht SiZe and other essays,* Oxford University Press, Oxford (1985), p. 149.
3. Denis Diderot, *D'Alembert's Dream* (1769).
4. Isadore Nabi, *correspondence*.

Chapter 5

1. Oliver Goldsmith, *The Deserted Village* (1770).

Chapter 6

1. Bernard Williams, in: D.S. Bendall (ed.) *Evolution from Molecules to Men,* Cambridge University Press, Cambridge (1983), p. 558.
2. Isadore Nabi, *On the Tendencies of Motion* (no date).
3. Fernand Braudel (1984), p. 65.
4. Eric Wolf (1982), p. 3.

Chapter 7

1. Rosario Morales, *Getting Home Alive,* Firebrand Books, Ithaca, New York (1986).
2. Mary Douglas (1975), p. 231.
3. Herman Melville, *Moby Dick* (1851).
4. Susan George (1988), p. 270.
5. Yoko Ono, *Insound/Instructure,* Exhibition catalogue, Henie Onstad Arts Centre, Hovikodden, Norway (1990).

Bibliography

Allen, T.F.H. and Starr, T.B. (1982) *Hierarchy: Perspectives for ecological complexity*. University of Chicago Press, Chicago.

Anderson, P. (1974) *Passages from Antiquity to Feudalism*. New Left Books, London.

Andersson, M. (1976) 'Population ecology of the long-tailed skua (*Stercorarius longicaudus*)'. *Journal of Animal Ecology* 45:537–59.

Aristotle (1964) *Prior and Posterior Analytics*, translated by J. Warrington. J.M. Dent & Sons, London.

Åström, S. (1978) *Natur och byte. Ekologiska synpunkter på Finlands ekonomiska historia*. Söderström & C:o, Helsingfors.

Beck, U. (1986) *Risikogesellshcaft. Auf dem Weg in eine andere Moderne*. Suhrkamp Verlag, Frankfurt am Main.

Bernal, J.D. (1954) *Science in History*, vols 1–4. C.A. Watts & Co., London.

Birks, H.H., Birks, H.J.B., Kaland, P.E. and Moe, D. (eds) (1989) *The Cultural Landscape. Past, Present and Future*. Cambridge University Press, Cambridge.

Birks, H.J.B. (1986) 'Late-Quaternary biotic changes in terrestrial lacustrine environments, with particular reference to north-west Europe', pp. 3–65 in B.E. Berglund (ed.) *Handbook of Holocene Palaeoecology and Palaeohydrology*. John Wiley & Sons, New York.

Bleier, R. (1984) *Science and Gender. A Critique of Biology and Its Theories on Women*. Pergamon Press, New York.

Bookchin, M. (1982) *The Ecology of Freedom*. Cheshire Books, Palo Alto, California.

Boserup, E. (1965) *The Conditions of Agricultural Growth. The Economics of Agrarian Change under Population Pressure*. George Allen & Unwin, London.

Boyte, H.C. (1984) *Community Is Possible. Repairing America's Roots*. Harper & Row Publishers, New York.

Boytel, F. (no date) *La Geografia Aeolica de Orieste*. Planning Board of Santiago, Cuba.

Braudel, F. (1981) *Structures of Everyday Life. Civilization & Capitalism 15th–18th Century. Vol 1*. William Collins Sons & Co., London.

Braudel, F. (1982) *The Wheels of Commerce. Civilization & Capitalism 15th–18th Century. Vol 2*. William Collins Sons & Co., London.

Braudel, F. (1984) *The Perspective of the World. Civilization & Capitalism 15th–18th Century, Vol 3*. William Collins Sons & Co., London.

Brewster, B. (1987) *TE MOA. The life and death of New Zealand's unique bird*. Nikau Press, Nelson, New Zealand.

Brunov, B.B. (1980) 'O nekatoryh faunisticheskih gruppah ptits taigi Evrazii', pp. 217–54 in A.G. Voronov and N.N. Drozdov (eds) *Sovremennye problemy zoogeografii*. Nauka, Moskva.

Calow, P. and Berry, R.J. (eds) (1989) 'Evolution, ecology and environmental stress'. *Biological Journal of the Linnean Society* 37:1–187.

Caplan, A.L. (1988) 'Rehabilitating reductionism'. *American Zoologist* 28:193–203.

Carnap, R. (1938) 'Logical foundations of the unity of science'. *International Encyclopedia of Unified Science*, vol. 1. University of Chicago Press, Chicago.

Carson, R. (1962) *Silent Spring*. Fawcett Publications, Greenwich, Conn.

Caswell, H. (1989) *Matrix Population Models: Construction, Analysis and Interpretation*. Sinauer, Sunderland, Ma.

Caufield, C. (1986) *In the Rainforest*. Pan Books, London.

Chernov, Y. (1985) *The Living Tundra*. Cambridge University Press, Cambridge.

Clark, G. and Piggott, S. (1965) *Prehistoric Societies*. Hutchinson, London.

Commoner, B. (1971) *The Closing Circle*. Knopf, New York.

Connell, J.H. (1978) 'Diversity in tropical rainforests and coral reefs'. *Science* 199:1302–10.

Connell, J.H. and Slatyer, R.O. (1977) 'Mechanisms of succession in natural communities and their role in community stability and organization'. *American Naturalist* 111:1119–44.

Coope, G.R. (1987) 'The response of late quaternary insect communities to sudden climatic change', pp. 421–38 in J.H.R. Gee and P.S. Giller (eds) *Organization of Communities. Past and Present*. Blackwell Scientific, Oxford.

Cox, G.W. and Atkins, M.D. (1975) 'Agricultural ecology'. *Bulletin of the Ecological Society of America* 56(3):2–6.

Cronon, W. (1983) *Changes in the Land. Indians, Colonists, and the Ecology of New England*. Hill and Wang, New York.

Cronon, W. (1991) *Nature's Metropolis. Chicago and the Great West*. W.W. Norton & Co, New York.

Crosby, A.W. (1986) *Ecological Imperialism. The Ecological Expansion of Europe, 900-1900*. Cambridge University Press, Cambridge.

Davis, M.B. (1986) 'Climatic instability, time lags, and community disequilibrium', pp. 269–84 in Jared Diamond and Ted J. Case (eds) *Community Ecology*. Harper & Row, New York.

Delcourt, R.H., Delcourt, P.A. and Webb, T. (1983) 'Dynamic plant ecology: the spectrum of vegetational change in space and time'. *Quaternary Science Reviews* 1:153–75.

Douglas, M. (1975) *Implicit Meanings. Essays in Anthropology*. Routledge & Kegan Paul, London.

Douglas, M. and Wildavsky, A. (1982) *Risk and Culture. An Essay on the Selection of Technological and Environmental Dangers*. University of California Press, Berkeley.

Dyke, C. (1988) *The Evolutionary Dynamics of Complex Systems. A Study in Biosocial Complexity*. Oxford University Press, Oxford.

Egerton, F.N. (1973) 'Changing concepts in the balance of nature'. *Quarterly Review of Biology* 48:322–50.

Ehrlich, P. (1969) Reissued in G.A. Love and R.M. Love (eds) *Ecological Crisis. Readings for Survival*. Harcourt Brace Jovanovich, New York (1970).

Ellen, R. (1982) *Environment, Subsistence and System. The Ecology of Small-scale Social Formations*. Cambridge University Press, Cambridge.

Enemar, A., Nilsson, L. and Sjöstrand, B. (1984) 'The composition and dynamics of the passerine bird community in a subalpine birch forest, Swedish Lapland. A 20-year study'. *Annales Zoologici Fennici* 21:321–38.

Engels, F. (1986) *The Origin of the Family, Private Property and the State*. Penguin, Harmondsworth.

Enzensberger, H. (1973) 'Zur Kritik der politischen Ökologie'. *Kursbuch* 33.

Everest, L. (1985) *Behind the Poison Cloud*. Banner Press, Chicago.

Finley, M.I. (1983) *Politics in the Ancient World*. Cambridge University Press, Cambridge.

Forsman, E.D., Meslow, E.C. and Wight, H.M. (1984) 'Distribution and biology of the spotted owl in Oregon'. *Wildlife Monographs* 87:1–64.

Foucault, M. (1970) *The Order of Things. An Archaelogy of the Human Sciences*. Tavistock, London.

Foucault, Michel (1980), *Power/Knowledge. Selected Interviews and Other Writings 1972–1977*. Pantheon, New York.

Frege, G. (1892) 'Über Sinn und Bedeutung'. *Zeitschrift für Philosophie und philosophische Kritik* 100. English translation in H. Feigl and W. Sellars (eds) *Readings in Philosophical Analysis*. Appleton-Century-Crofts, NY.

Galeano, E. (1973) *The Open Veins of Latin America: Five Centuries of the Pillage of a Continent*. Monthly Review Press, New York.

George, S. (1976) *How the Other Half Dies: The Real Reasons for World Hunger*. Penguin, Harmondsworth.

George, S. (1988) *A Fate Worse than Debt*. Penguin, Harmondsworth.

Goonatilake, S. (1982) *Crippled Minds. An Exploration into Colonial Culture*. Vikas Publishing House, New Delhi.

Goonatilake, S. (1984) *Aborted Discovery. Science & Creativity in the Third World*. Zed, London.

Gowan, P. (1990) 'The pressure on East Europe'. *New Left Review* 182:63–82.

Greenway, J.C. (1967) *Extinct and Vanishing Birds of the World*. Dover, New York.

Grene, M. (1990) Perception and human reality, pp. 17–22 in Roy Bhaskar (ed.) *Harré and His Critics*. Blackwell, Oxford.

Griffin, S. (1978) *Woman and Nature: The Roaring Inside Her*. Harper & Row, New York.

Grime, J.P. (1989) 'The stress debate: symptom of impending synthesis?' *Biological Journal of the Linnean Society* 37:3–17.

Habermas, J. (1970) *Toward a Rational Society. Student Protest and Politics*. Beacon Press, Boston.

Hacking, I. (1975) *Why Does Language Matter to Philosophy?* Cambridge University Press, Cambridge.

Hacking, I. (1983) *Representing and Intervening. Introductory Topics in the Philosophy of Natural Science*. Cambridge University Press, Cambridge.

Haila, Y. (1983) 'Land birds on northern islands: A sampling metaphor for insular colonization'. *Oikos* 41:334–51.

Haila, Y. (1986) 'On the semiotic dimension of ecological theory: the case of island biogeography'. *Biology & Philosophy* 1:377–87.

Haila, Y. (1990) 'Toward an ecological definition of an island: a northwest European perspective'. *Journal of Biogeography* 17:561-8.

Haila, Y., Hanski, I.K. and Raivio, S. (1991) 'Turnover of breeding birds in small forest fragments in southern Finland: the "sampling" colonization hypothesis corroborated' (manuscript).

Haila, Y. and Järvinen, O. (1990) 'Northern conifer forests and their bird species assemblages', pp. 61–85 in Allen Keast (ed.) *Biogeography and Ecology of Forest Bird Communities*. SPB Academic Publishing, The Hague.

Haila, Y., Järvinen, O. and Kuusela, S. (1983) 'Colonization of islands by land birds: Prevalence functions in a Finnish archipelago'. *Journal of Biogeography* 10:499–531.

Hämet-Ahti, L. (1981) 'The boreal zone and its biotic subdivisions'. *Fennia* 159:69–75.

Hanski, I.K. and Haila, Y. (1988) 'Singing territories and home ranges of breeding Chaffinches: visual observation vs. radio-tracking'. *Ornis Fennica* 65:97–103.

Hansson, L. and Henttonen, H. (1985) 'Gradients in density variation of small rodents: the importance of latitude and snow cover'. *Oecologia (Berlin)* 67:394–402.

Hansson, L. and Henttonen, H. (1988) 'Rodent dynamics as a community process'. *Trends in Ecology and Evolution* 3:195–200.

Haraway, D.J. (1985) 'A manifesto for cyborgs: Science, technology, and socialist feminism in the 1980s'. *Socialist Review* 15(2):65–108.

Harding, S. (1986) *The Science Question in Feminism*. Open University Press, Milton Keynes.

Hare, F.K. (1954) 'The boreal conifer zone'. *Geographical Studies* 1:4–18.

Hassan, F.A. (1979) 'Demography and Archaeology. *Annual Review of Anthropology* 8:137–60.

Haukioja, E., Neuvonen, S., Hanhimäki, S. and Niemelä, P. (1988) 'The autumnal moth in Fennoscandia', pp. 163–78 in A.A. Berryman (ed.) *Dynamics of Forest Insect Populations. Patterns, Causes, Implications.* Plenum Press, New York.

Haukioja, E. and Niemelä, P. (1979) 'Birch leaves as a resource for herbivores: Seasonal occurrence of increased resistance in foliage after mechanical damage of adjacent leaves'. *Oecologia (Berlin)* 39:151–9.

Haukioja, E., Niemelä, P. and Sirén, S. (1985) 'Foliage phenols and nitrogen in relation to growth, insect damage, and ability to recover after defoliation, in mountain birch Betula pubescens spp tortuosa'. *Oecologia (Berlin)* 65:214–22.

Heinselman, M.L. (1973) 'Fire in the virgin forests of the Boundary Waters Canoe area, Minnesota'. *Quaternary Research* 3:329–82.

Helle, P. (1985) 'Habitat selection of breeding birds in relation to forest succession in Northeastern Finland'. *Ornis Fennica* 62:113–23.

Henttonen, H., Oksanen, T., Jortikka, A. and Haukisalmi, V. (1987) 'How much do weasels shape microtine cycles in the northern Fennoscandian taiga?' *Oikos* 50:353–65.

Hintikka, M.B. and Hintikka, J. (1986) *Investigating Wittgenstein.* Blackwell, Oxford.

Hobsbawm, E.J. (1962) *The Age of Revolution.* Weidenfeld and Nicolson, London.

Hobsbawm, E.J. (1975) *The Age of Capital 1848-1875.* Charles Scribner's Sons, New York.

Holling, C.S. (1973) 'Resilience and stability of ecological systems'. *Annual Review of Ecology and Systematics* 4:1–23.

Horsfall, J.G. and Cowling, E.B. (eds) (1977) *Plant Disease: an Advanced Treatise. Vol. II. How Disease Develops in Populations.* Academic Press, New York.

Hubbard, R., Henifin, M.S. and Fried, B. (eds) (1982) *Biological Woman – the Convenient Myth. A Collection of Essays and a Comprehensive Bibliography.* Schenkman, Cambridge, Ma.

Huntley, B. and Birks, H.J.B. (1983) *An Atlas of Past and Present Pollen Maps for Europe: 0–13000 Years Ago.* Cambridge University Press, Cambridge.

Hustich, I. (1974) 'Common species in the northern part of the Boreal Region of Canada. An essay'. *Rep. Kevo Subarctic Research Station* 11:35–41.

Illich, I. and Sanders, B. (1989) *The Alphabetization of the Popular Mind.* Penguin, Harmondsworth.

Iversen, J. (1941) 'Land occupation in Denmark's stone age'. *Danmarks Geologiske Undersogelse II* 66:1–68.

Jacob, F. (1982) *The Logic of Life. A History of Heredity.* Pantheon Books, New York.

Janzen, D. (1988) 'Ecological characterization of a Costa Rican dry forest caterpillar fauna'. *Biotropica* 20:120–35.

Järvinen, O. and Väisänen, R.A. (1976) 'Species diversity of Finnish birds, II: Biotopes at the transition between taiga and tundra'. *Acta Zoologica Fennica* 145:1–35.

Johnson, R.B. (1986) 'Human disease and the evolution of pathogen virulence'. *Journal of Theoretical Biology* 122:19–28.

Jussila, R. and Nuorteva, P. (1968) 'The ichneumonid fauna in relation to an outbreak of Oporinia autumnata (Bkh.) (Lep., Geometridae) on subarctic birches'. *Annales Zoologici Fennici* 5:273–5.

Kallio, P., Niemi, S. and Sulkinoja, M. (1983) 'The Fennoscandian birch and its evolution in the marginal forest zone'. *Nordicana* 47:101–10.

Kant, I. (1953) *Prolegomena to Any Future Metaphysics that Will be Able to Present Itself as Science*, translated by P. Gray Lucas. Manchester University Press, Manchester.

Karasek, R. (1989) 'Political implications of psychosocial work redesign: a model of psychosocial class structure'. *International Journal of Health Service* 19: 481–508.

Keller, E.F. (1985) *Reflections on Gender and Science*. Yale University Press, New Haven.

Kingsland, S.E. (1985) *Modeling Nature. Episodes in the History of Population Ecology*. University of Chicago Press, Chicago.

Kingsland, S.E. (1986) 'Mathematical figments, biological facts: Population ecology in the thirties'. *Journal of the History of Biology* 19:235–56.

Kirch, P.V. (1984) *The Evolution of the Polynesian Chiefdoms*. Cambridge University Press, Cambridge.

Kirikov, S.V. (1960) *Izmeneniya zhivotnogo mira v prirodnyh zonah SSSR*. Izd-vo AN SSSR, Moskva.

Kirikov, S.V. (1983) *Chelovek i priroda stepnoj zony, konets X – seredina XIX v (evropeiskaya tsastj SSSR)*. Nauka, Moskva.

Klausnitzer, B. (1988) *Verstädterung von Tieren*. A Ziemsen Verlag, Wittenberg Lutherstadt.

Koponen, S. (1976) 'Spider fauna (Araneae) of Kevo area, northernmost Finland'. *Rep. Kevo Subarctic Research Station* 13:48–62.

Koponen, S. and Linnaluoto, E.T. (1979) 'Flight periods and abundance of some moths caught by light traps in subarctic Finnish Lapland, 1972–78'. *Rep. Kevo Subarctic Research Station* 15:19–26.

Korpimäki, E. (1986a) 'Niche relationships and life-history tactics of three sympatric Strix owl species in Finland'. *Ornis Scandinavica* 17:126–32.

Korpimäki, E. (1986b) 'Gradients in population fluctuations of Tengmalm's owl *Aegolius funereus* in Europe'. *Oecologia (Berlin)* 69:195-201.

Kouki, J. and Häyrynen, U. (1991) 'On the relationship between distribution and abundance in birds breeding on Finnish mires: the effect of habitat specialization'. *Ornis Fennica* 68 (in press).

Koyré, A. (1965) *Newtonian Studies*. Johns Hopkins University Press, Baltimore.

Kuhn, T.S. (1962) *The Structure of Scientific Revolutions*, University of Chicago Press, Chicago.

Kuhn, T.S. (1977) *The Essential Tension. Selected Studies in Scientific Tradition and Change*. University of Chicago Press, Chicago.

Kujala, V. (1926) 'Untersuchungen über den Einfluss von Waldbränden auf die Waldvegetation in Nord-Finnland'. *Comm. Inst. Quaest. Forest. Finlandiae* 10(5):1–41.

Kuleshova, L.V. (1981) 'Ekologicheskie i zoogeographicheskie aspekti vozdejstvijah pozhzarov na lesnyh ptits i mlekopitayushsih'. *Zoologicheskij Zurnal* 60:1542–52.

Kullman, L. (1987) 'Long-term dynamics of high-altitude populations of Pinus sylvestris in the Swedish Scandes'. *Journal of Biogeography* 14:1–8.

Laine, K. and Henttonen, H. (1983) 'The role of plant production in microtine cycles in northern Fennoscandia'. *Oikos* 40: 407–18.

Laine, K. and Niemelä, P. (1980) 'The influence of ants on the survival of mountain birches during an Oporinia autumnata (Lep., Geometridae) outbreak'. *Oecologia (Berlin)* 47:39–41.

Larkin, P.A. (1978) 'Fisheries management – an essay for ecologists'. *Annual Review of Ecology and Systematics* 9:57–73.

Leeds, A. (1980) 'Systems level interaction in the Texas hill country ecosystem: structure, history and evolution', in *Beyond the Myths of Culture*. Academic Press, New York.

Leiss, W. (1972) *The Domination of Nature*. George Braziller, New York.

Levandowsky, W. and White, B.S. (1977) 'Randomness, time scales, and the evolution of biological communities'. *Evolutionary Biology* 15:69–161.

Levins, R. (1966) 'The strategy of model building in population biology'. *American Scientist* 54:421–31.

Levins, R. (1968) *Evolution in Changing Environments*. Princeton University Press, Princeton.

Levins, R. (1969) 'Some demographic and genetic consequences of environmental heterogeneity for biological control'. *Bulletin of the Entomological Society of America* 15:237–40.

Levins, R. (1973a) 'The limits of complexity', pp. 111–27 in Howard Pattee (ed.) *Hierarchy Theory. The Challenge of Complex Systems*. George Braziller, New York.

Levins, R. (1973b) 'Fundamental and applied research in agriculture'. *Science* 181:523–4.

Levins, R. (1974) 'Qualitative analysis of partially specified systems'. *Annals of the New York Academy of Sciences* 231:123–38.

Levins, R. (1986) 'Perspectives on IPM: From an industrial to an ecological model', in Kogan, M. (ed.) *Ecological Theory and Integrated Pest Management*. John Wiley & Sons, New York.

Levins, R. (1990) 'Eulogy beside an empty grave: Reflections on the future of socialism'. *Socialist Register*.

Levins, R. and Lewontin, R. (1980) 'Dialectics and reductionism in ecology'. *Synthese* 43:47–78.

Levins, R. and Lewontin, R. (1985) *The Dialectical Biologist*. Harvard University Press, Cambridge, Ma.

Lovelock, J.E. (1979) *Gaia: A New Look at Life on Earth*. Oxford University Press, Oxford.

MacArthur, R.H. and Wilson, E.O. (1967) *The Theory of Island Biogeography*. Princeton University Press, Princeton, N.J.

MacCormack, C. and Strathern, M. (eds) (1980) *Nature, Culture and Gender*. Cambridge University Press, Cambridge.

MacIntyre, A. (1985) *After Virtue. A Study in Moral Theory*. 2nd edn. Duckworth, London.

Mandelbaum, M. (1971) *History, Man, & Reason. A Study in Nineteenth-Century Thought*. Johns Hopkins University Press, Baltimore.

Marcuse, H. (1988) *Negations. Essays in Critical Theory*. Free Associations Books, London.

Martin, B. (1979) *The Bias of Science*. Society for Social Responsibility of Science, Canberra.

Martin, P.S. and Klein, R.G. (eds) (1984) *Quaternary Extinctions. A Prehistoric Revolution*. University of Arizona Press, Tucson.

May, R.M. (1973) *Stability and Complexity in Model Ecosystems*. Princeton University Press, Princeton, NJ.

Mayr, E. (1963) *Animal Species and Evolution*. Harvard University Press, Cambridge, Ma.

McKeown, T. (1976) *The Modern Rise of Population*. Edward Arnold, London.

Mead, M. (1950) *Male and Female: A Study of the Sexes in a Changing World*. Morrow, New York.

Merchant, C. (1980) *The Death of Nature. Women, Ecology and the Scientific Revolution*. Harper & Row, San Francisco.

Merchant, C. (1989) *Ecological Revolutions. Nature, Gender, and Science in New England*. University of North Carolina Press, Chapell Hill, NC.

Myers, N. (1980) *The Sinking Ark. A New Look at the Problem of Disappearing Species*. Pergamon Press, London.

Nagel, A. (1961) *The Structure of Science. Problems in the Logic of Scientific Explanation*. Routledge & Kegan Paul, London.

Neuvonen, S., Saikkonen, K. and Haukioja, E. (1990) 'Simulated acid rain reduces the susceptibility of the European pine sawfly (*Neprion sertifer*) to its nuclear polyhedrosis virus'. *Oecologia (Berlin)* 83:209–12.

Neuvonen, S. and Suomela, J. (1990) 'The effect of simulated acid rain on pine needle and birch leaf litter decomposition'. *Journal of Applied Ecology* 27:857–72.

Niemelä, J., Haila, Y. and Halme, E. (1988) 'Carabid beetles on isolated Baltic islands and on the adjacent Åland mainland: variation in colonization success'. *Annales Zoologici Fennici* 24:179–94.

Nitecki, M.H. (ed.) (1984) *Extinctions*. Chicago University Press, Chicago.

Nuorteva, P. (1972) 'A three-year survey of the duration of development of *Cynomyia mortuorum* (L.) (Dipt., Calliphoridae) in the conditions of a subarctic fell'. *Annales Entomologici Fennici* 38:65–74.

Odum, E.P. (1989) *Ecology and Our Endangered Life-Support Systems*. Sinauer, Sunderland, Ma.

Olson, S.L. and James, H.F. (1982) 'Fossil birds from the Hawaiian Islands: Evidence for wholesale extinction by man before western contact'. *Science* 217:633–5.

O'Neill, R.V., DeAngelis, D.L., Waide, J.B. and Allen, T.F.H. (1986) *A Hierarchical Concept of Ecosystems*. Princeton University Press, Princeton, NJ.

Pajunen, V.I. (1983) 'The use of physiological time in the analysis of insect stage-frequency data'. *Oikos* 40:161–5.

Park, T. (1962) 'Beetles, competition, and populations'. *Science* 138:1369–75.

Pietiäinen, H., Saurola, P. and Väisänen, R.A. (1986) 'Parental investment in clutch size and egg size in the Ural Owl Strix uralensis'. *Ornis Scandinavica* 17:309–25.

Pimentel, D. et al. (1987) 'World agriculture and soil erosion'. *BioScience* 37:277–83.

Popper, K.R. (1935) *Logik der Forschung*. Vienna.

Postan, M.M. (1972) *The Medieval Economy and Society*. Weidenfeld and Nicolson, London.

Preston, F.W. (1960) 'Time and space and the variation of species'. *Ecology* 41:611–27.

Price, P.W. (1980) *Evolutionary Biology of Parasites*. Princeton University Press, Princeton, NJ.

Prigogine, I. and Stenghers, I.(1984) *Order out of Chaos*. Fontana, New York.

Puccia, C.J. and Levins, R. (1985) *Qualitative Modeling of Complex Systems. An Introduction to Loop Analysis and Time Averaging*. Harvard University Press, Cambridge, Ma.

Punttila, P., Haila, Y., Pajunen, T. and Tukia, H. (1991) Colonization of clearcut forests by ants in the southern Finnish taiga: a quantitative survey'. *Oikos* 61:250–62.

Quine, W.V. (1961) *From a Logical Point of View. Logico-Philosophical Essays*. 2nd ed. Harper & Row, New York.

Raup, D.M. and Jablonski, D. (eds) (1986) *Patterns and Processes in the History of Life*. Springer Verlag, Berlin.

Rolstad, J. and Wegge, P. (1987) 'Distribution and size of capercaillie leks in relation to old forest fragmentation'. *Oecologia (Berlin)* 72:389–94.

Rorty, R. (1980) *Philosophy and the Mirror of Nature*. Princeton University Press, Princeton, NJ.

Rose, H. (1983) 'Hand, brain and heart: a feminist epistemology for the natural sciences'. *Signs* 9:73–90.

Rose, S., Kamin, L.J. and Lewontin, R.C. (1984) *Not in Our Genes. Biology, Ideology and Human Nature.* Penguin, Harmondsworth.

Ruben, P. (1980) *Dialektik und Arbeit der Philosophie.* Pahl-Rugenstein Verlag, Köln.

Salo, J., Kalliola, R., Häkkinen, I., Mäkinen, Y., Niemelä, P., Puhakka, M. and Coley, P.D. (1986) 'River dynamics and the diversity of Amazon lowland forest'. *Nature* 322:254–8.

Sarvas, R. (1937) 'Havaintoja kasvillisuuden kehityksestä Pohjois-Suomen kuloaloilla'. *Silva Fennica* 44:1–64.

Schnaiberg, A. (1980) *The Environment from Surplus to Scarcity.* Oxford University Press, Oxford.

Schoener, T. (1986) 'Mechanistic approaches to community ecology: a new reductionism?' *American Zoologist* 26:81–106.

Selye, H. (1989) In *Neuroendocrinology and Stess.* Springer Verlag, New York.

Shugart, H.H. (1984) *A Theory of Forest Dynamics. The Ecological Implications of Forest Succession Models.* Springer Verlag, New York.

Simon, H.A. (1977) *Models of Discovery.* D.Reidel, Dordrecht.

Slobodkin, L.B. (1953) 'An algebra of population growth'. *Ecology* 34:513–19.

Slobodkin, L.B. (1961) *Growth and Regulation of Animal Populations.* Holt, Rinehart and Winston, New York.

Spretnak, C. and Capra, F. (1985) *Green Politics. The Global Promise.* Paladin, London.

Stegman, B.K. (1938) 'Osnovy ornitogeograficheskaya deleniya Palearktiki'. *Fauna SSSR, Ptitsy, Tom 1, vypusk 2.* Izd. Akademii Nauk SSSR, Moskva. (Zusammenfassung: Grundzüge der ornithogeographischen Gliederung des palearktischen Gebietes.)

Strong, D.R. Jr. (1979) 'Biogeographic dynamics of insect–host plant communities'. *Annual Review of Entomology* 24:89–119.

Thomas, W.L., Sauer, C.O., Bates, M. and Mumford, L. (1956) *Man's Role in Changing the Face of the Earth.* University of Chicago Press, Chicago.

Tonteri, T. and Haila, Y. (1990) 'Plants in a boreal city: Ecological characteristics of vegetation in Helsinki and its surroundings, southern Finland'. *Annales Botanici Fennici* 27:337–52.

Underwood, A.J. and Peterson, C.H. (1989) 'Towards an ecological framework for investigating pollution'. *Marine Ecology – Progress Series* 46:227–34.

Vandermeer, J. (1977) 'Ecological determinism', in *Biology as a Social Weapon.* Edited by the Ann Arbor Science for the People editorial collective. Ann Arbor.

Van Straalen, N.M. (1983) 'Physiological time and time-invariance'. *Journal of Theoretical Biology* 104:349–57.

Virkkala, R. (1990) 'Ecology of the Siberian Tit Parus cinctus in relation to habitat quality: effects of forest management'. *Ornis Scandinavica* 21:139–46.

Wahsner, R. (1981) *Das Aktive und das Passive. Zur erkenntnistheoretischen Begründung der Physik durch den Atomismus – dargestellt an Newton und Kant.* Akademie–Verlag, Berlin.

Wallerstein, I. (1974) *The Modern World-System. Capitalist Agriculture and the Origin of the European World-Economy in the Sixteenth Century.* Academic Press, London.

Weber, B.H., Depew, D.J. and Smith, J.D. (eds) (1988) *Entropy, Information and Evolution. New Perspectives on Physical and Biological Evolution.* MIT Press, Cambridge, Ma.

Whittaker, R.H. (1953) 'A consideration of climax theory: the climax as a population pattern'. *Ecological Monographs* 23:41–78.

Wiens, J.A. (1981) 'Scale problems in avian censusing'. *Studies in Avian Biology* 6:513–21.

Williams, R. (1973) *The Country and the City.* Chatto and Windus, London.

Williams, R. (1980) *Problems in Materialism and Culture.* Verso, London.

Wimsatt, W.C. (1981) 'Robustness, reliability and overdetermination', pp. 124–63 in M. Brewer and B. Collins (eds) *Scientific Inquiry and the Social Sciences.* Jossey-Bass, San Francisco.

Wittgenstein, L. (1953) *Philosophical Investigations.* Blackwell, Oxford.

Wolf, E.R. (1982) *Europe and the People without History.* University of California Press, Berkeley, Ca.

Wright, H.A. and Bailey, A.W. (1982) *Fire ecology. United States and Southern Canada.* John Wiley & Sons, New York.

Zackrisson, O. (1977) 'Influence of forest fire on the North Swedish boreal forest'. *Oikos* 29:22–32.

Index